RACE AND THE UNDESERVING POOR

Building Progressive Alternatives

Series Editors: David Coates and Matthew Watson

Bringing together economists, political economists and other social scientists, this series offers pathways to a coherent, credible and progressive economic growth strategy which, when accompanied by an associated set of wider public policies, can inspire and underpin the revival of a successful centre-left politics in advanced capitalist societies.

Published

David Coates
Flawed Capitalism: The Anglo-American Condition and its Resolution

David Coates (editor)
Reflections on the Future of the Left

Robbie Shilliam
Race and the Undeserving Poor: From Abolition to Brexit

RACE AND THE UNDESERVING POOR

From Abolition to Brexit

ROBBIE SHILLIAM

First edition published in 2018 by Agenda Publishing

Agenda Publishing Limited
The Core
Science Central
Bath Lane
Newcastle upon Tyne
NE4 5TF
www.agendapub.com

ISBN 978-1-78821-037-9 (hardcover)
ISBN 978-1-78821-038-6 (paperback)

British Library Cataloguing-in-Publication Data
A catalogue record for this book is available from the British Library

Typeset by Out of House Publishing
Printed and bound in the UK by TJ International

For my father, born into a Midlands coal-mining family.

Livicated to the people of Grenfell Tower, in their pursuit of justice.

CONTENTS

ACKNOWLEDGEMENTS

My sincere thanks to the series editors, Alison Howson at Agenda Publishing, two anonymous reviewers, and to Gurminder K. Bhambra, Danny Dorling, James Dunkerley, John Holmwood, Engin Isin, the Pan African Society Community Forum, Daniel Renwick, Rick Saull, Lisa Tilley and Westway23.

FOREWORD

Matthew Watson

It should go without saying that it is always a dangerous predictions game to label something a "classic" upon its first publication. This is a judgement for people to make in the future, once they have seen the lasting impact that the book has made. I say all this now because I want to escape the charge of being wise after the event when classic status is subsequently ascribed to Robbie Shilliam's *Race and the Undeserving Poor*. Hindsight is indeed a wonderful thing, but its benefits are unnecessary to spot the potential legacies that this book might leave. They will, I am sure, be as clearly evident in other readers' first encounter with Shilliam's text as they were in mine.

The text itself rockets along at action-packed pace. This makes *Race and the Undeserving Poor* that academic rarity, because it has all the feel of a genuine page-turner. Yet the rush to find out what happens next only ever occupies part of the mind. The other part becomes increasingly fixated on unsettling questions that the reading experience throws up. The first one I kept coming back to as I made my way through the chapters was "why did I not know this before now?" The second elicited much more personal emotions. It felt as though I was being taken on a journey through my family's past and that I was being prompted to join the dots where my family's oral history draws a frustrating blank. That journey is from a racialized "other" to working-class "respectability" in what is now the archetypal Brexit county of small-town Lincolnshire. The second uncomfortable question accompanying my reading was therefore "why did I not know this *about me* before now?"

There might be a fairly straightforward answer to the first of these two questions. It is well documented that historians have generally been very slow to situate race at the heart of analyses of the British national past. It is as if a national society had formed – imperfectly and incompletely as all such processes necessarily are – that nevertheless asserts unproblematically an essential whiteness as its template. This might be thought of in terms of the originating myths on which popular conceptions of Britishness are based; the stories which link these myths to more distant events that are now typically seen as pre-emptive moves towards nation-building; the heroes whose actions drive a chronological narrative of British national achievements; or the events which appear in school textbooks as exemplary illustrations of the context in which the British national character was forged. All of these, along with many other similarly formative statements about what Britishness is and where Britain came from, tend to conflate historical agency with whiteness. There are exceptions, but to encounter them requires the reader to travel very much to the margins of British political history. To write from a perspective that situates race at the centre of the analysis means that it is always necessary to speak louder to make yourself heard.

The great merit to be found in Shilliam's book is just how clearly his voice comes across. He explores the lineage of repeated political attempts from the eighteenth century onwards to bracket off "the deserving poor" from the broader category of "the poor" in general. Some marker of difference must be called upon to distinguish those who do from those who do not merit political sympathy for their plight and state support to lessen their day-to-day grind of making ends meet. Shilliam shows that, often, the simple characteristic of what you look like was enough for a person of colour to be relegated from the deserving category. At other times, behavioural traits became the means of differentiation, but assumptions relating to the propensity to display proscribed behaviour have been so frequently racialized that this symbol of exclusion has also been reduced to the issue of skin colour. *Race and the Undeserving Poor* demonstrates how practices of British working-class respectability have historically been inscribed with underlying images of whiteness.

If it is to prove possible to build progressive alternatives as per the name of the series in which this book is published, the process will have to involve reflections on rejuvenating working-class political agency. Oppressive political structures have been institutionalized throughout the recent past that have increasingly removed from working-class communities the feeling that their destiny is in their own hands. Shilliam reminds us, however, to be attentive to the way in which constructions of working-class political identity in Britain have so often relied upon the deliberate projection of a racialized "other". He could not be any clearer – nor yet any more correct – in concluding that the working class is not an abstract category whose inherent whiteness can be accepted unquestioningly.

CHAPTER 1

INTRODUCTION

In 1885 influential jurist Albert Venn Dicey (1889: 38) defined Britain's parliamentary sovereignty as "the right to make or unmake any law whatever". For Dicey, the strength of this sovereignty was such that no person or group could "override or set aside the legislation of Parliament". Parliament's sovereignty was ill-disposed towards the sentiments of the "people" entering the halls of Westminster in an unmediated fashion. Rather, the people's representatives had to exercise independent reason in deliberation and decision making. For right or wrong, parliamentary sovereignty has always demanded representative rather than direct democracy. Except that when, in June 2016, the British public voted by 51.9 per cent to leave the EU, influential politicians and pundits claimed that the non-binding referendum result was a direct, unmediated expression of the "popular will". The government, they argued, was bound to legislate on this will.

In the months following the referendum, it became routine for politicians and pundits to claim that the will of "the people" was paramount, even over parliamentary sovereignty. In the first Conservative Party conference following the referendum, Theresa May (2016b) commanded her government to "respect what the people told us on the 23rd of June – and take Britain out of the European Union". When, in November, the Supreme Court of Justice ruled that parliament had to legislate on Brexit, the *Daily Mail* newspaper accused the judiciary of being "enemies of the people" (Phipps 2016). The justice secretary, Liz Truss, was noticeably slow to defend the judges.

1

Meanwhile, Nigel Farage of the United Kingdom Independence Party (UKIP) warned that a 100,000 strong "people's army" might march on the Supreme Court to ensure that the popular will was enacted (Payton 2016).

But who is morally worthy to count as "the people"? Pouring scorn on the European Parliament just days after the referendum, Farage (2016) argued that Brexit was the will of the "little people". Douglas Carswell (2016), UKIP's first elected MP, envisaged his party becoming the heir to the Chartists – a nineteenth-century labour movement for working-class suffrage and representation. Similarly, when introducing herself to the public as the new prime minister, May (2016a) appealed first and foremost to the "just about managing". In describing what she envisaged to be Britain's post-EU "shared society", May (2017) placed the "ordinary working class" as its prime deserving constituency.

What, then, counts as an "ordinary" member of the working class? To answer that question, it is useful to chart the re-entry of "class" back into the political grammar of mainstream media and debate. The language of class returned largely in the wake of the global financial crisis that took hold of Britain in 2008. A BBC poll conducted in March of that year for *Newsnight* found that 58 per cent of the "working-class" believed "nobody speaks out for people like me in Britain today". Accompanying the poll, a "white season" of shows was broadcast on the national network. The season controversially drew attention to a sense of unfairness amongst self-identifying white members of the working class in contrast to the positive discriminations purportedly enjoyed by Britain's Black and minority ethnic populations (Rhodes 2010: 83; Kenny 2012: 23).

Parliamentary politics responded. Looking ahead to elections in 2010, the Fabian Society, a gradualist and reformist left-of-centre organization, hosted a meeting at the 2008 Labour Party conference that sought to clarify for the party the putative demands of the "white working class" (Sveinsson 2009: 4). Phil Woolas, Labour's immigration minister, argued that skills shortages had to be met by better equipping Britain's "indigenous population" for work (Moore 2008). One year later, and to the delight of the *Daily Mail*, Hazel Blears, then communities secretary, acknowledged that lower-income white people felt their "acute fears" over immigration had been ignored (Reid 2009). Panicked by the possible loss of their voting base, in the last months of the election campaign Labour shifted back to associating social injustice with class rather than with race (BBC News 2010). Such a shift was consolidated under the new Conservative and Liberal Democrat coalition government and most commonly expressed in criticisms of education, a proxy for social mobility.

Even in 2008, education was considered a key arena wherein unfairness towards the "white working class" took hold. Then, a Department for Innovation, Universities and Skills report was released that primarily addressed gender gaps in higher education. However, the *Telegraph* seized upon a minor part of the report which mentioned the relative paucity of "white working class boys" attending university. These boys, the newspaper claimed, were "becoming an underclass" (Paton 2008; see also Gillborn 2010). In 2012, the *Telegraph* once more sounded the alarm that private school bursaries available to poor pupils were increasingly – and by implication unfairly – being claimed by children from "Asian, Afro-Caribbean and Eastern European families" (Paton 2012). Shortly afterwards, in 2013, David Willetts, universities minister, suggested that when it came to higher education, "white working class" boys should be targeted in the same way as other "disadvantaged groups" were by the Office for Fair Access (Silverman 2013).

These concerns continued to be voiced during the next Conservative government. In 2015, newspapers picked up on a report by the Equality and Human Rights Commission that "white working class" boys were falling further behind other social and ethnic groups at school (*Telegraph* 2015). In February 2016, four months before the EU referendum, David Cameron wrote an article for the *Sunday Times*, which drew attention to the relative paucity of Black and minority ethnic students in prestigious universities. The *Spectator* took issue with Cameron's focus: "But he is wrong about the ethnicity of those students and wrong about where the problem lies. It's working-class white boys who fare the worst, not Black boys" (Young 2016). In March 2016, three months before the referendum date, Liam Fox, a Conservative MP (soon to become a key Brexit minister in May's government), opined: "Everyone talks about the need for diversity and yet nobody seems to worry about poor white boys. We need to stop obsessing with particular minorities" (Charlotte Street Partners 2016).

3

What might be drawn out from these commentaries and debates? Fundamentally, this: in the years preceding the global financial crisis, inequality was rarely spoken of – or legislated on – in the language of class but rather through proxy concepts such as "social exclusion" (Griffith & Glennie 2014); since then, class has returned to the diet of parliamentary and public discourse as a constitutively racialized phenomenon. By "racialization", I refer to the way in which racist attributes and hierarchies come to determine the everyday meaning and common sense valuation of an entity or phenomenon. Criticisms have gathered over the often glib or metaphorical use of "racialization" (Murji & Solomos 2005). My use of the term in this book is specifically concerned with the shifting distinctions between those considered deserving and undeserving of an acceptable level of social security and welfare.

With this in mind, consider the way in which class has returned, racialized, as the white working-class. At a minimum, whiteness infers respectability. Yet by the 2000s poor residents of council estates were explicitly racialized as white at a time when whiteness normatively inferred *middle-class* respectability. This white "underclass" was thereby imbued with a hyper-visible social dysfunctionality and a moral character undeserving of welfare (see Lawler 2012). Now contemplate May's recent comments, which normalize the working-classness of whiteness. Indeed, in the years leading up to Brexit, the "white working class" have been more and more defined as the deserving people that neoliberal politicians and global business has unfairly "left behind" (Open Society Foundations 2014).

Despite these recent shifts in meaning, the racialization of the working class is not a new phenomenon. Neither has the "white working class" always been considered a constituency indigenous to the British Isles. In actuality, the category of the "white working class" has a much longer genealogy, one that is embedded in a colonial past, and thus requires us to gazette a historical field wider than that of an "island story".

For much of the twentieth century the "white working class" was part of an analytical vocabulary used by socialists and anti-colonial activists to investigate the racialized division of labour in the United States and apartheid South Africa. Oftentimes the category was deployed in arguments over the possibility of class unity (for example Johnson 1936; Kennedy & Leary 1947; see also Roediger 1991). For instance, James S. Allen (1938: 44), member of the Communist Party USA, wrote on the eve of the Second World War of the "special task of the white workers", who had to "wipe out all traces of the white superiority idea in themselves and be the first to demand and fight for the special demands of the Negro people".

In South Africa, Isaac Tabata (1945) of the Non European Unity Movement argued that the "white worker" had "so long fed on colour prejudice, that he has been completely blinded to his real position as a worker and has aligned himself with the exploiter". By the 1970s, academic critiques of racialized class structures had spread to discussions of the struggles over quasi-apartheid rule in neighbouring Southern Rhodesia (now Zimbabwe), whose white settler elite had broken away from British dominion (for example Wolpe 1972; Maxey 1976).

In Britain, the category of the "white working class" gained prominence through all these vectors as well as via the influence of the global Black Power movement in the era of decolonization. Black Power was met positively by many young Black scholars and activists in the late 1960s, and woven into existing traditions of struggle transmitted from Caribbean and South Asian heritages. Activists and intellectuals questioned prevailing concerns for the orderly integration of non-white Commonwealth immigrants and framed the problem, instead, in terms of the structural racism of British society (see Allen & Smith 1974). For instance, commenting upon racism in English trade unions in 1973, Black activist and Pan-Africanist Cecil Gutzmore argued that: "The white working class tend to be more or less willing agents of the ruling class in regard to Blacks, which is precisely why one section of the working class finds it is necessary to use industrial action against another" (Bailey 1973). By the early 1980s the mildly liberal Institute of Race Relations had been transformed into a radical organization. Its new journal, *Race and Class*, became a key forum for discussing the "white working class" and its hierarchical relationship to the Black working classes within British imperialism.

The evidence is striking: decades before the global financial crisis, the category of the "white working class" had already become regular currency in scholarly and activist debates over racism and neo-imperialism. Then, the "white working class" was a fundamental part of a race–class equation, and a term that signified a hierarchy of oppression within a division of labour that exceeded the British Isles. This historical debate, with coordinates embedded in Britain's past imperial hinterland and postcolonial present, prefigures but is also silenced by contemporary debates. Today, the "white working class" is introduced as a forgotten indigenous constituency, independent of colonial pasts, and unfairly displaced by multi-coloured newcomers. This disjuncture should give us pause for thought about the claims being made on behalf of a deserving "white working class" in distinction to undeserving others.

In the following pages I seek to demonstrate that the "white working class" is neither an indigenous constituency, nor its own progenitor, but a constituency produced and reproduced through struggles to consolidate and defend British imperial order, struggles that have subsequently shaped the contours of Britain's postcolonial society. To be crystal clear, I am arguing that the "white working class" is not a natural or neutral category of political economy. As a constituency, the "white working class" has rarely been self-authored, self-empowered or self-directed. Rather, this constituency must be apprehended as an elite artefact of political domination.

Over the course of the book, I will utilize "elite" in a purposefully capacious rather than sociologically exacting fashion. This is because I wish to demonstrate how race cuts across – or at the very least problematizes – common sense political divisions between left and right, as well as common sense distinctions between the domains of politics, law, economy, culture and knowledge-production. Furthermore, even on those occasions when non-elites have been actively involved in processes of racialization, I will argue that they have been guided for the most part by the directions laid down by elites. My core argument, then, is that elite actors have racialized and re-racialized the historical distinction between the deserving and the undeserving poor through ever more expansive terms that have incorporated working classes, colonial "natives" and nationalities. Elite actors have always been driven in this endeavour by concerns for the integrity of Britain's imperial – and then postcolonial – order. That has been the case from abolition to Brexit.

Nonetheless, I would not presume to tell a smooth story of political domination. Instead, the book seeks to chart the consistent shifting of these racialized coordinates by connecting various moments of struggle and crisis across British empire and postcolonial

Britain: namely, the abolition of slavery and poor law reform (1780s–1830s); Anglo-Saxon empire, eugenics and national insurance (1840s–1910s); welfare and colonial development (1890s–1950s); universal welfare, trade unions and Commonwealth migration (1940s–1970s); social conservatism, workfare and the emergence of the white "underclass" (1970s–2000s); and, ultimately, the rise of the "white working class" as a deserving constituency in the years leading to Brexit.

Throughout the narrative, special attention is given to the Caribbean – and Black peoples more generally – in the racialization and re-racialization of the distinction between those considered deserving and undeserving of social security and welfare. As will become clear, there is a solid historical reason for such a methodological bias. Briefly put, the enslavement of Africans was a fundamental reference point for the initial racialization of deserving and undeserving characteristics, with the "slave" – and thereby the condition of blackness – exemplifying the latter. At various points in the argument I shall demonstrate how other subjects of empire were "blackened" in the process of also being made to carry undeserving characteristics. In all this, there is a moral relationship – but not quite co-incidence – between whiteness and deserved-ness and blackness and undeserved-ness.

Additionally, the book's focus in Britain narrows to the English context due to the country's dominant position within the Union and its empire. This and the focus on Black subjects strengthen the thread of the argument. But the story I tell certainly needs to be tempered through more expansive histories of empire's dominions and mandates, of Ireland, Northern Ireland, Scotland and Wales, and of refugees and asylum seekers too.

In summary, this book narrates a history of political domination told through the moralizing discourses and rhetoric of the undeserving poor. The narrative places these discourses and rhetoric in a shifting constellation of legal, economic, cultural and political structures full of contentious interests. Via this strategy the reader will gain a sense of the stakes at play in the various racializations of the undeserving poor over centuries of British imperial history. The book's point of departure concerns the deserving and undeserving poor as adjudicated by eighteenth-century poor relief. But before long, the scope of this adjudication widens to attend to the political order required to balance the tensions and duplicities of capitalism in its imperial and postcolonial determinations. Principally, I claim that crucial to this adjudication of order has been the racialized distinction between those deserving and undeserving of social security and welfare, including the most recent return of the "white working class" as a deserving constituency.

The title of the series in which this book is published, *Building Progressive Alternatives*, speaks to the fact that Brexit has placed social justice back on the political agenda, albeit precariously. So why is this book primarily a story of political domination and not devoted to scoping out alternatives in the current conjuncture? For my part, I am concerned with how Brexit has at the same time revealed an entrenched inability by Britain's elites to consider justice outside of the normalization of race and empire. Hence, this book is designed to complicate and challenge any present-day attempt to pursue social justice in the name of the "white working class", whether implicitly or explicitly. Because this constituency is an artefact of political domination, I have felt it necessary to devote the book to exposing its imperial and postcolonial histories. Such a task, I believe, is a necessary requirement for any critical pursuit of social justice in our Brexit era. I do, though, finish by laying out two principles through which these histories and complicities might be confronted for the sake of building progressive alternatives.

CHAPTER 2

ENGLISH POOR LAWS AND CARIBBEAN SLAVERY

INTRODUCTION

Since at least the Elizabethan era, poor laws marked a formal dis-tinction between those deserving of relief – the lame, impotent, old or blind – and those who were able-bodied yet idle or vagrant and undeserving. To the deserving poor, relief was provided in the form of money, food or clothing. The undeserving were often sent temporarily to houses of correction. The poor laws were inher-ently patriarchal in their assumptions and applications. The fate of women and children was by and large determined by the character of their husband/father. Implemented locally, at parish level, the poor laws were secularized instruments of religious charity, framed by moral commandments. By the late eighteenth century, poor laws had become indispensable to the maintenance of political order in Britain's fast-evolving "commercial society".

Customary tenures in England had long guaranteed use and access rights to land while defining reciprocal (albeit uneven) obligations between lord and subject. From the later 1600s, however, a variety of means were utilized by large landowners to force peasants to sell their customary tenures in order to consolidate land holdings into private property. These "enclosures" cut personal ties to local parishes and led to a growth of "masterless men" who threatened the political order of the rural idyll. Enclosure facilitated the "marketization" of agriculture, which can be understood for our purposes as a shift from moral obligations regarding the provision of subsistence to a far less personal and amoral mechanism of supply and demand. Concerns over "masterless men" led many to ask whether poor laws could check the apparent disintegration of rural order. Regardless, in 1773 parliament passed an Enclosure Act by which common lands would ostensibly be better cultivated, "improved" and regulated. However, by this point in time the political problem posed by England's rural poor was already being apprehended in more expansive terms, referencing African enslavement and the plantation economies of the Americas.

In the first part of this chapter I explore late eighteenth-century claims as to the distinctive political heritage of England, said to be characterized as a tradition of orderly independence. Moral philosophers and legal scholars argued that at the foundation of political order lay England's common law, which guaranteed private property rights and patriarchal inheritance. Under common law, England's subjects were embedded in paternalistic hierarchies that connected the lowest servant to the highest master through dependent relations. The good servant was said to be comprised of characteristics associated with the deserving poor – industriousness, prudence and patriarchy. But I also examine arguments by abolitionists who perceived plantation slavery in the American colonies as a threat to such hierarchies. While in common law the lowest servant could be a small patriarch himself, through commercial law the male slave, being the property of another, could not fulfil such a function and hence severed paternalistic hierarchies. In the aftermath of the American War of Independence, I argue that the Caribbean slave took on all the characteristics associated with the undeserving poor: idleness, licentiousness and anarchy.

What if Caribbean slavery came to England? In the second part of the chapter, I turn to this question, mainly by addressing the work of William Cobbett, a famous defender of the rural poor. Cobbett railed against enclosure, the marketization of agriculture and the destruction of the old cottage economy. I show how Cobbett presented this process as one wherein English rural labourers were reduced to the status of slaves, thereby undermining England's paternalistic hierarchies and patriarchal foundation. I make the case that Cobbett analogized the English poor with Black slaves. Through analogization, Cobbett argued that marketization unjustly cut the deserving poor from their patriarchal filiations, condemning them to social death. I also detail how Cobbett's arguments resonated with the wider and growing movement against factory work. It was from this position that Cobbett attacked the proposed changes to poor laws in the early 1830s, claiming that such changes would further reduce the status of the deserving poor to that of slaves. Finally, I examine how the commissioners tasked to scope out the changes to poor relief in the early 1830s also used the slave analogy. Yet unlike Cobbett, they claimed that the existing poor laws had already induced slave-like characteristics in the rural population, namely, idleness, licentiousness and poor parenting.

This chapter therefore presents slavery and abolition as a foundational moment in the racialization of the distinction between the deserving and the undeserving poor. In the course of the argument I introduce some key concepts that I will return to regularly in following chapters: the "English genus", the "little platoons", the "slave analogy" and the "blackening of the poor".

PROPERTY, PATRIARCHY AND SLAVERY

An early poor law – the Vagrancy Act of 1547 – imposed slavery as a punishment for refusal to work (Davies 1966). Notwithstanding this short-lived instrument, "villeinage" was the closest legal approximation to slavery in England, pertaining to a bonded tenant who could not leave his lord's land without consent; 1618 saw the last recorded case wherein a villein had been set free (Drescher 1999: 17). And as the suffering of this form of slavery receded from jurisprudence, the condition of liberty gained clarity by way of the common law tradition.

Writing his definitive commentaries on this tradition in the 1760s, jurist William Blackstone argued that liberty's defence lay fundamentally in the inalienable ownership of inherited property. Blackstone's argument reflected a gradual political realignment whereby a landed-interest gained increased independence from monarchical and aristocratic dominion, especially through the appropriation of private property via enclosures. For Blackstone, the focus on the right to inherit private property – and its productive potential – was a claim to the liberty of property owners based upon an independent political and legal identity (Michals 1993: 200).

Individual liberty under common law was deeply qualified by the patriarchal order and paternalistic hierarchies that made the inheritance of property possible. Blackstone (1766) was explicit that the right to inherit property under common law pertained to the father/ husband alone. Upon marriage, a woman would lose the right to own property to her husband; and this held even if the husband was himself dependent upon a patriarch (Michals 1993: 202–3). Patriarchal inheritance therefore depended upon paternalistic hierarchies that bound all together in various levels of dependency. An un-propertied man, unable to meet his family's subsistence needs independently, could rightfully enter into a dependent relationship of master and servant wherein his benefactor would also be his moral guide (Blackstone 1766; Stanley 1998: 11).

By this logic, even though common law outlawed slavery it did not equate a man's property in himself to freedom from servitude. Both political freedom and economic unfreedom could codetermine a man's status. In short, common law assured the sanctity of private property through the rule of the patriarchal household. Crucially, the paternalistic stewardship of the property-owning master was supposed to cultivate in his free-labouring servant and dependents deserving characteristics: a rational response to material needs in the form of self-interest; a commitment to improving productivity through industrious activity; and a deferral of gratification for the prudential management of meagre resources. Above all, the servant would learn to become a small patriarch, taking his orderly place in the hierarchy of paternalistic dependencies.

Increasingly, then, the deserving poor normatively referenced those servants whose labour contributed to the enrichment of the proprietor and who accepted their relationship to that proprietor as one of paternalistic dependency. The characteristics borne by the undeserving poor threatened this order and its values, whether it be due to idleness (failure to produce), impropriety (disrespect of property) or licentiousness and vagrancy (i.e. failing to uphold the patriarchal order). In this respect, the deserving/undeserving distinction became the normative calculus that underpinned what scholars had begun to call "commercial society" and what we would now call capitalism.

Enclosures were one of the key elements in the rise of the landed-interest, whose inherited property common law protected even against appropriation from monarchy and aristocracy. At the same time, enclosures threatened to unravel the patriarchal order and paternalistic hierarchies that ensured such inheritance by creating "masterless men". Hence, while the poor laws had initially consolidated as an instrument to calculate the just receipt of Christian benefaction, they came to serve as a legal device to discipline the working poor even as economic conditions progressively destabilized the political order. Key to such discipline was the moral distinction between the deserving and the undeserving poor. The distinction itself was wielded as an instrument of political domination.

England, though, was already a colonial power when it joined Scotland in the 1707 Acts of Union. In fact, empire was considered, in Blackstone's era, to be a civic analogue of the paternalistic relationship of British father (king) and British child (colony). The drama over the deserving and the undeserving poor played out on this wider field. If enclosures threatened the patriarchal order within England's countryside, African enslavement did the same on England's world stage (Brown 1999: 282–3).

Concerned with the abuse of monarchical and aristocratic power, Blackstone argued that common law explicitly outlawed "pure and proper slavery" that gave "absolute and unlimited power" to the master. He additionally claimed that English soil could not abide slavery, unlike in the Caribbean where, even if repugnant, the practice was possible (Michals 1993: 204). The principles of common law espoused by Blackstone could not conceive of the legal status of enslaved Africans in the Americas, which alternatively fell entirely under commercial law. Yet not even commercial law possessed the specific category of a commodity that was also a person. Such law had to be innovated such that a person could be robbed of any claim to legal personality (Bush 1993: 443).

So long as enslaved Africans remained in colonies across the Atlantic they presented no direct challenge to the principles of English common law. But their presence on English soil upset common law's delicate compact between liberty, property and patriarchy. In 1772, an enslaved African called Somersett was brought to London from the American colonies by his master, Charles Steuart (see Drescher 1987: 16–19). Somersett promptly escaped, but then was recaptured. Before his ship was due to return to the colonies an application of *habeas corpus* was made by his supporters. Granville

Sharp, a prominent abolitionist, used the force of common law to argue against Somersett's detention on English soil. Key for Sharp was the political danger that slavery posed to the traditional liberties of the English subjects of common law (Davis 1975: 375, 392).

Against the claim to Somersett by his "master" as a purchased piece of property, Justice Mansfield, presiding, ruled that Somersett was to be freed on the basis of common law having no precedent for the return of a slave from English shores. But while Mansfield's ruling targeted the unlawful detention and potential deportation of Somersett, it was ambivalent over explicitly outlawing slavery in Britain (Hulsebosch 2006). A similar ambivalence can be identified 15 years later, across the Atlantic, when James Madison wrote Federalist Paper No. 54, an essay discussing the apportioning of seats in the US House of Representatives. Madison confirmed that enslaved Africans should be considered property, albeit a peculiar property that possessed some sense of personhood, hence requiring their representation to be scaled down to three-fifths of a person.

Still, when it came to the English poor, common law did indeed make a fundamental distinction between servitude – which was accepted – and enslavement – which was outlawed. So why Mansfield's ambivalence? Consider the difference between common law and commercial law. When it came to enslaved Africans, commercial law had no legal conception of servitude, which is why slavery could not be considered a patriarchal relation, only a despotic one. Paradoxically, this meant that setting Somersett categorically "free" on English soil logically rendered him freed even from servitude. This was worrisome because servitude was the foundation of the patriarchal order and paternalistic hierarchies which gave integrity to inherited property rights. That is why Blackstone himself was compelled to argue, in a twist of legal fiction, that even English soil did not rescind the "contract" that the slave had apparently "made" in the colonies to serve his masters in perpetuity (Blackstone 1766: 412–13; Prest 2007: 111–15).

If we read the Somersett case as an early legal argument for the abolition of slavery, then it becomes clear that the category of "free" labour held significant ramifications for Britain's commercial society just as much as it did for plantation colonies. Crucially, Somersett's case suggests that fear of radically freed labour did not organically derive purely from England's enclosure movement; it derived conjointly from England's colonial project. Scottish philosophers such as Adam Ferguson, James Steuart and Adam Smith are well known to have inquired into the moral constitution of Britain's commercial society. What is less well appreciated is that by considering the prospects of the "freed" slave, abolitionists (including some of those Scottish philosophers) were already clarifying the political stakes at play in the regulation, through the poor laws, of masterless men.

In these ways, the dangerous logics of slave abolition, which targeted commercial law, implicated the problem of "masterless men", which referenced common law. As we shall now see, the distinction between the deserving and the undeserving poor began to be racialized by analogy to the Black slave.

Many early plans for the emancipation of enslaved Africans in British colonies did not so much dispute the need to sustain plantation production rather than question the form of labour deployed for this purpose. Key to these considerations was the extent to which characteristics associated with the deserving poor – industriousness, prudence, patriarchy – could be ingrained in emancipated labourers who had previously been enslaved. For instance, the first English publication to offer a concrete emancipation scheme, written in 1765 and published anonymously in 1772, suggested that young African boys could be taken from European trading forts on the African continent, educated in England, and then sent to North America. There, they would train emancipated Africans in the "spirit of industry and achievement" so that their work would be cheaper than that of slaves (cited in Brown 1999: 276–7).

Adam Smith, perhaps the most famous philosopher of "commercial society", took part in these debates over emancipation. While slavery might appear to be the cheapest form of labour, it was, Smith argued, costlier when it came to productivity. The slave could not acquire property because he was property himself and so had no interest other than to eat as much as possible and to labour as little as possible (Smith 1986: 488–9). In other words, in Smith's estimation, by working for the master the slave had no incentive to improve the land voluntarily. Whereas, a free labourer who had to pay rent to a landlord, would have far more rational interest in making the land productive (and indeed be paternally trained in this faculty by the landlord) (Smith 1978: 185–6). Through this logic, Smith argued – as did abolitionists – that the fear of hunger, prison and unemployment would affect a man's "rational nature" in ways that the fear of physical coercion could not (Davis 1975: 466). In short, for Smith and other abolitionist thinkers, slavery did not encourage the slave to cultivate deserving characteristics within himself.

Abolitionists shared with Blackstone a commitment to patriarchy as the order which best ensured private property inheritance. Like most abolitionists, Smith also believed that the successful cultivation of deserving characteristics in the slave depended upon the provision of a patriarchal order and the encouragement of marriage (see Smith 1976: 720). As property, argued Smith, the male slave could not marry and consequently could not be a patriarch (Smith 1978: 176–8). Rather, slavery broke the chain of paternalistic hierarchies between male servant patriarchs and master patriarchs, that "beautiful gradation", wrote colonial administrator and writer William Burke (1760: 118), "from the highest to the lowest where the transitions all the way are almost imperceptible". This "natural inequality", as abolitionist James Ramsay put it, was considered to positively restrain the actions of all men (Davis 1975: 378). In the absence of such gradation, prostitution, vice and debauchery would grow amongst all of the poor of the colonies, white and Black (Burke 1760: 120; Smith 1978: 178).

But what if abolition was pushed forwards by the enslaved themselves, without the paternalistic supervision prescribed by white abolitionist and moral philosopher? This was the question that forcefully presented itself with the beginning of the Haitian Revolution in 1791. Authored by the enslaved themselves (Shilliam 2017), the revolution in the French colony of St Domingue was in part a strategic response to the twists and turns of the French Revolution, begun two years earlier. These regicidal developments across the English Channel disturbed many English commentators who saw in the growing Jacobin disposition an anarchical promotion of radical equality shorn of orderly hierarchies. Interestingly, as early as 1792, some English pamphleteers were characterizing white abolitionists as the "Jacobins of England" (Turley 2003: 183). The association of Jacobinism with slavery is instructive. For in the opinion of many, the logical conclusion to the French Revolution lay in the Haitian one.

Two commentators deserve attention in these respects. Edmund Burke, travelling compatriot of William Burke, was an influential MP and a political theorist who is retrospectively considered a father of conservatism. Henry Brougham was a founder of the whiggish *Edinburgh Review*, an abolitionist and future Lord Chancellor during the 1833 Abolition of Slavery Act. While evincing somewhat different political persuasions, both Burke and Brougham looked upon the Haitian Revolution with the same trepidation. What they feared, above all, was the self-authored destruction by slaves of all ties of servitude and slavery, to be replaced by an anarchical, absolute freedom.

In his critique of the French Revolution, Burke contrasted the "selfish and mischievous ambition" of the French revolutionaries to the public affections generated by membership of England's "little platoons" (Burke 1910: 44). By this term, which later gained greater currency in conservative thought, Burke identified a political order that was underwritten by a set of local filiations that together comprised the paternalistic hierarchies of patriarchy. Burke believed that reform had to be predicated upon a defence of England's patriarchal order undertaken by the little platoons and their extension into Britain's colonies. In his estimation, it was the "spirit" of Christianity and of the nobility that enabled commercial society to progress in a civilized rather than anarchical fashion. Effectively, Burke shared the abolitionists' solution to slavery: the paternalistic treatment by masters of their charges and the concomitant training in slaves of a civilized, patriarchal and proprietary sensibility (see Kohn & O'Neill 2006).

Thus, Burke presumed that the "little platoons" could carry the English genus into the world at large, even if by way of colonialism. These two interlinked terms – "little platoons" and "genus" – are quite central to the argument of this book. Let me here explain my use of the latter. "Genus" glosses a heritable root, a legacy transmitted through birth. In Burke's time, this filial legacy was apprehended via a patriarchal and civilizing moral discourse; but as we shall see in the next chapter, the same legacy could also be apprehended through the race science of eugenics. In any case, defenders of the English genus always referenced its exceptional ability to engender in its members (the "little platoons") an orderly independence at every level in the grand hierarchy, as opposed to the disorderly and anarchical terror of revolution.

It is no surprise, then, that Burke was bitterly opposed to the "regicide" in France. But what is of especial interest is how his famous reflections on the French Revolution were given, at crucial points, political salience via an analogy to the Haitian Revolution (see Wood 1999). By analogy, I mean the identification of correspondences between seemingly disparate entities. For instance, at one point, Burke compels the reader to imagine an England that has suffered the Jacobin fate – its royalty and aristocracy executed, its proper-tied classes expropriated, and its Christian laity disbanded. Asking whether, in this condition, England should be considered less a geographical space and more of a heritable root, Burke follows the imagined refugees of Jacobin atrocities – the English nobility and gentry – who seek succour elsewhere in Europe. How might we feel, Burke asks, if, instead, these refugees were to be:

> taken prisoners ... delivered over as rebel subjects, to be condemned as rebels, as traitors, as the vilest of all criminals, by tribunals formed of Maroon negro slaves, covered over with the blood of their masters, who were made free and organized into judges, for their robberies and murders?
>
> (Burke 1796: 90)

Here, the destruction of commercial society is analogically envisaged by Burke as undertaken by slaves. Rather than be guided by their masters to develop deserving characteristics, slaves self-author their own anarchical freedom and hold the English genus ransom.

In 1803 Henry Brougham wrote a tract that sought, in part, to clarify the ramifications of the Haitian Revolution for England's colonial policy. Arguing, similar to Burke, that "filial submission" was the root of political order, Brougham (1803: 145–6) identified the terror of the French Revolution as arising from the unavoidable fact that the stability of civilized government required "hereditary succession". More worrying for Brougham was the sense that slavery had arrested the civilizing process amongst Africans; and here he echoed the sentiments of his fellow Scottish moral philosophers with regards to the civilizing effect of free labour and patriarchal marriage (Brougham 1803: 144). Without being inducted into these arrangements the "tribes of St Domingo [St Domingue]", who were in the process of gaining their independence, would be capable of governing only through "the caprice and violence of the human passions" (Brougham 1803: 148). Moreover, Brougham (1803: 153–4) worried that the enslaved Africans in British colonies would learn from "the example of Haiti". Hence, "African barbarism" might spread over "the fairest portions of the New World" (Brougham 1803: 183).

For both Burke and Brougham, then, the threat of the French Revolution to the English genus was given political salience through the problem of slavery. It is telling that abolitionists also looked towards Haiti in the aftermath of revolution and asked the question: might those self-authored free men still be amenable to instruction from England in the deserving qualities of industriousness, prudence and patriarchy? Elizabeth Heyrick, an original member of the Anti-Slavery Society, replied positively and argued for immediate and not gradual emancipation. Her support was based on her assessment that, after the revolution, Haitians demonstrated the deserving characteristics of industriousness and orderly independence (Heyrick 1837: 9–10).

Thus, in the various debates for, against and over abolition we can identify three broadly accepted propositions, albeit mobilized for different purposes. First, slavery preserved and even promoted the qualities associated with the undeserving poor. Second, abolition necessarily required the instruction of slaves in the qualities of the deserving poor – industriousness, prudence, patriarchy. And, third, self-authored freedom of the enslaved would, in the absence of proper instruction, threaten to unleash a mass of indolence, licentiousness and anarchy. In the era following the abolition of the slave trade (1807) these considerations subtly came to frame political debate around the undeserving poor in England, especially with regards to the poor law amendments of 1834.

ENGLAND'S POOR AND THE SLAVE ANALOGY

Confronted with increases of malt tax, enclosures and a decline of poor relief, rural labourers in the South and East of England rose up in 1830. On behalf of a fictional Captain Swing they destroyed threshing machines, workhouses and other objects associated with rich farmers and poor-law guardians (Dyck 1993: 185, 195). William Cobbett, a self-made man born to a farmer and publican, is best known for his ethnographies of early nineteenth-century rural England, and for his qualified support of the Captain Swing riots.

Cobbett's sympathies ensued from his abiding concern for the rural labourer and the food scarcities and pauperism that they increasingly suffered due to enclosures and the marketization of agriculture. Against these trends Cobbett defended the moral economy of the traditional English farming community.

In what follows I will provide an extended engagement with Cobbett, who has been lauded even from a leftist position as one of the seminal defenders of the nineteenth-century English poor (Rustin 2003). But Cobbett's writings are instructive for another reason. They demonstrate the extent to which a putatively anti-elite stance can incorporate so many fundamental coordinates of the elite distinction between the deserving and the undeserving poor, including, especially, the racialization of this distinction. As we shall see later, Cobbett pre-empted the duplicities found in much of the twentieth- and twenty-first-century labour movement: a commitment both to social justice and to racialized hierarchies of labour.

At one point in his early life, Cobbett was favourable to Reverend Thomas Malthus's proposition to limit the birth rate of poor populations. By 1807, however, Cobbett had denounced Malthusianism as a scheme that allowed the real producers of misery – politicians and profit-mongers – to reproduce unchecked. Crucially, Cobbett criticized one key instrument that Malthus had proposed for checking the population growth of the poor: making marriage conditional, not a duty. Cobbett identified in such a move the forced introduction of undeserving characteristics amongst the poor. Instead of "kind husbands, virtuous wives, affectionate parents and dutiful children", Cobbett prophesized that England would become "one great brothel of unfeeling paramours, shameless prostitutes, and miserable homeless bastards" (Kegel 1958: 253). Indeed, Cobbett bemoaned any intervention that might cut off "the chain of connection between rich and the poor" (Cole 1924: 266–7).

In these respects, Cobbett's defence of the rural economy incorporated Burke's conception of the English genus, albeit placing the poor labourer to the fore. For Cobbett, the countryside was composed of "little platoons" bound through the paternalistic hierarchies of labourers, tenant farmers and landlords (see Dyck 1993). But this defence depended upon a specific rhetorical strategy: the analogizing of the Caribbean slave to the English rural poor.

Let us briefly consider Cobbett's public life prior to being the champion of the English rural poor. Writing as "Peter Porcupine", and influenced by Burke's tirades (see Wood 1999), Cobbett spent the revolutionary years of the 1790s on the east coast of the United States publishing pro-monarchist and pro-slavery material. Like Burke, Cobbett was outraged by the Haitian Revolution and especially what he perceived to be an inadequate response to it by the white world. He warned that the revolution would lead to revolts in the South spearheaded by a united front of Black, Jacobin and Irish insurrectionaries (Scherr 2003: 8–9, 13). For Cobbett, not only did the Haitian Revolution reveal the unreconstructed indolence and anarchism that lay at the heart of the slave's being, the Revolution's message of radical equality even threatened to undermine the patriarchal order that disciplined metropole and colony, white and Black, master and servant, and male and female relations. In various articles Cobbett imagined the pubescent English girl as desiring of Black men, with the effeminate Jacobin/abolitionist-inclined white husband unable to intervene (Scherr 2003: 16–18).

Upon returning to England in 1800, Cobbett reinvented himself as pamphleteer of the rural poor. But his work as Peter Porcupine still informed these latter travelogues and commentaries principally by framing the challenges facing the English rural idyll through the spectre of Caribbean slavery. This is immediately evident in straightforward political economy terms, for example, in his linking of the taxation burden suffered by the "helpless people of England" to the need to maintain the Caribbean colonies (Cobbett 1912: 2:7). However, I want to focus on the normative register of Cobbett's critique, wherein he analogizes the disintegration of the cottage economy with the introduction of Black slavery.

In *Rural Rides*, an anti-Malthusian travelogue, Cobbett (1912: 2:43) describes the English rural diet most beneficial to maintaining the autonomy of the cottage economy; it includes "none of the slave produce". He also comments positively upon the working people of Worcester and notes that the pursuit of glove-manufacturing, unlike that of "cottons", does not "make who do the work slaves". Here, he notes, "there are no masses of people called together by a bell, and 'kept toil' by a driver" (Cobbett 1912: 2:121). Obversely, in describing the decline visited upon Withington by "tax-eaters", "loan-mongering robbers" and "blaspheming Jews" who now control the land, Cobbett

(1912: 2:130–1) depicts the rural labourers as more completely slaves "than the Blacks are the slaves of the planters in Jamaica", with the farmers acting "in a capacity corresponding with that of the negro-drivers there".

With these various examples Cobbett makes a normative distinction between the detrimental dependency produced by capitalist incursion and the dignified autonomy of the traditional cottage economy. This distinction, though, is mediated through an analogy to plantation slavery, an especially powerful one whenever Cobbett utilizes it to point towards the disintegration of the patriarchal order. For instance, in "cutting off the chain of connection between rich and the poor", Cobbett worries that marketization is intent upon "reducing the community to two classes: masters and slaves". Notably, Cobbett contrasts these two classes with the common law arrangement of "master and man" (Cole 1924: 266–7).

Cobbett's analogizing of the English poor with the Black slave was by no means exceptional or idiosyncratic to the times he lived in. Between 1807 (the year of the abolition of the slave trade) and 1834 (the year of the Poor Law Amendment Act) abolitionism featured centrally in British debates over labour and the poor. Anti-slavery sentiment was in fact well established within the labour leadership of the Factory Movement, which agitated for the reduction of working hours and amelioration of conditions in the cotton mills of the North. Many in the movement considered the abolition of slavery and amelioration of the working conditions suffered by the English poor to be complementary – if not identical – issues. As Seymour Drescher notes, it was "almost impossible to find a meeting petition or tract in favour of the Ten Hours Bill which did not borrow from antislavery" (Drescher 1981: 11–12). Here lay the wellsprings of a worker's abolitionism.

Alternatively, some supporters of labour reform charged middle-class abolitionists with obfuscating the terrible condition of England's own labourers (see especially Hollis 1980). Furthermore, they often chose to accept propaganda spread by pro-slavery voices that depicted the Caribbean slave-owner as a diligent father to his Black dependents, meeting all their basic needs adequately. There was a corollary to this defence of slavery. As slave-trader and polemicist, Gilbert Francklyn argued back in 1789, because the English labourer was "free", he was paradoxically a "slave to necessity", and necessity was deemed a "harder task-master than the African finds in the West Indies" (cited in Davis 1975: 462). Such pro-slavery reasoning was deployed by Chartists and "Tory radicals" alike, the latter evoking the long-held fear that slavery threatened to break the chain of patriarchal order.

Consider, for example, Samuel Roberts, a campaigner against the use of child chimney sweeps. Roberts berated Sheffield abolitionists who waxed lyrical about the separation of child and parent in the slave markets in North America but who lay silent on the fate of "kindred" children of their own "form and colour" bought and sold as chimney sweeps. "This is no nigger", remonstrated Roberts, "[no] piccaninny sold by a strange slave trader in a foreign market". Still, he despaired, children were being enslaved "in this land of liberty, in this slavery-detesting town" (Smith 1834: 230–2). Similarly, Richard Oastler, Tory radical, famously criticized the despotism that factory owners exercised over child labour to the detriment of filial (if poor) patri-archal authority. For Oastler, the despotic owner should be considered akin to the plantation master. The pithy term "wage slavery" began life here, as a rhetorical analogue (see especially Persky 1998).

Although his principal concern was for the rural labourer rather than factory worker, Cobbett positioned himself against the missionary philanthropy of middle-class abolitionists and undertook parliamentary campaigns against anti-slavery (Thorne 1997: 308). Cobbett also drew generously upon pro-slavery stereotypes of "fat and lazy and laughing and singing dancing negroes" in order to judge the Black slave as undeserving of any pity (Drescher 1981: 16). Writing to William Wilberforce in part about the Factory Movement, Cobbett pleaded, "will not the anxiety of a really humane Englishman be directed towards the Whites, instead of towards the Blacks[?]" (Cole 1924: 259). Cobbett also decried the £20 million compensa-tion granted to slave-holders in the 1833 Abolition of Slavery Act as compensation for the loss of their "property". Why, he asked, should poor Britons ultimately pay for the freedom of "comfortable" West Indian slaves (O'Connell 2009a: 96)? Only by this logic, combined with pressure from his North of England constituency while he was an MP, did Cobbett at one point support emancipation without com-pensation in 1833 (Scherr 2003: 20).

So far, I have shown how Cobbett clarified the political stakes at play in the destruction of the cottage economy via an analogy to plantation slavery. But the attentive reader will have noted that slavery, for Cobbett, performed a double function. First, the slave was a figure composed by undeserving characteristics and coloured as Black. Second, to be reduced from an English freeman to a slave speaks to a distinct injustice, a sullying of the English genus.

These functions come to the fore in Cobbett's *Advice to Young Men and (Incidentally) Young Women*, published on the eve of the 1830 Swing riots. Cobbett consistently advises his interlocutor to live as an independent, self-determining being. In his *Advice*, the figure of the "slave" takes form as the opposite to this being. A slave, for Cobbett, is the condition that results from abject poverty – "bare bones and rags" – and especially the lack of owning property in one's own labour. "He who lives upon anything except his own labour", claims Cobbett, must rely upon servility for survival; and servility breeds "idleness". To be a slave, then, is to inhabit a condition that robs the human of his moral character. Slaves, argues Cobbett (1829: 144), "are always lazy and saucy; nothing but the lash will extort from them either labour or respectful deportment". Slaves are also "frequently well fed and well clad" but only on condition that they "dare not speak; they dare not be suspected to think differently from their masters" even if they are in possession of "superior understanding". Such a state of "idleness with slavery", deems Cobbett, is "fit only for the refuse of nature ... the unhappy creatures whom nature has marked out for degradation" (Cobbett 1829: 15, 55, 344). The slave is constitutively undeserving.

In this line of argumentation, Cobbett presents slavery less as an external imposition and more as a choice determined by character. To be fed and kept healthy by the will of another is to make oneself a "white slave". Let this peculiar kind of slave, spits Cobbett, "no longer affect to commiserate the state of his sleek and fat brethren in Barbadoes and Jamaica; let him hasten to mix the hair with the wool, to blend the white with the black, and to lose the memory of his origin amidst a dingy generation" (Cobbett 1829: 350). To be clear, Cobbett's "white slave" is neither a slave under commercial law nor Black; analogue is not equivalence. Instead, through analogical miscegenation, Cobbett makes the English subject invest himself with the undeserving characteristics of the Black slave. To be a slave and English is to be blackened. To be blackened is to sully the English genus, its patriarchal inheritance and its common law traditions.

Through the slave analogy, Cobbett racializes the undeserving poor of England.

Cobbett's decision to present blackening in his *Advice* as a voluntary procedure is strange considering his focus elsewhere on the imposition of slavery on the English poor. This, though, was a rhetorical device, with Cobbett attempting to press a political point. For if the slave stands in all its horror as the abrogation of morality, of independence, of the English genus itself, then who would possibly dare to *force* enslavement upon Englishmen? Cobbett accused those who wished to reform the poor laws of pursuing precisely such a heinous act.

In *Advice*, Cobbett provides a genealogy of the poor laws from ancient common law to church canons and finally to its return as acts of parliament in the Elizabethan era. Cobbett thereby renders seminal to English tradition not simply parliamentary sovereignty but also the "legal and secure provision for the poor, so that no person, however aged, infirm, unfortunate, or destitute, should suffer from want" (Cobbett 1829: 14–15). In other words, the poor laws cannot be considered a mere "gift to the working people", as suggested by "greedy landowners"; they encode, rather, the fundamental "right of the [English] poor" to be protected against destitution (Cobbett 1829: 3, 16). Crucially, because their governance is localized at the parish level, the poor laws, for Cobbett, strengthen the paternalistic hierarchies of the "little platoons". With this argumentation, he renders the provision of poor relief organic to the English genus as a supportive structure for the maintenance of orderly independence. If slavery promotes undeserving characteristics, the poor laws reinforce deserving ones. For this reason, the English rural labourer, in Cobbett's opinion, should be considered:

> the most orderly, the most independent, yet the most obedient; the best fed and the best clad, and, at the same time, the most industrious, and most adroit working people that ever lived upon the face of the earth, being, along with these qualities, the best parents, the best children, the most faithful servants, the most respectful in their demeanour towards superiors, that ever formed a part of any civil community.　　　　　　　　　　　　　(Cobbett 1872: 3)

To better understand why Cobbett believes that poor law reform will turn free and orderly Englishmen into slaves we must pay attention to a certain thread of reasoning in his *Advice*. Cobbett argues that under slavery it is not the "flesh and blood and bones" that are bought and sold but the "labour of man". In the case of the "Black slave-trade" specifically, it is even "an advantage to the slave to be private property" because "the owner has then a clear and powerful interest in the preservation of [the slave's] life, health and strength" and so the master will provide adequately for his basic needs. By contrast, "public property is never so well taken care of as private property; and this, too, on the maxim, that 'that which is every body's business is nobody's business'" (Cobbett 1829: 345).

A number of elements comprise this argument which are worth highlighting. First, Cobbett wrongly codes the status of enslaved Africans through common law, not commercial law. This is a cru-cial – perhaps intentional – slippage. In common law, labour power might be "commodified", i.e. bought and sold, albeit as part of a rela-tion of servitude; yet the person cannot be sold; while in commercial law it is the labour *and* flesh, blood and bones that are commodified. Second, Cobbett softens Atlantic slavery further by reciting pro-slavery propaganda that enslaved Africans are well kept by a pater-nalistic master (Cobbett 1829: 345). It should be noted that this was always a fallacious claim. Only in the South of the United States – and only after a certain period – did policy shift towards "breeding" a population of enslaved Africans, and then only by nefarious means most of which could hardly be called paternalistic. In most other plantation economies across the Americas such populations were sustained only by buying in new bodies.

Through these faulty elements, Cobbett contrasted the com-fortable "private" nature of African enslavement with the far more "uncaring public" nature of enslavement, which poor law reforms would promote. Therefore, it is by presenting the English poor as the real victims of slavery, and hence deserving of poor relief rather than discipline and punishment, that Cobbett became a key sym-pathizer of the Swing riots of 1830. Accounting for the riots and uprisings, Cobbett argued that rural labourers were being reduced to "land slaves".

But what was so worrisome for Cobbett about the proposed reforms to poor relief? The 1834 Poor Law Amendment Act abolished outdoor poor relief to able-bodied men and their dependents who, if they lacked work, were instead forced into workhouses. Concomitantly, the living conditions of those who occupied the workhouse were kept below the poorest of "free" labourers so that only truly destitute persons would voluntarily enter. In this way, the workhouse threatened to break the patriarchal order and its paternalistic hierarchy.

Often located far from home, Cobbett (1872: 17) argued that the workhouse had the effect of separating "man and wife completely" as well as "the children from the parents". Stripping away the protective paternalistic hierarchies of the "little platoons", Cobbett claimed that the workhouse effected a "public" slavery worse than the "private" slavery of the Caribbean by inducing what would later be called a "social death". What is more, Cobbett analogized this death as a blackening of the rural labourer: "[upon their demise] the keeper of the workhouse who may be a negro-driver from JAMAICA, or even a NEGRO, [will] dispose of the body to the cutters up, seeing that it cannot be claimed by the kindred of the deceased" (Cobbett 1872: 17). In Cobbett's estimation, then, the poor law reforms – especially (but not only) the compulsion to enter the workhouse – would turn deserving English poor into blackened slaves and transform the rural idyll into a plantation more despotic than the Caribbean.

What, then, of the authors of poor law reform? How did they conceive of the distinction between the deserving and the undeserving poor? As Peter Mandler (1990) has argued, most of the commissioners' intellectual dispositions had been formed through a combination of natural theology and political economy. They accepted that the marketization of agriculture was a process that could not be stopped. Yet they also determined that the existing patriarchal order had to be force-fitted into the new conditions. For these conservatives (as they mostly were) progress was not determined by material comfort but by higher levels of virtue. In order to advance this providential movement, deserving characteristics had to be rewarded and undeserving ones punished.

Hence, when it came to the poor laws the commissioners were mostly convinced that the relief that paupers received must not make them more comfortable than independent labourers; the going-rate for wages would determine the rate of poor relief. And if the unwise and careless application of paternalism had heretofore produced this destabilizing state of affairs, the market had to be relied on as a corrective influence that underwrote political order. In fine, the natural system of just desserts had to be turned into an instructive – if painful – resource for developing a virtuous character fit for commercial society. That was the purpose of poor law reform, made all the more pressing by the Swing riots and uprisings of 1830.

However, the report of the Royal Commission was written at a time when domestic legislation in general was heavily influenced by the politics of empire. Close to home, the Irish Repeal Association attempted to rescind the Act of Union. Meanwhile, parliamentary debates over the poor law resonated across the empire and especially in its settler colonies such as Cape Colony and Canada (see Magubane 2004: 51–2; O'Connell 2009a). But of overriding importance was the issue of legal emancipation. The momentous Baptist War of 1831 in Jamaica, led by Sam Sharpe, only emboldened abolitionists to argue for the urgency of their cause (see Taylor 2003). The work of the Commission was largely contemporaneous to the Select Committee on the Extinction of Slavery and both projects shared an imperial and paternalistic framework of "improvement" (see especially O'Connell 2009b).

The key commissioners, such as Nassau William Senior (the first university chair of political economy in Britain), wrote much of their report prior to the collection of evidence. Interestingly, the documented evidence is often at odds with the arguments of the commissioners. Nonetheless, both evidence and argument demonstrate how the racialization of deserving/undeserving characteristics by way of the slave analogy was not idiosyncratic to Cobbett but widely shared amongst England's elites – provincial and metropolitan. Let us first engage with some of the collected evidence.

It is notable that the dispossession of labourers' access to land was often likened to enslavement. "We can do little or nothing to prevent pauperism", noted one member of a propertied family: "the farmers will have it; they prefer that the labourers should be slaves" (House of Commons 1834: 35). Many witnesses also disapproved of any changes to poor relief that might undermine the independence of the rural labourer. One Thomas Batchelor from Lidlington articulated the effect of such changes as "transferring something very much like West Indian slavery into English villages; viz, compulsory labour, enforced by fines and penalties, instead of the Negro-driver's whip"

(House of Commons 1834: Appendix B, 5a). Thomas Saunders from Allhallows the Great described any compulsion to enter the workhouse as "tending to that species of slavery which is much decried in our colonies, without possessing its only redeeming quality, viz. that the master has the greatest interest in the life and health of his slave" (House of Commons 1834: Appendix B, 110). Considering the integrity of the poor man's patriarchal authority, some magistrates compared the parish apprentice – usually a child bound at nine years of age without consent from parents – to "a slave attached to the soil" and often "treated worse than slaves" (House of Commons 1834: Appendix A, 430).

Crucially, some commentators drew alarm towards the potential response by the rural labourer to increased poverty and dependence. Robert Bevan, magistrate at Bury St. Edmunds, described such a labourer as "a mean discontented slave, ready to cut his master's throat" (House of Commons 1834: Appendix C, 456). One respondent at Whitburn contextualized the matter in light of the Swing riots, which he directly connected to the Baptist War in Jamaica: "The destruction of the property of the Slave-holder [in the South of England], as in the West Indies, was, and ever will be, the inevitable result, soon or late of man's inhumanity to man" (House of Commons 1834: Appendix B, 165). Notable, here, are echoes of Burke, Brougham and Cobbett's framing of the meaning of the French Revolution through the fear of the Haitian Revolution, now sounding an alarm over Captain Swing.

The commissioner's actual report shared the analogical logic of Cobbett's writings, and especially the pro-slavery propaganda concerning the paternalistic master and the well-fed slave. Echoing Cobbett's normative distinction between the private slavery of the Caribbean and the public slavery of rural England, the report opined that "the slave at his sale has at least the satisfaction of knowing that success in the biddings consists inobtaining him: the pauper at the appeal knows very well that the common objects of the litigating parties is to reject him" (House of Commons 1834: Appendix C, 551). Resonant, again, with Cobbett's definition of slavery, the report described the effect on the character of the labourer thus:

> The constant war which the pauper has to wage with all
> who employ or pay him, is destructive to his honesty and

his temper; as his subsistence does not depend on his exertions, he loses all that sweetens labour, its association with reward, and gets through his work, such as it is, with the reluctance of a slave. (House of Commons 1834: 49)

Despite the shared logic, the commissioner's argument was the antithesis of Cobbett's: it was the existing poor laws that had already fostered undeserving characteristics amongst the rural population. Poor relief, argued the report, tended to improve the condition of the pauper over that of the independent labourer such that relief became "a bounty on indolence and vice" (House of Commons 1834: 28). Overall, while the application for parochial aid was at one time considered by the poor themselves to be "very discreditable" presently the poor had lost their "conscious independence" and had instead become "the slaves of pauperism" (House of Commons 1834: Appendix C, 20). Incidentally, Nassau William Senior repeated this argument seven years later in a reflective note for the *Edinburgh Review*. There he argued that the prior practice of providing poor relief to the labourer and his family at home (rather than in the workhouse),

placed [him] in the condition, physically and morally, of a slave – confined to his parish, maintained according to his wants, not to the value of his services, restrained from misconduct by no fear of loss, and therefore stimulated to activity and industry by no hope of reward.
(Levy 2002: 54 note 28)

In sum, opponents against and supporters for poor law reform both racialized the distinction between the deserving and the undeserving poor via the slave analogy. Where they differed was with regards to the effect of the *existing* poor laws on the character of the rural labourer. Cobbett argued that these laws had up to that point provided for the orderly independence of the poor man, and that the increased disciplining of the rural poor in line with market interests would destroy such deserving qualities and enslave the rural population. Alternatively, the Royal Commission argued that existing poor relief had already degenerated the character of the rural labourer to such an extent that they acted as slaves. No matter how painful, reform was required, if needs be by utilizing the logic of the market, in order to cultivate their deserving characteristics.

CONCLUSION

Most of the politicians, judges, power-brokers and intellectuals that I have recounted in this chapter were concerned primarily with the problem of political order presented by the growing number of "masterless men" created by enclosures, the work-house and revolution. Concerned with maintaining order in dis-orderly times, the racialization of the distinction between the deserving and the undeserving poor was made in the service of political domination. This was just as true of abolitionists in so far as they distrusted the anarchical propensity of enslaved Africans. It was even true of the defender of the English rural poor, William Cobbett, in so far as his defence sought to protect the English genus from being blackened.

While they differed significantly on the nature of the poor laws, tellingly, both Cobbett and the Commission racialized those who were falling into pauperism or had become paupers. Of course, these English poor were never legally coded as Black in the same way that commercial law encoded the enslaved African as a commodity. Yet, in the arguments on both sides, it seemed as if one section of the English poor had lost – or were threatened with losing – their fili-ation to the English genus. Having become undeserving, whether wilfully or unjustly, they were not considered to be indigenously white. Whether they deserved it or not, they were blackened. This racialization did not emerge purely out of poor law debates, but out of the integration of these debates into broader problems of colonial rule, chief of which being the nature and consequences of abolition.

There are two points I wish to end this chapter with. First, in the era of abolition and poor law reform, elite commentators conceived of the moral worth and measured the political agency of the poor through a colonial cartography that exceeded the British Isles. If different laws pertained in England and the Caribbean, the problem space of the undeserving poor conjoined colony and metropole. Slavery and the figure of the Black slave were intimately known to those who pondered the fate of the English poor in an era of agricultural marketization and rural change.

Second, poor law reform in many ways marked a new era wherein the cottage economy and parish community were slowly disassembled by industry and urbanization. We shall turn to these new processes in the next chapter. But few commentators identified an indigenous working class making the transition from an old to a new world. Rather, they assayed the poor as a racialized and morally bifurcated agglomeration: the deserving poor – English; and the undeserving poor (by choice or imposition), who, if not Black, were certainly not white and had perhaps even lost their English filiation.

CHAPTER 3

ANGLO-SAXON EMPIRE AND THE RESIDUUM

INTRODUCTION

How did the changing contours of British empire affect the racialization of the undeserving poor? And how did the changing demographic of England's own working poor impact the integrity of empire? In the last chapter I detailed the ways in which the deserving/ undeserving distinction was formatively racialized. In this chapter I interrogate the shifting racialization of this distinction beyond the classic concern for the parish poor as Victorian Britain's imperial project responded to several significant challenges.

In the first part of the chapter I turn to the post-emancipation era and the way in which the political franchise in Britain was framed by the politics of abolition and empire. I begin by interrogating the humanitarianism that abolition sired, which presented empire as one human family. Questions remained as to whether the now-freed Black man could cultivate deserving characteristics or would instead be unable to shirk the undeserving essence of the slave. I then examine the 1865 Morant Bay uprising in Jamaica and its pivotal influence in undoing the humanitarianism that conceived of empire as a human family. I argue that the fallout from Morant Bay decisively re-racialized the imperial family. An Anglo-Saxon family was now envisioned, stretching from metropole to settler-colonies, which faced an agglomeration of non-white colonial subject populations that required discipline. I then make sense of the 1867 Reform Act by reference to these racial politics. The Act enfranchised a portion of the working class into the English genus and hence into the Anglo-Saxon family. In this double movement, the "deserving" took on a new form: skilled and settled working men were re-racialized as an Anglo-Saxon constituency.

What of the undeserving English poor? In the second part of the chapter I address this question. From the 1840s onwards, considerations shifted geographically to focus upon urban landscapes, especially the slums of London. The populations that inhabited these areas – part-vagrant, casual and unskilled workers – were given a new name – the residuum, or "left behind". I consider how the residuum was racialized by analogy to savages and slaves. But I also track how the problem of the residuum was increasingly parsed through the race science of eugenics. I then explore interventionist policies in the areas of family life, reproduction, hygiene and employment, all of which sought to quarantine the enfranchised working "stock" from the undeserving residuum. However, I show that the eugenicist project to preserve good racial stock was bound up in the need to preserve the integrity of British empire in an era of increased inter-imperial competition. The difficulties of defending British possessions, demonstrated by the Boer War, provided the eugenics project an urgent gravitas. I finish by charting how all this led to the first National Insurance Act of 1911.

In this chapter I introduce some more key concepts to the argument. The English genus takes on an imperial formation as the "Anglo-Saxon family". The slave analogy, although not disappearing, becomes in large part displaced by the turn towards eugenics as a science of race. The undeserving poor, heretofore having a rural and/or parish provenance, now become primarily an urban problem to be known as the "residuum".

EMANCIPATION AND THE MAKING OF THE ANGLO-SAXON FAMILY

Missionary philanthropy had come to the fore in the moral space created by late eighteenth-century abolitionism. Its basic aim, spiritual conversion, was pursued, in England, by a middle class who often functioned as itinerant missionaries. During the revolutionary period, missionary philanthropy moved overseas, targeting not just white settlers but also "natives" (see especially Thorne 1997). After the final legal emancipation of enslaved Africans in 1838, abolitionism decisively morphed into an imperial humanitarian project, determined to save the inhabitants of Africa (especially), Asia and Oceania from the despotism of British "enslavers" and commercial interests (see Heartfield 2015). The missionary impetus to convert souls remained implicated in this project and led to an obsession with "heathenism" and its social malignancies. These obsessions returned to England via various travel exhibitions, lectures, speaker meetings and missionary texts (see Huzzey 2012). The abolitionist conception of the Black slave continued to inform humanitarian approaches to the plight of continental Africans well into the mid-Victorian era due to the fact that legal emancipation did not occur in the United States until 1865 (Lorimer 1978: 70).

For all these reasons abolitionism remained even in the post-abolition era as a central moral framework through which middle-class reformers classified the colonial native and home poor for various social interventions (Thorne 1997: 248–9; Magubane 2004: 42, 47–8; Lorimer 1978: 71). I now want to consider four coordinates of this abolitionist disposition.

First, amongst abolitionists, the "negro" was widely considered to be human and not an animal or a thing. Such was the claim of the Ethnological Society of London, which emerged in 1843 from the Aborigines' Protection Society, itself borne out of the abolition movement as empire widened its contours. Fittingly, ethnologists understood their object of inquiry to be the family of humanity. Edward Tylor, the first anthropologist to hold a chair in British academia, was influenced by this intellectual tradition. In 1871 he no doubt made William Cobbett turn in his grave when he boldly stated that, when it came to human evolution, "we may draw a picture where there shall be scarce a hand's breadth difference between an English ploughman and a negro of Central Africa" (Tylor 1920: 7).

Second, though, opposition to such claims of racial equality, although in the minority, persisted. Most famous were the polemics of philosopher Thomas Carlyle. Commenting on the aftermath of emancipation, and writing in the tradition of Edmund Burke, Carlyle argued that the negro had no ability to adjust his savage calculus to the virtuous laws of "supply and demand" which free labour had to abide by. Setting the negro free therefore courted, in Carlyle's words, "Black anarchy and social death" for the white race. It is notable that Carlyle used the same terminology as William Cobbett when he had warned of the despoiling of the English genus that would take place with poor law reform. Central to Carlyle's position was a defence of the white patriarchal order from being sullied by the social or reproductive inter-mixing of races and the "unnameable abortions" and "wide-coiled monstrosities" that would eventuate (Carlyle 1899: 529–32).

Third, even those who espoused racial equality shared something with Carlyle, and that was a commitment to the idea of civilizational hierarchy. Consider the 1833 Abolition of Slavery Act, which did not straightforwardly free the enslaved, but rather transmuted their chattel status to that of apprenticeship. Evident in this Act is a generalized doubt of the capacity of enslaved Africans to become orderly-and-free labourers without guidance from their white Christian patrons (see Drescher 1981: 17–18; O'Connell 2009b). This sentiment was especially pronounced in Harriet Beecher Stowe's incredibly popular American novel *Uncle Tom's Cabin*. Some even read into this story the requirement for the white English Christian to paternalistically enfold the junior negro Christian into his house-hold. Take, for instance, the suggestions of the author of *Uncle Tom's Cabin Almanack*: "Admit a negro family into your home; treat them in a Christian spirit, let them eat your bread and drink of your cup, you can no longer doubt of their essential equality with yourself" (Lorimer 1978: 74–5).

Fourth, advocates of the old Factory Movement continued to call out the hypocrisy of middle-class philanthropy and sympa-thies expressed towards distant Black peoples living across the oceans. *Reynolds's Newspaper*, the self-styled "leading working man's newspaper", regularly castigated middle-class do-gooders for failing to address the conditions suffered by their own immediate subordinates: "Which is the better lot of the two – that of the slave embellished with the name of freeman [the English worker], or that of the slave who is openly and honestly called a slave [the American negro]?" (*Reynolds's Newspaper* 1850).

Pulling these four strands together we might say that even after emancipation the *de jure* equality of the negro could never be abso-lutely proclaimed in Britain absent of qualifications of hierarchy, pater-nalism and racial affiliation (see in general Huzzey 2012). It should be no surprise, then, that turns of fate could quickly shift sentiments amongst humanitarians away from the hallowed ground of equality. This was to be the precise effect of the 1865 Morant Bay uprising in Jamaica.

The economy of post-emancipation Jamaica was marked by growing poverty and unemployment for the Black majority. Despite being a principle desire of the population, no major land redistribution had been undertaken after 1838, and reparations for slavery were only delivered to slaveholders for loss of their "property". As the sugar industry continued to decline, the prevalence of absenteeism amongst remaining landlords meant that the island's affairs were administered by a white managerial class. Although the vote was opened to Black and mulatto subjects from 1840, property qualifications ensured that in practice Jamaican government remained an instrument of the plantocracy. Representing this interest in Britain, the West Indian lobby remained somewhat influential in parliament, albeit less to do with its economic importance and more to do with the island's strategic value in checking American expansion into the Caribbean (Smith 1994: 132–3).

In the early 1860s a series of petitions were made by various groups in Jamaica urging for the alleviation of grinding poverty and pointing to the difficulties in obtaining justice through the local courts. Dr Edward Underhill, an English Baptist minister who had recently visited Jamaica, passed on these concerns to his acquaintance Edward Cardwell, then secretary of state for the colonies. Cardwell subsequently passed Underhill's letter to Edward John Eyre, the colonial governor of Jamaica. Underhill attributed the deterioration of living conditions to the policies of the Jamaican Assembly and the Colonial Office in London (Holt 1992: 270). Eyre's response, however, attributed the cause of decline to Black pathologies. In Eyre's judgement, which matched Carlyle's invective, Black people had not been able to cultivate deserving characteristics upon being freed and had retained their "natural disposition to indolence and inactivity" (Winter 2016).

Officially, Eyre's position won out. Henry Taylor, a veteran colonial officer, drafted the queen's response to the petitions. Her Jamaican subjects were instructed to work for wages "not uncertainly, or capriciously, but steadily and continually"; for only by "adding prudence to industry" could they meet their needs (Holt 1992: 277–8). Such a patronising response ultimately resulted in October 1865 with an uprising of Black peasantry in St Thomas parish, its epicentre being Morant Bay. Although the insurrectionists embarked on minimal violence as they temporarily took over the parish, Eyre authored an entirely disproportionate response that included the indiscriminate slaughter of hundreds and the arrest and execution of hundreds more without trial. Responsibility for the uprising was placed upon two prime suspects – a Black Baptist deacon named Paul Bogle and a former member of the House of Assembly and fellow Black Baptist, George William Gordon. Eyre ensured that both were executed.

The uprising and especially Eyre's bloodthirsty response produced a major crisis of conscience in Britain's political and polite society. Anti-Eyre demonstrations began in Britain in November and a coalition of religious and intellectual personalities formed the Jamaica Committee one month later with a mission to bring Eyre to justice. The Committee's membership included notables such as John Stuart Mill, Charles Darwin, John Bright MP, Herbert Spencer, John Ludlow (leader of the Christian socialists) and Charles Buxton, son of Thomas Buxton, founder of the Anti-Slavery Society.

The committee formed to defend Eyre included just as many notables, such as Charles Dickens, John Ruskin and Charles Kingsley (another Christian socialist). Eyre's defenders worked in the tradition laid out by Burke, Cobbett and Carlyle, the latter being an active supporter of the embattled colonial governor. Key to their defence was the claim that Morant Bay demonstrated the unchangeable and undeserving character of the negro, whose freedom had only provided a licence for anarchy (see Huzzey 2012: 811). In this regard, the spectre of the Haitian Revolution haunted Eyre's supporters. Eyre himself had justified the extremity of his response to the uprising by claiming that the island was in danger of becoming "a second Haiti" (Winter 2016). In November, *The Times* newspaper attributed the cause of the uprising to agitators from Haiti who had "broken out" the nature of "Africa", "hitherto dormant" in the lazy Jamaican (Erickson 1959: 111).

Crucially, the contention over Eyre's response to the Morant Bay uprising brought into sharp relief a deep fissure that had begun to grow in the governance of Britain's empire. From the 1850s onwards, parliament debated the growing autonomy of white settler colonies and how this process might logically conclude (Eldridge 1973: 30–2).

Concomitantly, by the 1860s, the filial lines of "Englishness" had become rearticulated in a diasporic framing of belonging, owing much to the proclivities of colonial settler elites. At this point, the English genus took on a decisively imperial constitution through the label "Anglo-Saxon" (see for example Young 2008: 179–81).

In 1868, Charles Dilke published *Greater Britain* wherein he influentially argued for a federation of racially distinct and civilizationally superior "Anglo-Saxon" polities (Dilke 1869: 346–7; see in general Bell 2007). Dilke's text is testament to the ascendency of the presumption that white and non-white parts of the British empire deserved different levels of autonomy, self-government and equality (see Madden 1979). Outside of the Anglo-Saxon community of equals, Dilke and others expected that non-white colonies and the Indian empire would still be governed through a hierarchical civilizing mission that, only in the long run, might eventually plant "free institutions among the dark-skinned races of the world" (Dilke 1869: 348; see also Eldridge 1973: 49). In any case, the pursuit of this civilizing mission had been brought into question by a series of "native" uprisings that required military responses – in Cape Colony against Khoi Khoi and Xhosa in the early 1850s, in India against the Sepoys in 1857, in 1860 against Māori in New Zealand, in 1863 against Ashanti in the Gold Coast, then in Jamaica against Bogle and his followers in 1865.

Much closer to home, and occurring just after Morant Bay, the Fenian uprising in Ireland provoked analogies regarding the disorderly nature of Irish and Black. The Earl of Kimberley, Lord Lieutenant of Ireland at the time, isolated the cause of the problem in the "character of the Irish race" and especially their inclination towards vulgarity, violence and fickleness. Kimberley even considered there to be strong parallels between negros and Irish (Smith 1994: 139). The racial character of the Irish had also been one of Carlyle's obsessions. Although Carlyle strongly favoured British union, he enjoyed a good relationship with some of the Young Irelanders who worked towards national independence and whom he met and conversed with in 1846. His *Discourse on the Nigger Question* was, in fact, written after a second tour of Ireland in 1949.

Carlyle considered Black peoples to be incapable of the rationality required to live as free labourers. But his *Discourse* was also designed to critique – in a manner akin to Cobbett – the marketization of agriculture as well as the "dismal science" that promoted it, i.e. political economy. For this double-task, Carlyle presented the future of the free Caribbean as that suffered by Ireland – starvation: "To have 'emancipated' the West Indies into a Black Ireland" (Carlyle 1899). Certainly, Carlyle racialized the Irish as Celtic and thus inferior to the civilized Anglo-Saxon. (Conveniently, he tied his own Scottish ancestry to Anglo-Saxon settlers.) Nevertheless, he judged the Celt to be more redeemable than the Black. For Carlyle, Black was a fixed position, constituted in slavery, and formative of undeserving characteristics (see also Dugger 2006). But because Carlyle blackened the Celt, there was a small possibility of that race's redemption that was not granted to the Black.

Suspicion of the resolutely undeserving nature of Black people provides a clue as to why, while Ireland was a far closer problem of geopolitical order for the British empire, it did not emote the kind of response reserved for Morant Bay. In November 1865, *The Times* made an especially telling argument. The editorial argued that Morant Bay disproportionately evoked disappointment and damaged Britain's pride. "Jamaica is our pet institution", argued the paper, "and its inhabitants are our spoilt children" (Holt 1992: 77). As I have noted, the grammar of imperial humanitarianism was fundamentally abolitionist and thus predicated upon a paradoxical support of both human equality and civilizational hierarchy. Because abolitionism in Britain enjoyed a historically special relationship to the Caribbean, the Morant Bay uprising was proof to many that the great abolitionist experiment to paternalistically cultivate the ex-slave into a subject deserving of freedom had failed (see in general Moore & Johnson 2004). If humanity was a family organized through racial hierarchy, its youngest children had proved wayward in the extreme. Perhaps blackness was unredeemable, after all.

To understand how such sentiments had gained political salience we must turn to the aims of the Jamaica Committee. Soon after the uprising, Eyre had orchestrated the dissolution of the House of Assembly leading to a change in the status of Jamaica from a self-governing entity to a Crown Colony with an appointed legislature. One of the last acts of the House, however, was to sanction the state of martial law and indemnify all actions undertaken in the putting down of the uprising. In their capacity as private citizens, the Jamaica Committee sought to bring Eyre to trial for murder and subsequently to try the ex-governor for illegally proclaiming martial law and hence committing acts of oppression against British subjects. In other words, the Committee was most concerned with the procedural element of Eyre's actions and the degree to which they undermined rule of law (see especially Winter 2016).

Furthermore, the Committee's case unavoidably drew attention to the fact that British jurisprudence had heretofore developed no clear conceptualization of a "state of siege". Whilst rule over Ireland in the nineteenth century had occasionally required temporary and special legislation, it was in the overseas empire that martial law was most regularly proclaimed and enacted. What made martial law a grave challenge to common law was the fact that, under such circumstances, only the military could determine to resume rule of law. Strictly dire necessity therefore warranted such a turn of events. In the absence of necessity, argued the Jamaica Committee, martial law threatened the common law bedrock of British freedoms (Townshend 1982). Yet precisely by this logic, the Committee's argument invalidated the regularity with which martial law was invoked as a core element of colonial rule (Fraser 2011: 21). In short, the Committee's argument, taken to its jurisprudential conclusion, threatened to unravel empire. It could not be allowed to stand.

Crucially, the Committee's critique of martial law invoked the racialized constitution of Britain's imperial polity. For at the centre of their case lay the wrong that Eyre had committed *not* against the de facto leader of the uprising, Paul Bogle, but against George William Gordon. In order to execute Gordon, Eyre had him physically removed from Kingston, which was still under civil law, and transported to Morant Bay where martial law was in effect. Above all, Gordon was a mulatto. His mother had been enslaved; his white father had left an inheritance with which the son was at times able to leverage positions in the Jamaican legislature. Miscegenation, of course, had always been a vexed affair under slavery. But by the 1860s, "race mixing" deeply troubled the increasingly ambivalent relationship between the Anglo-Saxon family and the non-white subjects of empire (Watson 1997). Implicit in the debate over Eyre, then, was a question regarding filiation: were mulatto men competent enough to partake of the white patriarchal order, or were they too tainted with Black anarchy?

There existed a longstanding opinion that mulattos distinguished themselves through their white heritage. For example, commenting upon George Harris, her mulatto character in *Uncle Tom's Cabin*, Harriet Beecher Stowe mused that "half-breeds often inherit, to a great degree, the traits of their white ancestors" (Lorimer 1978: 85). Discussions around Gordon's parentage considered such racial proximity, with some reporting his "deferential regard" to his father, while Eyre insisted that "all feelings of delicacy towards Gordon's family must subside" (Watson 1997). John Stuart Mill cleaved to the former position in so far as he clearly considered Gordon's fate to be of *universal* concern. On behalf of the Jamaica Committee, Mill described the wrong done as "the illegal execution of a British subject" and called for the "obligation of justice and humanity towards all races beneath the Queen's sway" (Winter 2016). In this way, Mill presented empire as one human (if hierarchically ordered) family. Alternatively, John Tyndall, physicist and Eyre supporter, cleaved to the latter position: "we do not hold an Englishman and a Jamaica negro to be convertible terms, nor do we think that the cause of human liberty will be promoted by any attempt to make them so" (Winter 2016). For Tyndall, the rights pertaining to empire's subjects were racially distinct.

The Jamaica Committee lost their legal battles. But in this respect, they unintentionally settled the precedent that colonial subjects *could* suffer legislation that common law in England would not allow (see Handford 2008). What is more, the acceptance of Gordon's fate cemented a racialized differentiation of imperial possessions and populations. Since the first part of the eighteenth century, Jamaica had been formally categorized as a "settled" colony yet, unlike the Australian colonies, New Zealand and Canada, one in which the majority was composed of a Black population. However, the first governor of Jamaica as a Crown Colony, John Peter Grant, believed that self-governance was dependent upon racial qualities and that Jamaica's population were "thoroughly ill-suited" to such a system being that they exhibited "not one Anglo-Saxon characteristic" (Smith 1994: 140). The general principle was summed up, soon after the Eyre affair, by Arthur Mills, barrister, MP and expert on colonial systems of governance. Mills conceded that it was "hopeless to transplant institutions slowly grown in Europe to uncongenial places or people", and that the negro was the "the most conspicuous example" of the "stationary races" (Smith 1994: 140).

And so, as the nineteenth century progressed, the abolitionist disposition shifted. The idea of imperial humanity being one family lost integrity to the idea of a discretely Anglo-Saxon family. Anglo-Saxon settler colonies received more of the rights of governance enjoyed by Britain's own citizens and they shared in – at times led – franchise reforms. In distinction to this Anglo-Saxon family, other non-white colonies were placed on a different developmental trajectory. Their populations, being governed by London-centred autocracies backed by military might, benefited little from political reforms even if they were also subjects to the same crown (Bolt 1971: 90–1; Mantena 2008: 122; Fraser 2011: 23).

As the fallout from Morant Bay made its way through the halls of parliament, so did legislation intent on expanding suffrage in England. For some years the Chartist movement had built a popular movement across Britain for political enfranchisement. The banning of a demonstration by the Reform League in Hyde Park in 1866 led some to suggest that Eyre's treatment of Black Jamaicans through the imposition of martial law was now finding an opening in England. Certainly, the problems of empire did not influence franchise legislation with the same intimacy as had been the case in the 1830s (Middleton 2017; Smith 1994: 136; Himmelfarb 1966: 100). Nevertheless, Catherine Hall's (1994) suggestion of the entanglement of Morant Bay and franchise reform remains an astute one. For franchise reform effectively transformed those who had in the past political lexicon been considered "deserving poor" into a deserving constituency of skilled and settled workers. In the same movement, these workers were adopted into the Anglo-Saxon family at the same time as this family distanced itself from troublesome non-white colonial populations.

Although initially spearheaded by the Liberal Party, the Second Reform Act of 1867 was pushed through by Benjamin Disraeli, Chancellor of the Exchequer, under a minority Conservative government. The Act effectively doubled the English and Welsh electorate by giving the vote to male urban householders and lodgers who paid £10 rent per annum or more, as well as to agricultural landowners and tenants with small land plots. While the rent sum was vociferously debated, parliament ultimately enfranchised what, in its member's estimations, was a set of workers who demonstrated deserving characteristics: skilled and industrious, settled, small patriarchs. In making this distinction amongst workers in general, politicians were effectively following the arguments that guided popular protest. By the 1860s, many of the provincial movements that had inherited the Chartist mantle argued for enfranchisement on the basis of the contribution that specifically skilled labour made to the nation's wealth; and such skills were linked predominantly to trades that employed no women (Chase 2017: 20–1).

Regardless, significant contention surrounded the expansion of the franchise. Prominent voices expressing disquiet at the possibility that reform might break paternalistic hierarchies. Tellingly, the anarchy potentially unleashed by political equality was often apprehended through the well-worn analogy to the slave. Take, for example, a poem published in the April 1866 edition of the popular magazine *Punch*:

> We lately heard the Working Men
> Called 'fellow-creatures,' but, what then?
> Why, so'a [*sic*] the grinning African!
> (Lewis 2012: 539)

Carlyle provided the most influential and polemical rebuttal of this kind in his *Shooting Niagara*. Contextualizing the Reform Act within other notable events such as the American Civil War against slavery and the Jamaica Committee's attack on Eyre, Carlyle's chief concern – as it had been with abolition and even the Irish question – was with the disastrous effects caused by levelling the relationship between "servantship and mastership". (It will be recalled that this same issue lay behind Carlyle's disgust of the political economy.) Instead, and looking to the future, Carlyle (1867: 21) placed hope in the chivalrous and magnanimous character of the "English Nobleman".

Those who demurred from Carlyle's assessment placed their faith in the character of the working men who were to be enfranchised. John Ludlow, supporter of the Jamaica Committee and leader of the Christian Socialist Movement, addressed this issue in his *Progress of the Working Class*. Ludlow was at pains to demonstrate that working men had learnt the value of deference in their recent struggles. For evidence, he recalled a presentation made to Disraeli by G. J. Mantle, previously a vocal Chartist: "We offer to the throne the homage of our loyalty … We have as keen an appreciation of our country's honour as any other class of men ... The blood of working men, in times of trouble, has flowed as freely as that of the proudest peer of the realm" (Ludlow & Jones 1867: 285–6). But Ludlow (Ludlow & Jones 1867: 3) was also clear that he did not mean to include into this family the "poor" – those who could not maintain themselves other than by occasional efforts. Ludlow (Ludlow & Jones 1867: 252) expressly distanced the deserving working class from the "lowest classes" where the "real problem" lay in individuals and families "entangled in ... evil".

When it came to politicians, both sides of the House claimed the new deserving constituency not through the grammar of class hierarchy but, instead, of national belonging. For instance, William Gladstone, then one of the key Liberal proponents of reform, described the expanded electorate as "our fellow-subjects, our fellow-Christians, our own flesh and blood" (Himmelfarb 1966: 17). On the Conservative side, in assessing the danger of enfranchise-ment, Disraeli counted upon the paternalistic deference that in his estimation made England "safe in the race of men who inhabit her ... [and] safe in her national character, in her fame, in the traditions of a thousand years" ("Disraeli's Speech on the Reform Bill: 15 July 1867"). This was the "one nation" principle that Disraeli introduced to conservatism, which by endorsing the skilled and settled working man, presumed to have dispensed with class conflict.

Enfranchisement into the nation also presented the issue of enfranchisement into Anglo-Saxon supremacy. For instance, des-pite working on his book with Lloyd Jones, an Anglo-Irish socialist, Ludlow's position distanced English labour organization from its historical entanglement with Irish radicalism via Chartism. In this sense, Ludlow's confirmation of working-class loyalty inevitably courted anti-Irish sentiment that was so popular in the English press. Ludlow's pledge of loyalty can be contrasted to the radicalism of tex-tile labourers in Manchester, many of whom had recently agitated against the Southern interest in the American Civil War despite the detrimental impact of a cotton embargo on their livelihoods. The Morant Bay episode divided empire's humanity; yet Manchester workers seemed to think that humanity's fate was shared: "when the slave ceases to be and becomes an enfranchised free man", argued one of these agitators, "[then] the British workman's claim may be listened to" (cited in Rice 2010: 97).

The 1867 Act wedded the deserving characteristics heretofore signalled in poor law debates to a respectable constituency of working men (Hall 1994). This constituency, with its adherence to orderly independence, was claimed by conservatives, liberals and Christian socialists on behalf of the English genus. What defined this new constituency of working men was not class – and the disorderly struggles heretofore associated with labour organization – but rather the national family. Meanwhile, the English genus had been geopolitically expanded into an Anglo-Saxon formation. Morant Bay confirmed the abolition experiment to be a failure. Its fallout affirmed the re-racialization of the imperial family into an Anglo-Saxon family hierarchically differentiated from non-white colonial subjects.

From this viewpoint, as the deserving English working man became enfranchised they also became racialized as Anglo-Saxon. It is telling, in this respect, that from the 1860s onwards, and except for the case of worker's abolitionism, the public discussion over the meaning of citizenship focused less on the rights of the propertied individual and more upon the duties owed by the enfranchised to community, nation and empire (McClelland & Rose 2006: 84). In sum, the making of a "working class" constituency was firmly an act of political domination, with elements of the workers' movement complicit in its conscription.

THE EUGENICIST DEFENCE OF THE ANGLO-SAXON FAMILY

The question remains, though, as to the position of England's undeserving poor in this bifurcated empire. In the 1830s debates over poor law reform, those considered undeserving – by choice or imposition – were blackened via the slave analogy. Those debates focused upon the rural parish, artisan and agricultural worker. By the 1840s, attention had shifted towards the urban setting and industrial occupations. Yet even as it shifted away from the classic parish poor, the deserving/undeserving distinction remained racialized. By the 1850s, for instance, mining had come to be classified as the occupation of a race apart. Arthur Munby, barrister and famous diarist, fetishized the English colliery women – considered amongst the lowest occupation – by sketching them as black, heavy-framed, men (MacClintock 1995: 108, 114–15).

Despite its relative lack of industry *vis-à-vis* Birmingham and Manchester, London emerged as a prime location for investigating the undeserving poor. Perhaps the predominant reason for this focus is due to the predilections of London's middle classes who undertook ethnographic investigations. Many sought to replicate in their household the paternalistic hierarchies of the rural manor, even though London living stretched these hierarchies across wider affective and geographical distances (see Jones 1983). In fact, these hierarchies were also wilfully stretched beyond their past interpellations. For instance, it will be remembered that in the debates over abolition the difference between a master/servant and master/slave relationship was fundamental: the latter, unlike the former, was believed to break the paternalistic hierarchy. Notoriously, Arthur Munby married Hannah Cullwick, a housemaid resident in London, and the two secretly married; their relationship was marked by Cullwick blackening her skin and playing "slave" to Munby's "massa" (see Todd 2009). Aside from this striking instance, there is quotidian evidence to suggest that some of the urban middle classes nicknamed their servants "slaveys" (Lorimer 1978: 106).

Greater distances also affected the composition of Victorian London's working demographics, with small workshops instead of large factories predominating in its industrial topology. Hence, as the middle classes separated from workers, so did enfranchised workers divide from a vast array of semi- and unskilled labourers, many working irregularly, piecemeal or hardly at all (Jones 1983: 223). In the urban milieu, these poor who were believed to demonstrate undeserving characteristics – whether by fate or by fault – took on a new name. In 1854, Sir George Nicholls (1899: 4), a poor law commissioner appointed in the 1834 Act, spoke in the London context of a "residuum" – something that had been left behind. These "classes of men", Nicholls claimed, remained "in a condition of primitive poverty, ignorance and subjection, all the more aggravated because it can be contrasted with the higher possibilities of the civilized life". John Bright, in his arguments in parliament over the Reform Bill, also deployed the new term to identify those whom even "intelligent and honest working men" disavowed (Himmelfarb 1966: 126).

I argued above that deserving working men were enfranchised in 1867 not as a class per se, but as a national constituency and, moreover, a racialized one that could claim an Anglo-Saxon filiation.

So too did commentary on the London residuum rely not so much upon "class" distinctions but far more upon racialized distinctions. For instance, in his observations in the late 1840s, Henry Mayhew, co-founder of the satirical magazine *Punch*, noted that when it came to visiting London's working poor, it seemed "as if we were in a new land, and among another race" (1861: 233). As one *Saturday Review* essay put it in 1864, the residuum existed as a "caste apart, a race of whom we know nothing, whose lives are of quite different complexion from ours" (Lorimer 1978: 101). Take also the definition provided by Helen Bosanquet (née Dendy), leading light of the Charity Organization Society: "a race living … [with] no specialised skill … who yet have only the minimum of physical strength" and "a low order of intellect, and a degradation of the natural affections to something little better than animal instincts" (Bosanquet & Dendy 1895: 84, 89; Bosanquet 1902: 332).

Through these imagined cartographies the residuum was placed outside of – and in some ways presented as a threat to – the Anglo-Saxon family. In general, areas occupied by the residuum were regularly described in ethnographic commentaries as "wilds", "dens" and "a dark continent" populated by "wild races" and "wandering tribes" (Bonnett 1998: 322–3; Jones 1983: 183). The obsession of many such commentaries with the East End docklands is especially telling. The port areas, as evidenced in Joseph Conrad's *Heart of Darkness*, were apprehended as the "threshold space" between industrialism and empire, civilization and savagery (MacClintock 1995: 120).

The slave analogy had previously been mobilized to pursue the salvation of parish poor who were being cast into either the workhouse or the factory. The analogy accompanied the poor as they became the urban residuum. Sidney Webb, prominent intellectual of the Fabian Society to which we shall soon turn, described the hardest working and most cruelly treated labourers as "London's wage-slaves", reminiscing that "the horrors of the white slavery which made the fortunes of Lancashire have become terribly familiar to us" (Webb 1891: 73–4). Oscar Wilde's biographer, Robert Harborough Sherard (1897: 20), wrote about the "white slaves of England" and the "abominations in our midst which should make one ashamed of the name of Englishman". In a forceful jeremiad, William Booth, founder of the Salvation Army, challenged his reader to consider that a "darkest England" existed just as did a "darkest Africa", and he agitated for Christians to attend to the "colonies of heathens and savages in the heart of our capital" (Booth 1890: 11–12, 16).

But moral categorization of the urban poor was increasingly overtaken by the pursuit of a purportedly more "objective" methodology linked to the study of urban demography. Charles Booth's extremely influential and magisterial survey on *Life and Labour of the People in London* is a case in point. Categorizing residents into seven classes, Booth described the lowest parts of the residuum as "barbarians" or as living an "almost savage life" (Booth 1897: IX:421; Brown 1968: 351). Moreover, during this period the very study of race was being innovated in ways that would impact upon the assessment of the residuum and its relationship to the Anglo-Saxon family. While there are presidents dating back to the 1840s, the key intervention in the development of a "science" of race heredity was made by Francis Galton. In 1883 he introduced the term "eugenics". By the end of the decade, eugenics had become commonplace in public debate (MacKenzie 1976: 504).

Galton himself was an early proponent of the idea that urban living quickened the degeneration of a population's stock, and he utilized the categories provided in Booth's *Life and Labour of the People in London* in order to arrive at a demographic distribution of inherited civic worth (MacKenzie 1976: 513, 515). However, as Dorothy Porter (1991) argues, eugenics did not necessarily promote a Nazi-like aim of eradicating gene pools. Just as important as the extreme "positive" eugenics of this kind was a "negative" eugenics, a position that Galton progressively subscribed to (MacKenzie 1976: 512). Negatively, eugenics aimed to prevent the degeneration of stock through "social hygiene" interventions into education, health, sanitation, habitation and food (see Jones 1986).

If eugenics implied one thing, it was public intervention into the social and economic dimensions of urban living. Social Darwinism, with its partial dependence upon Malthusian logic, resonated strongly with commitments to economic laissez-faire. Alternatively, eugenicists fundamentally distrusted nature's given design. For this reason, eugenics became especially attractive to debates over poor relief, the language of which already resonated with a science of race. For example, two years before Galton coined the term, one speaker at a poor law conference claimed that vagrants were a "pedigree bred ... a race which has the very genius of not working in its bones and sinews" (Vorspan 1977: 72). Fabianism, with its project to achieve socialism through top-down, gradual and enlightened reform, also found the interventionist logic of eugenics attractive. So much so, in fact, that some Fabians such as Eden Paul confidently asserted that "unless the socialist is a eugenicist as well, the socialist state will speedily perish from racial degradation" (Paul 1984: 568; MacKenzie 1976: 507–11).

The eugenicist case for intervening into the lives of the residuum was made primarily with reference to the family and reproduction. To be fair, many eugenicists were ambivalent over the straightforward genetic inheritance of undeserving characteristics. Rather, they understood inheritance to be just as much transmitted through the intellectual aptitude of the mother and her educational level. But whether by nature or nurture or both, eugenic interventions were designed to reinforce the old patriarchal concern for moral parenting, which had been so central to the poor laws. For example, the Charity Organization Society can hardly be said to have eugenicist origins. Set up in 1869 to help identify those deserving of outdoor poor relief, the Society pioneered fine-grained case-study work into poverty stricken families. Nonetheless, charitable interventions of this kind could easily be made to serve the eugenics impulse. Later, the Society worked with the Eugenics Education Society to agitate for parliamentary reforms in mental health provision (Jones 1986: 27).

At the same time as eugenics pressed for more public intervention into family life and reproduction, debates over the prime cause of poverty – irregular or insufficient employment – mooted the necessity of national-scale interventions. James O'Grady's presidential address to the Trades Union Congress (TUC) in 1898 argued that "if ... the national prosperity depends on the well-being of the worker, the necessary corollary is that the state should care for him in sickness" (Mallalie 1950: 56). What is more, the entry into parliamentary politics by the Labour Party was accompanied by demands for a national "right to work" (see especially Hanagan 1997). Additionally, the idea that unemployment had to be addressed as an impersonal, national problem, grew in favour across the political spectrum and partially displaced the traditional focus upon moral character (see Taylor 2015).

The strongly interventionist science of eugenics was deeply implicated in the movement from provincial poor relief towards a system of national insurance and welfare, as demonstrated by the early work of perhaps the most influential British welfare reformer of the twentieth century. It was the "dysgenic effects" of the less-civilized urban industries that, in the opinion of a young William Beveridge, produced a "degenerate posterity" (Harris 2003: 104). By the 1920s, whilst Director of the London School of Economics, Beveridge was so convinced that social scientists should learn from the biological sciences that he pushed for a Department of Social Biology (see Renwick 2014).

As part of his intellectual development, Beveridge also shifted his concerns from the moral character of the unemployed towards unemployment as an impersonal "problem of industry" which required nationally coordinated – and eugenicist – policy interventions (Harris 2003: 95–7; Hanagan 1997: 466). This shift from moral to impersonal considerations carried with it the deserving/undeserving distinction. Beveridge worried that if skilled labourers lost their jobs they would have to fall back upon casual work – work that bred undeserving attributes. This degradation of work would also degenerate the English stock (Taylor 2015: 163). In many ways, Beveridge's concern for eugenics and for national regulation combined. For instance, instead of paternally addressing the unemployed man's moral character, Beveridge promoted the use of labour exchanges as an impersonal mechanism that might nonetheless discipline the work-shy (Harris 2003: 133).

When insurance and welfare provisions were mooted on a national scale they necessarily attracted considerations regarding imperial order. The last decades of the nineteenth century witnessed an intensification of inter-imperial competition, increased continental alliances, and a rise in protective instruments, such as the US McKinley Tariff Act that impacted upon British metal exports. Above all, the Boer War clarified the way in which the eugenicist interventions described above articulated with the defence of empire's integrity (see Thompson 1997).

At the start of the war in 1899, Joseph Chamberlain, secretary of state for the colonies, declined to force direct rule over the breakaway Transvaal (Quinault 1985: 637). But when hundreds of thousands of troops from across the empire saved Britain's dominion in South Africa, Chamberlain came to a "realization of that great federation of our race which will inevitably make for peace and liberty and justice"

(Zebel 1967: 141). Chamberlain was referring to the Anglo-Saxon family. Above all, it was widely believed that up to 60 per cent of English volunteers were rejected due to physical fitness (MacKenzie 1976: 515; see in general Semmel 1968). The realization, in the context of inter-imperial competition, that British rule had to count on the vitality of its imperial stock shocked most parties of the political establishment. In this way, the condition of the working class and its residuum in Britain was increasingly perceived as a threat to the integrity of empire (see in general Bonnett 1998).

Concern over the virility of Anglo-Saxon manhood accompanied the war. Robert Baden-Powell wrote his famous *Scouting for Boys* after encountering Lord Cecil's boy scout troop, formed during the Mafeking siege. Unapologetically promoting pioneer attributes, Baden-Powell's *Scouting* argued that "every boy ought to learn how to shoot and to obey orders, else he is no more good when war breaks out than an old woman" (cited in Mackenzie 1995: 176). But strong manhood required a strong patriarchal family. With the war in mind, Karl Pearson, protégé of Galton and creator of the academic field of mathematical statistics, lectured in 1900 on the connection between domestic eugenics and imperial integrity. "Selection of parentage", he argued, "is the sole effective process known to science by which a race can continually progress" (Stone 2001: 409). In 1907, John Frederick Sykes, Medical Officer of Health for St Pancras, London, claimed that "if we intend to remain an imperial race, we must restore to its imperial place the dignity of motherhood" (Porter 1991: 170).

Miscegenation was an unavoidable concern when it came to motherhood and racial integrity. This had been the case during the years of abolition as well as with the disputes over William Gordon's execution at Morant Bay. A few years after the end of the war, Robert Rentoul, another eugenicist and member of the Royal College of Surgeons, reminded his profession of the "terrible monstrosities produced by the intermarriage of the white man and the black". According to the learned surgeon, the negro "culminates his sexual furore by killing the [white] woman, sometimes taking out her womb and eating it" (Stone 2001: 399).

Hence, the Boer War clarified the extent to which eugenicist interventions were necessarily national *and* imperial in their import and extent. In 1904 the Inter-Departmental Committee on Physical Deterioration reported on their inquiry into the "deterioration of certain classes of the population as shown by the sizable percentage of rejections for physical causes of recruits for the Army". The language of the report, ostensibly addressing a national problem, was in fact principally addressed to the "deterioration of the race". The report explicitly refuted the Social Darwinian position of letting the unfit die, and instead embraced the utility of eugenicist interventions (Inter-Departmental Committee on Physical Deterioration 1904: 81). On this point, the report argued that urbanization had produced "consequences prejudicial to the health of the people", and advocated social hygiene policy in terms of housing, environment and employment.

The war therefore quickened proactive interventions into the reproduction of the British poor. Some argued that the state should treat as motherless those children who would only be brought up into a life of pauperism (Porter 1991: 167). After all, the maternity wards of workhouses were often associated with prostitution (Thane 1978: 39). In 1908 a royal commission introduced a new category – the feebleminded – that addressed the danger of those incapable of competing on equal terms for jobs or of managing their own affairs. Of special importance were women in receipt of poor relief and who had given birth to illegitimate children (Jones 1986: 29). Questions to do with marriage and fertility were thereafter included in the census, starting in 1911, the year of the National Insurance Act.

The Act itself was a cornerstone of social reforms pursued by Liberal governments from 1908 to 1916. David Lloyd George, then Chancellor of the Exchequer, was especially influential in these pursuits, and was further propelled by a desire to match the industrial vitality and stability of imperial Germany. The health provision of the Act included all manual workers and anyone who earned less than £160 per year. The unemployment provision was more particular, focusing on specific industries – building, construction, shipbuilding, mechanical engineering, iron founding and construction of vehicles and saw milling (Porritt 1912: 279). These trades were not only cyclical in nature (hence lending themselves to the necessity of insurance) but just as importantly were capital-intensive and required high-skill levels from their labourers. The employees and employers of such trades were able to form alliances in support of the Act, unlike labour-intensive and less-skilled sectors (Hellwig 2005: 119).

Most importantly, the actual provisions in Britain's first national system of social insurance accorded to the eugenicist logic developed in the decades before. The negative eugenics established in the Act sought to guard against a degeneration of the working stock in two ways: first, that the less skilled worker could benefit from basic social hygiene; second, that, due to the cycles of industry, the skilled labourer would not become destitute and degenerate into the residuum. Alternatively, married female labourers were excluded from nearly all provisions on the assumption that their earnings were supplementary to their husband's wage (Thane 1978: 33). Women in general were subject to a suspicion of idleness that men were not, for as Lloyd George stated as justification for their exclusion, there was "no way of checking [their] malingering" (cited in Porritt 1912: 263). This act of omission ensured that labouring women would not be able to recuse themselves of their imperial patriarchal duty to raise good English stock.

In sum, the 1911 National Insurance Act established the principle that employee, employer and state would contribute collectively to insurance against sickness and unemployment. But the Act did not dispense with the poor laws, nor with the distinction between those deserving and undeserving of social security and welfare. More accurately, the Act's logic sought to mitigate against the degeneration of deserving characteristics among English workers and ensure the reproduction of deserving stock. In these ways, the Act guarded against the race degradation represented by the urban residuum. National welfare manifested as a eugenicist enterprise – an act of political domination in service of empire's integrity.

CONCLUSION

The argument presented in this chapter suggests that it would be spurious to talk of an English "white working class" even at the high point of industrialization and empire. It would be more accurate to present Britain's division of labour at this time as bifurcated along racialized lines drawn in the nineteenth century as abolition humanitarianism was refuted and eugenics embraced. Those skilled and settled workers who had demonstrated deserving characteristics were inducted, through the franchise, into the English genus. But with the fallout out from Morant Bay, the English genus had taken on a decisively imperial formation as the Anglo-Saxon family. The nation was part of an imperial family. So even this enfranchised "working class" was not an indigenous constituency but was claimed as an orderly constituent of empire. It remained so for as long as there was an empire to substantively defend.

And the undeserving poor? As the abolitionist experiment fell apart under the professed weight of evidence that free Blacks could not cast off their slave essence, the Anglo-Saxon family separated itself from an agglomeration of non-white colonial subalterns. Even at this moment, the undeserving in England did not magically become white but were apprehended as a residuum, a stock that would corrupt the Anglo-Saxon breed. The residuum was not a colonial population, but its filiation to the Anglo-Saxon family was of a negative kind – a degenerative influence. The enfranchisement and racial salvation of the residuum would have to wait until the 1948 National Assistance Act formally revoked the poor laws and the moralizing distinction between those deserving and undeserving of social security and welfare. Yet as we shall now see, the celebrated "welfare state" did not emerge as an island affair. It, too, was conceived in relation to empire and in distinction to colonial development.

CHAPTER 4

NATIONAL WELFARE AND COLONIAL DEVELOPMENT

INTRODUCTION

By distinguishing between good stock – the enfranchised, skilled worker – and bad stock – the urban residuum – the National Insurance Act of 1911 institutionalized the eugenicist distinction between deserving and undeserving stock. In this chapter I explore the further racialization of the deserving/undeserving distinction through debates over colonial development and national welfare from *fin de siècle* to the Second World War. This chapter seeks to demonstrate that a quintessentially "national" arrangement, Britain's "welfare state", was actually bound up in imperial determinants that racialized those deserving and undeserving of social security and welfare.

In the first part of the chapter, I discuss how the 1867 Reform Act prompted a re-narration of the English genus such that organized labour could be considered amongst its "little platoons". I show how those who supported labour's advance argued that the provincial and patriarchal roots of nineteenth-century friendly societies had provided labour cooperation with the spirit of self-help, that is, of orderly independence. I then turn to debates over poor law reform between the Charity Organization Society and the Fabians. At stake was the viability of transplanting labour's cooperative spirit from its provincial wellsprings into an unforgiving urban environment, there to improve the character of the residuum. I demonstrate that central to these debates was the tension between the personalized nature of cooperative enterprise and the impersonalized nature of eugenicist interventions organized on a national scale.

In the second part of the chapter I turn to Britain's colonies. There, labour's cooperative spirit was looked upon with far greater suspicion. I detail how some Fabians initially turned towards the Caribbean and there identified the cooperative spirit in rural smallholdings outside of the plantation complex. These observations were then generalized into a policy for colonial development, which encouraged self-owner- ship via smallhold farming in opposition to the dependencies created by working on large plantations and in extractive industries. I chart how the latter model came to ultimately predominate in the interwar period. I consider how social anthropologists identified in the accom- panying urbanization a dissolution of tribal order and a potential for resistance to colonial rule. For similar reasons, the British government looked upon the possibility of transplanting labour's cooperative spirit to the colonies with increasing scepticism.

In the third part of the chapter I bring together two contempor- aneous reports: William Beveridge's 1942 report on Social Insurance and Allied Services, and Baron Moyne's 1940 recommendations on colonial development in the Caribbean. I demonstrate the eugenicist basis of Beveridge's report, with its principle aim being the repro- duction of good Anglo-Saxon stock. I then examine Moyne's wish to turn the institutions of colonial development towards the culti- vation of deserving characteristics amongst their Black populations. I specifically focus on Moyne's desire to induce Caribbean women into a proper patriarchy. I argue that both reports work together to defend empire's integrity. However, they do so by racially differenti- ating aims and expectations. On the one hand, England's coopera- tive spirit, being conservative and progressive, is conducive to the provision of universal insurance and welfare. On the other hand, the tribal spirit, being conservative and regressive, is not. This argument expands the claim I made in the last chapter that national welfare manifests as an act of political domination.

In this chapter, I once more conceptually extend the argument. While the deserving working *man* is affiliated to the Anglo-Saxon family with the 1867 Reform Act, by the end of the century *organized* labour is now affiliated on account of its orderly "cooperative spirit". In subsequent chapters we will see how labour's cooperative spirit is disassociated with the English genus under neoliberalism but then becomes reaffiliated in the years leading up to Brexit when the "white working class" is redeemed as a deserving constituency.

LABOUR'S COOPERATIVE SPIRIT

During the first half of the nineteenth century, the cooperative spirit of labour was by and large considered a force for disorder. For instance, the Combination Acts of 1799 and 1800 prohibited trade unionism for fear of the anarchical influence of revolutionary Jacobinism. But in 1859 ex-Chartist Samuel Smiles wrote a popular "self-help" guide for the skilled and settled working man. With his old movement in decline, Smiles preached not just industriousness and prudence but also the cultivation of "better habits, rather than greater rights". Moreover, it was through enriching the "collective character of a nation" that Smiles (1897) identified the new providential movement of the age. In 1867 the Second Reform Act enfranchised skilled and settled labour into the nation and Anglo-Saxon family. Come the 1870s, self-organized skilled labour had been granted de facto associational privileges in the halls of parliamentary governance (McKibbin 1984: 320). At this point, elites had rhetorically reconciled the cooperative principle of labour organization (self-help) with political order.

Such an embrace necessitated a reimagining of the English genus. Edmund Burke had believed that genus to be carried by the "little platoons" – local and personalized chains of paternalist filiation. William Cobbett identified these platoons in the paternalistic hierarchies of the cottage economy, including its rural poor. But by the 1860s the platoons were also being identified with the workers' cooperative movements, friendly societies and – albeit more guardedly – trade unions. Take, for instance, John Ludlow, head of the Christian socialists. In his *Progress of the Working Class*, Ludlow imputed a special significance to the growth of "Benefit Societies, Building Societies, Industrial and Provident Societies, Working Men's Colleges, Working Men's Clubs and Institutes, etc.", all of which generated "an ever-increasing number of meeting-points, material as well as moral, between class and class, which are gradually binding each to each by closer links of fellowship" (Ludlow & Jones 1867: 282). Far from intensifying class struggle, cooperative

59

values, for Ludlow (Ludlow & Jones 1867: 283), were responsible for the "growth of loyal national feeling among the working class".

There are two elements to this re-narration of the English genus that I wish to highlight. The first is reflected usefully in the work of Charles Fay. Nowadays a somewhat forgotten Cambridge economic historian, in the first part of the twentieth century, Fay was a public intellectual, enthusiast of cooperatives and friend to influential economists John Maynard Keynes and Alfred Marshall. In his popular economic history of Britain, Fay approvingly cited Austrian politician Joseph Baernreither's description of friendly societies and cooperatives as "the most conspicuous examples of English self-help" (Fay 1950: 406). Importantly, Fay located the wellspring of such organizations in provincial towns and villages, which were led by a "local spirit". Fay even argued that in the "very large towns", where workers did not know each other "so intimately", the development of such self-help organizations was "relatively backward" (Fay 1950: 425, 427). This was especially the case in London, the centre of which, Fay argued,was "barely touched" by this spirit even as late as 1914. In his estimation, the embrace of labour's cooperative spirit was at the same time a geographical embrace of the personal, local and/or provincial wellsprings of the English genus.

Fay was an advocate of women's rights. On this note, we should not forget that the cooperative movement had initially opened a radical space for non-patriarchal sexual and economic relations. But, and this is the second element, that space was quickly shut down. As they came together, artisans tended to defend their crafts by arguing that work demeaned women's morality, reduced men's wages and prevented the provision of a breadwinner's wage (see in general Clark 1997). The integrity of skilled labour was presented as a bulwark of "domesticity", thereby playing into the politics of patriarchal respectability (Rose 1993: 155). Take, for instance, one contributor to the *Trade's Newspaper* in 1825 who agitated for the withdrawal of women and children from the labour market so as to "establish the authority of fathers" and make "each man responsible for the comfort, respectability, and the education of his family" (Clark 1997: 203). Such arguments were given extra strength by the Factory Movement's use of the slave analogy, which, as we have seen in Chapter 2, identified in female and child factory labour the arrival of Black anarchy.

Patriarchy and provincialism were often identified as the core qualities that underwrote labour's cooperative spirit, and it was these qualities that allowed proponents to advocate for self-organization as a deserving characteristic of English working men. This is the logic by which Burke's little platoons could be reconciled with labour's cooperative spirit across the ideological spectrum from conservatives to socialists. With this in mind, I now want to turn to Helen Bosanquet of the Charity Organization Society and Beatrice Webb of the Fabians, both of whom were key protagonists in *fin de siècle* debates over poor law reform. Both drew upon labour's cooperative spirit in their arguments concerning the urban residuum.

In 1902 Bosanquet wrote *The Strength of the People*, a text that underlined the importance of charitable interventions in the alleviation of urban poverty. Bosanquet framed part of the argument by reference to the contrast between "town and country". Why is it, she asked, that "we accept it as a sort of law of nature that in the country a man can bring up a family successfully upon half what is considered the Poverty Line in London?" (Bosanquet 1902: 103). Eschewing a straightforward economic analysis, Bosanquet focused on the malformation of the moral character of poor wives and husbands in the urban milieu. Specifically, Bosanquet (1902: 104–7) argued that, lacking appropriate experience, poor wives could not transmit the virtues of prudence, patience and planning to their progeny. This deficit was compounded by the fact that their husbands had also "missed the interests and companionship and assistance which should have come to him from his friendly society or trade union or co-operative store".

Bosanquet's (1902: 122) point was that the residuum's male had only ever been in a position of receiver rather than co-instigator of aid. Because of this circumstance, he had degraded his character to the point where he could not function as a small patriarch. Indeed, Bosanquet attributed much of the progress of the labourer in the nineteenth century to "the growth of the modern Friendly Society, the institution by means of which a group of men combine for mutual aid in times of sickness". She also lauded the cooperative as "a means of making [the working man's] earnings more effective". Finally, Bosanquet affirmed the edifying effect of the trade union, which proved that "the workers of the country are not naturally or necessarily without the qualities which make for independence, and the strength to maintain themselves" (Bosanquet 1902: 168–70).

While Fabians differed to the charity approach by agitating for a stronger public administration role in poor relief, they too identified in labour's cooperative tradition the source of their socialism. In her influential tract on the cooperative movement, Beatrice Webb (née Potter), directly invoked Henry Brougham's treatises on the revolutionary era (which, it should be remembered from Chapter 2, were distinctly negro-phobic). Via Brougham, Webb compared the "complete separation of the higher and lower orders, leading inevitably to anarchy and despotism" with the emergence of the "new spirit" of association (Potter 1904: 38). Webb followed this "inborn capacity of Englishmen for self-government" through the religious dissent of the eighteenth century into the mutual improvement clubs, benefit societies and union shops of the nineteenth century (Potter 1904: 36–8). The spirit of cooperation, argued Webb, had "one aim and one motive ... the desire on the part of a majority to regulate and to limit the exploitation of their labour by a powerful and skilled minority" (Potter 1904: 39). Beatrice and Sidney Webb (Webb 1891) sought to transplant this spirit into the urban milieu in the form of "municipal patriotism".

It is remarkable the degree to which Fabianism echoed the ethical concerns of William Cobbett. Recall that in Cobbett's estimation, the parasitical interests of capitalist farmers and their urban co-conspirators threatened to turn the rural labourer into a slave, hence horrifically blackening the English genus. Now consider the musings of G. D. H. Cole, notable Fabian intellectual of the early twentieth century, and biographer of Cobbett. In melancholic tones redolent of Cobbett, Cole hoped that the contemporary urban worker might not exist as a "desiccated townsm[a]n, remote from the life of field and village, but [as a] countrym[a]n in mind, wherever [he] live" (Griffiths 1999: 101). So, in the Fabian narrative of labour's cooperative spirit, the English genus now became identified in local and provincial self-help organizations, which protected workers from the possibility of race degeneration in their migrations to urban metropoles. At the end of the Victorian era, Fabians hoped to transplant that spirit of independence into the unforgiving urban milieu.

But it was not at all clear whether a successful transplantation of labour's cooperative spirit was possible. In fact, by the late nineteenth century migration to the urban milieu had emerged as a general concern for political order. A movement even gathered pace for the nationalization of rural land. The Land Reform Union and other proselytizers urged government to properly utilize such land in order to attenuate the flow of poor people into cities (see in general Ridley 1987). Charles Booth, the premier urban demographer, suggested that casual workers could be removed to domestic labour colonies. In 1904 William Beveridge advocated for permanent and compulsory colonies for the undeserving unemployed, and free colonies for the "genuine casual labourer" (Brown 1968: 356). In 1909, David Lloyd George, as Chancellor of the Exchequer, legislated for the reclamation of rural land in England upon which portions of the urban poor would be set to work in labour colonies (Cowen & Shenton 1991: 147). Several colonies were actually set up by charitable organizations.

In eugenicist terms, the rural idyll came to be considered a conducive environment for the strengthening of Anglo-Saxon stock. But the urban milieu complicated eugenicist interventions. For, as will be remembered from the last chapter, industrialization had mooted new national scales and modes of social interventions. In this context, both Bosanquet and the Webbs struggled to answer a fundamental question: would the national dispensation of welfare along impersonal, eugenic lines undermine efforts to induct the urban poor into the personal and provincial nature of labour's cooperative spirit? Debate over this question was met through the Royal Commission on the Poor Laws, which gathered evidence between 1905 and 1909. The commission split into a majority report, effectively taking the Charity Organization Society's position, and a minor report espousing the Fabian view.

The majority report was especially concerned with assaying the extent to which intervention into family life was warranted so as to support the self-help principle amongst the individuals concerned (Vincent 1984: 362). Considering various commentaries on the Commission, Bernard Bosanquet, husband of Helen, sought to clarify the majority position by normatively framing his argument in terms of "democratic citizenship". Bosanquet envisaged a franchise wherein no class would be dependent upon another and whereby "obligations and liabilities", except for within the family, would be "reciprocal and voluntary". In this respect, Bonsanquet circumscribed active citizenship to the male head-of-household, whose independence required a degree of material success but owed primarily to moral character (Bosanquet 1910: 397). To the extent that Bosanquet's vision disavowed class hierarchy it nonetheless affirmed the Disraelian notion of "one nation", or more accurately, "one Anglo-Saxon family". Similar to William Beveridge's eugenicist argument for national insurance, Bosanquet proposed that to "restore" the weak citizen was a positive duty of social policy, while to support the independent citizen was a preventative duty (Bosanquet 1910: 399).

The minority position had already been communicated in an 1891 Fabian pamphlet. According to Fabian logic, the poor law failed because it discouraged "provident saving" and "degenerated" the moral character of English people (Fabian Society 1891: 3). Fabians did not wish to do away with relief, but rather agitated for its public administration rather than rely upon the voluntary nature of private charity (Fabian Society 1891: 4). For this purpose, intervention had to be scaled up to the national level and administered to whole classes of paupers. By this reasoning, the Fabians considered the personalized case-by-case assessment model of the Charity Organization Society to be inadequate to the eugenic challenge (Fabian Society 1891: 7). In reporting on the work of the Commission, Sidney Webb believed that the existing poor laws acted as an "anti-eugenic influence", especially when considering how outdoor relief was even given to "mentally and morally degenerate" childbearing women (Webb 1910: 232–3).

Both majority and minority reports agreed that poor laws had to be reformed. Both intellectual positions identified in labour's cooperative spirit the deserving characteristics that had to be transplanted into the urban milieu. What distinguished them, though, was the centrality that they accorded to personalized interventions. The Bosanquets saw their charitable work as intervening primarily in the cultivation of moral character. And they believed that the best method was case-specific where regular home visits would eventuate in a conducive, paternalistic relationship that approximated the old parish hierarchies. In many ways, the social visit was designed as a substitute for direct involvement in cooperative enterprises. For the Webbs, "municipal patriotism" advocated a far more impersonalized administration of reform efforts. They even appealed for a functional differentiation of efforts such that discrete government bodies would address child, mental and physical health issues (Vincent 1984: 347).

The Webbs' position was far more conducive than the Bosanquets' to the interventionist demands of eugenics. After all, the quality of Anglo-Saxon stock could only be addressed at the level of nation and empire. Yet the Webbs' method ran counter to the cultivation of labour's cooperative spirit, whereas the Bosanquets sought to transplant this spirit into the urban milieu through personalized and paternalistic family intervention. These unavoidable lines of tension ultimately influenced the administrative structures of the National Insurance Act of 1911.

The economist William Braithwaite, who was heavily involved in drafting the health provisions of the Act, conceived its administration of funds as a balancing act. On the one hand, Braithwaite understood the importance of promoting the deserving characteristics of organized labour to the rest of the working poor. On the other hand, he was aware that pursuing this aim could destroy the very bases of voluntarism and self-help (Harris 1992: 78). As a compromise, the Act placed the public administration of the insurance scheme with government-approved societies. Still, this did not stop a conflict emerging between friendly societies (exemplars of the cooperative spirit) and commercial life insurance companies who sought to leverage the provision of health services (see Alborn 2001). At stake was the eclipse of the personal and provincial provision of insurance by an impersonalized and commercialized insurance industry. The secretary of the Charity Organization Society, C. S. Loch, even pronounced the Act as the "death warrant of the friendly societies" (Finlayson 1990: 185–6).

In the last chapter I argued that national insurance in Britain manifested as a eugenicist enterprise. So far in this chapter I have examined how labour's cooperative spirit was considered central to this enterprise. The provincial and personal wellsprings of this spirit were favourably identified by most commentators as giving rise to a form of self-help conducive to orderly independence. In short, labour's cooperative spirit was presumed to strengthen the English genus. Henceforth, the transplantation of this spirit into the urban milieu was considered necessary in order to address the weakness of empire's stock that lay in the residuum, and which we discussed in the last chapter. However, in so far as the eugenicist interventions that might direct this transplantation were national in scale and impersonalized in application, they paradoxically threatened to undermine the provincial and personal wellsprings of labour's cooperative spirit.

As the issue of rural land reform gained some traction in Britain, cognate concerns over demographic transitions were mooted in *fin de siècle* colonial policy. But while the concerns were cognate, their articulation and implications were differentiated along lines of race.

THE COOPERATIVE SPIRIT IN THE COLONIES

Let us first turn to the most famous social imperialist at *fin de siècle*, Joseph Chamberlain. Having undertaken a stint as the president of the Board of Trade in the 1880s, Chamberlain suggested that, when it came to the Anglo-Saxon family that was spread across empire, "one should feel what the other feels … all should have a share in the welfare, and sympathize with the welfare of every part" (Zebel 1967: 133). Upon becoming secretary of state for the colonies in 1895, Chamberlain turned his attention to the decimation suffered by the sugar industry in Britain's old Caribbean crown colonies – in his words, Britain's "undeveloped estates" (Will 1970: 129–31).

Chamberlain's apprehensions of empire implied that those filiated to the Anglo-Saxon family should receive an equitable share of welfare, while Britain's other subjects would require development. George Bernard Shaw's contemporaneous manifesto on empire, putatively on behalf of the Fabians, suggests that Chamberlain's split between welfare and development relied upon older distinctions forged in the Morant Bay controversy. Responding to the Boer War, Shaw proposed that "native races" be either protected "despotically by the Empire or abandoned to slavery and extermination". When it came to white European subjects, Shaw ruled out long-term rule by martial law and instead agitated for the safeguarding of democratic rights in settler colonies through common law (Shaw 1900: 22, 31–3).

But what course might the cooperative spirit take in developing the colonies? This was, in fact, a popular concern which initially complicated the racialized division between Anglo-Saxon welfare and colonial development. Take, for instance, the Cooperative Union of Manchester, which in 1900 passed a resolution urging the legislative and executive councils of the Caribbean colonies to encourage the growth of friendly societies there. Such a shift, the Cooperative

Union (1900) argued, would improve the social and economic position of the natives. Additionally, the Union noted that in comparison to the "capitalist planters" who cast "longing eyes upon the United States" the Black labourers of the British Caribbean had proven to be staunchly patriotic. Certainly, they had proved themselves to be "better-conducted, more habitually honest, moral, law-abiding" than any other Black peoples (Wolf 1900). In partial response to the resolution, and despite supporting the sugar industry, Chamberlain agreed on the desirability of encouraging friendly societies ("Minutes, 5th April" 1900).

The legacies of the plantation system featured centrally in subsequent discussions over colonial development and the wellsprings of labour's cooperative spirit. As did input from the Fabian Society. One Fabian, Sydney Olivier, made an especially influential contribution. Prior to joining the Society in 1885, Olivier had been a member of the Land Reform Union, there engaging with the prospect of better developing Britain's rural lands. He was then colonial secretary to Jamaica and its acting governor at various times between 1900 and 1904 before returning to the colony as governor in 1907. Olivier shared the Fabian desire for colonies to be governed for the improvement of the whole empire. He was, though, far more concerned than Shaw to address the ways in which colonial development had so far failed the native.

To understand Olivier's ideological position, it is useful to turn to his slightly later reflection on the debates over Morant Bay. In *The Myth of Governor Eyre*, Olivier (1933: 7) recalled that before he resided in Jamaica he too had associated the island with "blackness and horror, infested by murderous natives". But Olivier's experience as governor compelled him to write against Carlyle's hagiography of Eyre and its "strangely anomalous and fantastically unconvincing" depiction of the peoples of Jamaica (Olivier 1933: 17). The root of the uprising, for Olivier (1933: 19–20), lay not in the blackness of Jamaica's population, but in their exclusion from land ownership and occupation. This injustice had continued post-emancipation with parliament's consistent support of absentee landlords and the plantocracy.

Strikingly, Olivier reserved special praise for those Black Jamaicans who managed to subsequently erect "hamlets, villages and towns" in the "interior and mountains" (1933: 28, 34–5). So taken was Olivier with the industriousness and "exceedingly temperate" nature of "West Indian country negroes" that he even considered drunkenness to be a "Nordic, rather than an African, racial vice". So, when it came to Jamaica, Olivier identified a tenuous wellspring of cooperative spirit outside of the plantations, in the provincial settlements of smallholdings that peppered the marginal lands of the hilly interior. It was in these sites that the Jamaican population were cultivating deserving characteristics. Olivier was adamant that no such wellsprings could arise from the plantation, an extractive system long considered to breed anarchy and indolence. "For the negro and collie to develop at all", argued Olivier in 1898, "they must come out of the plantations system and become small owners and cultivators for themselves" (cited in Cowen & Shenton 1991: 152).

At one point in his biography of Eyre, Olivier (1933: 24) likened the continued exclusion of Black peoples from land ownership to a "practical restoration of slavery". Pointing towards the expropriation of land in South Africa and Kenya, Olivier suggested that the same process would be "familiar to our own generation in African 'development' policy" (1933: 24). In other words, Olivier posited Jamaica as a model by which to frame the pitfalls involved in developing Britain's colonies on the African continent (Cowen & Shenton 1991: 153): smallholding encouraged the cultivation of deserving characteristics; the plantation arrested any such cultivation. Olivier's position resonated strongly with the early work of Arthur Lewis, an influential development economist hailing from St Lucia. In a book published by the Fabians in 1938, Lewis (1977: 48) spoke of the "shadow" of plantation "serfdom". In the absence of a democratization of property holding, Lewis argued that the plantation would always demean the labourer's "sense of dignity and independence".

The analytical transposition of the Caribbean plantation to a general problematic of colonial development gained traction in the aftermath of the First World War. During its first parliamentary government, the Labour Party's Advisory Committee on Imperial Questions considered colonial development along two models. A "capitalist policy" was represented by the plantation economy of Kenya and the alienation of peasantry from the land by white settlers; a (West) "African policy" encouraged the native to "make the most economic use of his land" (Kelemen 2007: 78–9; Cowen & Shenton 1991: 163). The latter – and preferable – policy was buoyed by Lord Lugard's thesis on the "dual mandate" of colonial rule for West Africa. Writing in 1922, Lugard advocated for the economic strengthening of empire and the simultaneous development of the African native's competencies.

Lugard's thesis was soon compromised by the 1929 Colonial Development Act, which provided regular funds principally for the "purpose of aiding and developing agriculture and industry" with a specific view to "promoting commerce with or industry in the United Kingdom". In brief, the Act effectively ignored the need to develop colonial subjects themselves. By the 1930s, the Labour Party had accepted the reality that no colonial economy could be sheltered from the growth of wage labour arising from an increase in plantation projects and extractive industries (Kelemen 2007: 78). Come the Second World War, the development of the native's character was a prospect that met with increased scepticism (see for example Orde Browne 1941).

Over the course of two decades growing scepticism soured hope that native communities might organically cultivate the cooperative spirit. With the arrival of the Labour Party's first government in 1923, Leonard Woolf, then chairperson of the Party's Advisory Committee on Imperial Questions, suggested that colonial governments might encourage "co-operative societies" as an element of development (Davies 1963: 80–1). The next Labour government in 1929 gave the same encouragement (Kelemen 2007: 80). But by the 1930s, the national government valued the supposed stability of tribal life as a counter-weight to the the flux and flow of townships linked to extractive industries. This was the position taken by James Griffiths, the secretary of state for the colonies in Labour's first postwar government (Kelemen 2007: 85–6).

Some still held out for a resolution to the tension between the development of labour's cooperative spirit and the development of extractive industries. William Macmillan, a historian, soon to become a war-time member of the Fabian-led Colonial Office Advisory Committee on Education, published a *Warning from the West Indies* in 1938. Macmillan shared Olivier's position that the West Indies experiment demonstrated the social problems that were introduced by the "planter, farmer, settler, as the case may be, in the West Indies, South Africa or Kenya". For Macmillan it was the insecure economic position of this white agent that drove the demand for cheap Black labour, subsequently leading to both social and economic stagnation. But he also mooted the emergence of a "new planter" and looked towards the "self-reliance of the intelligent, progressive smallholder, usually but not necessarily an owner" (Macmillan 1936: 187). Attentive to the need for colonial development to economically benefit the imperial centre, Macmillan (1936: 187) argued that the real issue was how to blend the productive efficiency of the plantation model with the "agency of free self-reliant workers".

These paradoxes created by colonial development ran historically parallel to the paradoxes created by national insurance. For the latter, the issues were intellectually explored by charity organizations and left-liberal policy makers; for the former, social anthropologists took the intellectual lead. Hence, I want to turn now to the work of Bronisław Malinowski, a professor of the London School of Economics, as well as the most influential and representative voice of his field during the interwar years.

Over the course of the interwar and war years, Malinowski and other anthropologists increasingly cast their gaze upon the African settler-colonies, especially Kenya, North and South Rhodesia, and South Africa. Malinowski was especially concerned with the ways in which the increase in extractive industries around townships had encouraged native urbanization. To gauge these tendencies, he identified three broad typographies: European districts, tribal reserves, and then the urban areas. In the latter, Africans and Europeans "collaborated" and depended upon each other directly (Malinowski 1945: 9). Through interaction, he suggested, a "new type of human being" was being produced.

Malinowski proposed that this "westernized" or "educated" African evolved through a number of stages. First, as the native took up waged labour and European schooling he began to detribalize. Second, the native, "overwhelmed" by the superiority of European ways, would enter the European or American university system. Upon return to the colony the native would experience a colour bar in white-dominated occupations and positions. The colour bar had the effect of fundamentally rebuffing the native's aspirations to assimilate, and in response, the native would try to fall back upon African beliefs and values. Failing to do so completely, Malinowski claimed, the native mutated Europe's superior political structures so as to create tribal, regional and Pan-African nationalisms, or, as he put it elsewhere, "Black bolshevism" (Malinowski 1929: 25–8).

It is instructive to compare Malinowski's narrative of Africa's tribal spirit to the narrative of labour's cooperative spirit in England. Recall that the wellsprings of this spirit were identified in the personalized and patriarchal affiliations of workers, which cultivated deserving characteristics, principally self-help. In this case, the challenge was to find ways to transplant the provincial cooperative spirit into the unforgiving urban milieu. When it came to England, reformers did not laud the cooperative spirit for its fundamentally "modern" disposition, but rather for its potential to deliver the tradition of orderly independence into a quintessentially modern milieu (the urban). Malinowski also identified in the tribal spirit a traditional disposition – provincial and personal. But in the colonies, the traditional was coded specifically as "primitive" in comparison to the European-induced urban milieu. Because of this primitiveness, Malinowski assumed that the tribal spirit could only rebel when it encountered the "modern" urban. This rebellion signalled the degeneration of the tribal spirit.

Why did Malinowksi attribute degeneracy not to the urban milieu (as Beveridge and many others had done in Britain) but to the tribal spirit? Similar to many social anthropologists of the era, Malinowski assumed that the native possessed a "primitive psychology". His teacher, Charles Seligman, was convinced that the division between the conscious and unconscious was "specially pervious in primitive peoples" leading to a far more "instinctual" temperament resulting in "sudden tempestuous fits of anger", "suggestibility" and sexual "liberty" (Seligman 1932: 204, 219). In his earlier work in the Trobriand Islands, Malinowski (1954) argued that the function of myth in primitive psychology was not symbolic but rather a "direct expression" of its subject matter. In other words, and cognate to his teacher, Malinowski believed that when it came to the primitive psyche, only a thin and fragile wall separated the unconscious and conscious. Hence, rather than attribute to the urbanizing African an ability for adaptation, Malinowski saw in this transplantation the eruption of Black unconsciousness, manifest as unrestrained resentment. It is, then, possible to glean in the "primitive" psyche a social anthropological interpretation of the Black license and anarchy that Burke, Cobbett and Carlyle feared so much.

Fear of Black license became increasingly prominent in the governing mindset when it came to addressing the urban, industrial and national dimensions of colonial development. Take, for instance, Arthur Creech Jones, founder of the Fabian Colonial Bureau. Creech Jones was especially concerned with the effect of the "colour-bar" on the ability of colonial subjects to learn the practice of responsible self-government in industry ("Empire – A Bi Monthly Record of the Fabian Colonial Bureau 4 (1)" 1941: 4). Creech Jones (1945: 71) argued that successful development relied on the "British ability to inspire in the people a great measure of social responsibility and moral integrity". Yet as secretary of state for the colonies in Clement Attlee's postwar Labour government, Creech Jones also warned of too quickly increasing raw material production to bolster Britain's economic recovery for fear of destabilizing tribal life.

Similar scepticism was also more and more evident in plans to use white labour organizations to guide the formation of trade unionism in non-white colonies. As secretary of state for the colonies in Labour's second government, Sidney Webb passed the 1929 Memorandum on Native Policy in East Africa which reaffirmed a commitment to the protection of "native interests" but also encouraged the registration of trade unions through constitutional channels. The Fabian concern for "responsible" trade unionism quickly became a fixture of colonial policy, and the TUC itself joined the Colonial Labour Advisory Committee. Subsequently, the TUC sent officials to various colonies to help focus unionism strictly on wage improvement and the amelioration of work conditions (Kelemen 2007: 84; see also Davis 2010). However, the capacity of the African to follow even this guidance ultimately came under question. In 1955, three years into the colonial war against the Kenya Land and Freedom Army, one member of the Royal Commission on East Africa opined that "unsophisticated Africans" were by and large unable to pattern their efforts on the British trade union model ("Colonial Labour Advisory Committee – Draft Mintues of Meeting September 29th" 1955b).

All these discussions were shaded by the prospect of independence. In Britain, the narrative of labour's cooperative spirit had served to reorient political sensibilities after the enfranchisement of skilled and settled working men into the Anglo-Saxon family. No such enfranchisement was offered to the African colonies. In 1946, George Hall, secretary of state for the colonies, claimed that "thrift, self-help, fair-dealing and above all a practical training in the working of the democratic process are all encouraged by association" (Kelemen 2007: 85). Nonetheless, the Clement Attlee government – the government that would implement universal welfare for residents of Britain – accepted the utility of promoting in its African colonies cooperatives, trade unions and limited local self-governance, but emphatically *not* parliamentary forms of rule (Kelemen 2007: 82–4). Again, we can contrast this locking in of political dependency to the effective independence now enjoyed by white dominions.

In sum, by the arrival of the Second World War a consensus had emerged that the tribal spirit could not be conducive to colonial development in the same way that England's cooperative spirit could be conducive to the defence of empire. In Britain, the aim of imperial defence, being the strengthening of Anglo-Saxon stock, necessitated expanded public interventions in the form of national insurance. In opposition, colonial development ended up pointing towards a distrust and disillusionment of Black/African cooperation and, as we shall now see, an accompanying curtailment of the provision of social welfare. The political salience of these divergent trajectories is testified to in the contemporaneous publication of two influential reports on welfare policy.

THE BEVERIDGE AND MOYNE REPORTS

In 1942 William Beveridge published *Social Insurance and Allied Services*. The report backed a universalization of social insurance that had, in 1911, been partial in terms of its reach and application across industries and occupations. Mindful of the tensions that informed the 1911 Act, Beveridge trod the fine line between consolidating the national administration of universal welfare and preserving the provincial wellsprings of labour's cooperative spirit. "My plan", he emphasized, was "insurance not charity" (Beveridge 1944: 12). As a partial solution to these tensions, Beveridge cleaved strongly to the principle of a national minimum of living standards. This principle allowed for a cooperative enterprise to be struck between state responsibility and voluntary action (Beveridge 1948: 8–9). It was the stipulation of a minimum rather than maximum that incentivized each man to make extra provisions for his family by voluntary insurance or saving (Beveridge 1944: 12).

Universal social insurance was to be supported by a system of "allied" welfare services that were distinctly eugenicist in their purpose. Beveridge's eugenicist leanings are most evident in his thinking on the family. Take, for instance, a 1942 address, wherein he (1943: 36) responded to five peace points set out by Pope Pious XII. Beveridge was especially taken by one proposed principle that "every child, regardless of race or class, should have equal opportunities of education, suitable for the development of his peculiar capacities". In his response, Beveridge strongly opposed the destruction of the family because, through its organization, selfish individuals learned to cultivate a sense of "service" to a common human heritage. He also clearly accepted the heredity principle of family and its production of inequality of opportunity along distinctly "race or class" terms, in so far as "more capable parents will have more capable children". By supporting the family unit, Beveridge (1943: 36) refused to accept that he was articulating a "doctrine of aristocratic exclusiveness". Rather, he argued, the state had to be conceived of as the "general parent of all children". Effectively, Beveridge believed that the state should intervene only when the natural family failed, therein providing opportunity regardless of race or class.

Notable in Beveridge's response to the pope was a desire to address equality of opportunity in strictly eugenicist terms: good stock would be allowed to breed, while bad stock would be ameliorated through state intervention. This was precisely the logic that underpinned his argument in favour of a universal children's allowance (Beveridge 1943: 150). Preparing for his Galton lecture to the Eugenics Society in 1943, Beveridge noted that such allowance would support "the skilled wage earners", who represented "probably the largest store of heritable ability in the country and a store which it is vital to keep as large as possible" (Beveridge 1943: 159–60). Addressing the tendency for the more-skilled and more-affluent to have fewer children, Beveridge (1943: 152) argued that it was not so important that universal provision might support the "thriftless and careless". It mattered far more that the economic system should no longer "favour breeding from those who are less successful than from those who are more successful in rendering services to the community" (Beveridge 1943: 161).

Beveridge's report owed much to *fin de siècle* interventions – eugenicist and otherwise – concerning the urban residuum. But the mandate that the report gave to pursue universal insurance and welfare must be contextualized within the late nineteenth-century imperial division between Anglo-Saxon family and colonial subject. For instance, Beveridge (1943: 150) explicitly identified the beneficiaries of his plan as the "British race". Moreover, he affirmed "pride of race" to be "a reality for the British as for other people", who had a duty to "maintain their breed at its best" (Beveridge 1943: 161). Beveridge's key concern, in this respect, was that at its "present rate of reproduction" the race could not continue (Beveridge 1943: 150). Therefore English mothers had "vital work to do in ensuring the adequate continuance of the British race and British ideals in the world" (Harris 2003: 402). By this eugenicist logic, Beveridge implicated the preservation of empire in the universal provision of social insurance and welfare in Britain.

Furthermore, Beveridge's geopolitical sensibility resonated with Disraeli's notion of "one nation", wherein class had been subordinated to national-racial affiliation. In an address at Oxford in 1942, Beveridge spoke of postwar planning in terms of prioritizing Britain's own challenges, and by addressing specifically the needs of the British worker. "It's often been said", he noted in an aside to Marx, "that the worker has no country. That has never been true of British workers" (1943: 94). Beveridge acknowledged that it was impossible to think of this Britain without its Commonwealth, meaning the white-settler dominions – i.e. its Anglo-Saxon family. Tellingly, Beveridge also noted that "certain parts of the world ... are not yet able or fit to govern themselves from within". Trusteeship, rather than democracy, was to be their postwar fate (Beveridge 1943: 94).

But would trusteeship necessitate a similar impulse to provide universal insurance and welfare? Beveridge did not directly address this question. Nevertheless, I want to follow Denise Noble's (2015) assertion that Beveridge's intervention should be apprehended as part of an imperial constellation of policy on welfare and development. It is towards another element of this constellation that we must now turn.

The Italian invasion of Ethiopia in October 1935 impacted significantly upon the British Caribbean. A desire to defend sovereign Ethiopia against a fascist European power merged with existing discontent in the islands over living conditions and political representation. Much of the resulting anti-colonial energy was channelled through (and co-opted by) local unions and continued for years. In response, a West India Royal Commission, led by Baron Moyne, was tasked with surveying social conditions in the colonies, beginning with Jamaica in 1938. The bulk of the report was considered so damning that it would aid Nazi propaganda and thus remained unpublished until 1945. But even the recommendations published in 1940 signalled a significant shift in imperial policy (one also represented in the 1940 Colonial Development and Welfare Act). Instead of the predominant focus on economic extraction, the report agitated for a much more interventionist approach towards colonial welfare.

The Moyne recommendations admitted a "pressing need" for the imperial centre to financially support the development of social services – especially, education, health and housing – and land settlement ("Recommendations of the West India Royal Commission" 1940: 1–2). Education was considered crucial for cultivating appropriate habits with regards to speech, hygiene and diet. A negative eugenics principle, similar to the preventative hygiene measures of *fin de siècle* Britain, underpinned recommendations for public health and urban housing initiatives ("Recommendations of the West India Royal Commission" 1940: 3–5). The recommendations also encouraged responsible unionism as a crucial factor in the regulation of wages and conditions of employment. In colonies that could afford it, unemployment insurance might be considered, albeit only in those industries that provided regular employment ("Recommendations of the West India Royal Commission" 1940: 7–8). In all these ways, Moyne's recommendations spoke of the need to task Caribbean institutions with the cultivation of deserving characteristics amongst their subjects.

But most important, for Moyne, was the need to install an orderly patriarchy. Joan French (1988) argues that Moyne identified the root of social problems not so much in poverty and/or land access but rather in the position of poor Black women. Moyne apprehended this position in terms of a dichotomy: there was either white sanctioned patriarchy or there was Black licentious anarchy. But consanguinity in the Caribbean was far more complex than Moyne could accept. Historically, extended family arrangements (including childcare) and the involvement of women in agriculture guaranteed that mothers retained a necessary degree of self-reliance and self-help (Chamberlain 2002). The Moyne report entirely obfuscated such values and contributions by instead complaining of a lack of monogamous, nuclear family life.

Against the flexibility of existing arrangements, Moyne advocated a division of labour between the male breadwinner and dependent housewife. Moyne also recommended that (relatively) middle-class Caribbean women should become voluntary social workers for poor women and might even embark on a Church-supported "organized campaign ... against the social, moral and economic evils of promiscuity" (French 1988: 9). Moyne's disciplining of Caribbean women was shared by Sir Frank Stockdale, Comptroller of Development and Welfare, a position set up through subsequent reforms (Chamberlain 2002: 189).

Denise Noble (2015) insightfully points out that, when read together, Moyne and Beveridge's reports sketched out an imperial patriarchy that ultimately supported the preservation of good English stock. While Beveridge commanded the white British woman to produce strong Anglo-Saxon stock for nation and empire, Moyne commanded Black women to retreat to the house to raise orderly colonial subjects who would produce for empire. Tellingly, the nature of both interventions diverged along the lines of imperial differentiation between the Anglo-Saxon family and non-white colonial subjects. The welfare challenge in Britain was to provide impersonalized national services without under-mining labour's cooperative spirit. In distinction, the development challenge in the colonies, and in the Caribbean especially, was to mobilize welfare provision expressly towards the establishment of small patriarchs.

In the last chapter I argued that national welfare manifested as an act of political domination in service of empire's integrity. Beveridge's and Moyne's reports can also be read together as another such act of political domination, that is, as addressing perceived weaknesses in the reproduction of empire's stock. Crucially, the reports pursued different aims towards empire's Anglo-Saxon family and its devel-opmental subjects. The political salience of this racial differentiation can be clarified by examining concerns over the reception of the Beveridge report in the colonies.

The report was sent almost immediately upon publication to colonial administrators with advice from Whitehall on how best to explain its contents to their populations. Above all, London officials hoped to contain the "vague but strong desire for social security" across the empire that was "stimulated" by the report (Epps 1943). Whitehall strongly suggested a reading of the report that focused upon the importance of cultivating deserving characteristics, or, at least, checked any expectations of welfare that might encourage idleness and dependency. For instance, discussion of the "national minimum" would have to make it clear that "insured persons" must not feel "that income for idleness, however caused, can come from a bottomless source" (Beveridge 1942).

It is useful at this point to recall that the Bosanquets and Webbs had identified the wellsprings of labour's cooperative spirit in Britain's personal and provincial idyll. Alternatively, Fabians and colonial administrators had become deeply sceptical about the possibility that Africa's tribal interiors could ever bring forth such a spirit without its importation via British agents. This difference in expectation was affirmed in Whitehall discussions over the viability of importing Beveridge's schema. London argued strongly that the universal scope of Beveridge's suggestions were "manifestly inappropriate" in most of the colonial world (Epps 1943). Not only did commentators unanimously point out the prohibitive cost of social security for colonial economies. Just as evident was a concern over the social readiness of colonial populations to receive such security ("Social Security in the Colonial Territories (Draft)" 1943: 11).

While in Britain, labour's cooperative spirit was deemed to be both conservative and progressive, in Africa the tribal spirit was increasingly seen to be conservative and regressive. This difference of opinion was evident in debates over the applicability of Beveridge's report for the colonies. Yet by the same ascription of backwardness, tribal life was presented as a bulwark against the social collapse impelled by the modern forces of urbanization ("Social Security in the Colonial Territories (Draft)" 1943: 10–11). Henceforth, "traditional methods" of social security and welfare were to be "preserved" in the colonies even as modern industrial methods might be carefully adopted in circumscribed areas. As one member of the Colonial

Labour Advisory Committee to the new Colonial Development and Welfare Act of 1955 put it, in lieu of the formation of a "homogenous society", "tribal society" could still provide the old-aged with security ("Colonial Labour Advisory Committee – Draft Mintues of Meeting 10th November" 1955a).

CONCLUSION

In the aftermath of the Second World War, any hope that labour's cooperative spirit might be universalized so as to embrace the whole of empire was largely abandoned. In its place, attention turned towards the preservation of a fractured and depleted set of arrangements in the face of precocious independence movements. Instead of providing universal welfare, attendees of the 1954 Ashbridge Conference on Social Development identified an overriding need to preserve the "moral responsibility" of colonial subjects as traditional values and sanctions inevitably weakened under the dull impulse of urbanization. As was the case in the Moyne and Beveridge reports, attendees targeted family life as the arena wherein these disorderly impulses would have to primarily be combated ("Report of the Ashridge Conference on Social Development – 3rd–12th August" 1954). Rural grandparents would henceforth take the strain of colonial development, whereas in Britain the load could at least in principle be spread through the welfare system.

In Chapter 3 I claimed that the eugenics project rendered the urban residuum a different or lesser-part-of-the race to that of the skilled and settled worker who had been enfranchised into the Anglo-Saxon family. What this chapter has suggested is that such a process of racialized differentiation within England must be more expansively contextualized within British empire. As two world wars ground on, and as British empire came to rely upon its colonial hinterlands outside of India, it became clear to many that labour's cooperative spirit could only be positively directed amongst and by Anglo-Saxons. Beveridge supported the universalization of social insurance and welfare in Britain because he was confident that the self-help principle was sufficiently embedded amongst its labouring population to offset any encouragement of dependency. No such confidence could be placed in non-white colonial labour. As we shall now see, with the inauguration of universal welfare, the "white working class" was finally given life, but as a constituency firmly installed within imperial coordinates and their racist determinations.

CHAPTER 5

COMMONWEALTH LABOUR AND THE WHITE WORKING CLASS

INTRODUCTION

In the last chapter I argued that William Beveridge's report on universal welfare had to be contextualized in relation to Baron Moyne's report on colonial development. In this chapter, I contextualize the implementation of universal welfare in postwar Britain *vis-à-vis* the racialized response to the arrival of Commonwealth labour. Up until this era, the deserving/undeserving distinction had a formalized nature, being embedded in various poor law provisions. With the 1948 National Assistance Act, the poor laws were formally rescinded. But the deserving/undeserving distinction was preserved through informalized "colour bars" that stretched across industry and beyond.

Those who contributed to this re-racialization of the deserving/undeserving distinction included Conservative and Labour politicians as well as trade unions. Their policies and rhetoric moulded the "white working class" into a viable constituency. This constituency defined itself not in the opposition between enfranchised English labour and its residuum, but rather in the opposition between deserving whites and undeserving Black and Asian Commonwealth immigrants. So, in this chapter I examine how organized labour was complicit in an elite exercise of political domination that sought to preserve the fraying integrity of empire even as British society took on postcolonial coordinates.

In the first part of the chapter I examine political and socio-economic responses to Black immigration in the postwar period.

After 1948, the universal provision of welfare formed part of a national compact between state, business and labour. I argue that this compact was not simply national but racialized as such, and in a paradoxical way. Britain's postwar economic recovery required labour to be sourced from the colonies. However, this requirement raised the spectre of an uncontrollable immigration of Black and Asian peoples to Britain. I then chart how academic responses to the growing issue of "race relations" drew upon existing social anthropological work. By these means, the threat of disorder mooted by Black migration from the rural to the urban in the colonies (an issue we encountered in the last chapter) informed the perception of Black migration from the colonies to Britain's towns and cities. I document how informal colour bars were erected across industry and society via the mechanisms that underpinned the compact between state, business and labour. Within this racialized division of labour, Black and Asian arrivals were considered undeserving of social security and welfare, and came to disproportionately occupy the worst jobs and receive the worst provisions of public goods.

As empire underwent progressive decolonization, and as the Anglo-Saxon Commonwealth increasingly became a composite of white, Asian, Black and other independent polities, the problem of Black immigration in Britain evolved into a problem of permanent Asian and Black presence. That is the focus of the second part of the chapter. In this context, Enoch Powell emerged as a voice of English "reason". I unpack Powell's ideological position and focus upon his wish to redeem an unsullied English genus from the disaster of empire. In purifying the genus from such contaminants, Powell also implicated its degenerate attachment to labour's cooperative spirit. In other words, I argue that Powell's populist nationalism was (again, paradoxically) both racist and anti-immigrant *and* opposed to the national compact which relatively privileged white labour. I consider how Powell received significant support from white labour, many of whom identified in his position a defence of their racial interest against Commonwealth immigration. I finally turn to an autonomous resistance movement of Black and Asian workers who confronted the colour bar with a different aspiration: to universalize social security and welfare beyond race and empire's strictures. From this position a critique of the "white working class" gained traction.

In this chapter, I introduce some new concepts. The "national compact" pertains to the arrangement between state, business and labour, necessitated by postwar recovery. The national compact was racialized such that "informal colour bars" were crucial to its integrity. I also add to or take away from the ensembles that I have built into concepts over the last few chapters. For instance, Powell's politics of race gives rise to a "populist nationalism" that in many ways replaces the older imperial "Anglo-Saxon family", which had defined English belonging. Additionally, while in the last chapter I showed how labour's cooperative spirit became affiliated to the English genus, in this chapter I examine Powell's attempt to disaffiliate this spirit from the genus. This disaffiliation is key to understanding the rise of social conservatism and the Thatcher revolution that we will encounter in the next chapter.

BLACK IMMIGRATION

As I argued in Chapter 3, the National Insurance Act of 1911 was partial in its coverage, focusing, for instance, on unemployment cover for skilled workers in industries prone to cyclical unemployment. I also detailed how the raising of some welfare functions to a national level of administration was met with concern over its negative impact upon labour's "self-help" principle. The 5th of July 1948 made for a striking contrast with past legislations and apprehensions. On this day, all the elements of what would be termed the "welfare state" became active. Henceforth, the provision of insurance and allied services was universalized, with such provisions being made principally a national responsibility (albeit administered locally).

The 1948 National Assistance Act is worthy of special attention in so far as it formally rescinded the poor laws. A National Assistance Board replaced poor law governance structures, and provided maintenance for those who could not receive sufficient insurance benefits to assure an adequate level of subsistence. Oftentimes, the subjects who came under the consideration of the Board were traditionally associated with undeserving characteristics, for example, families of unemployed men, abandoned wives and single mothers (Hill 1969: 81). Still, policy makers hoped that the National Assistance Act might "destroy the prejudices and free assistance from the old and unhappy associations" (Wolton 2006: 455). The new arrangements also dramatically expanded the reach of existing arrangements. The white paper on social insurance, written in September 1944, embraced "the solidarity and unity of the nation which in war have been its bulwark against aggression and in peace will be its guarantee of success in the fight against individual want and mischance" (Fraser 2009: 204). Here, the ideological affiliation to the nation prompted by the "war spirit" exceeded the strictures of the 1867 Reform Act, which had enfranchised only the skilled and settled working man.

So, in 1948 a nationally administered welfare system came into effect whose constituency was no longer adjudicated along deserving/ undeserving lines but was delineated, instead, in universalistic terms as the resident nation. It has since become commonplace to narrate postwar British citizenship in terms of a national compact between government, labour and business. Universal welfare took its place in this compact as a means to "socialize" the cost of reproducing labour power, hence mitigating class conflict (see Wolton 2006: 457; Bakshi *et al.* 1995). One might assume, then, that the formal dissolution of the distinction between those deserving and undeserving of social security and welfare would end the racialization of the poor. Yet this was not the case.

In Chapter 3 I detailed the fallout from the Morant Bay uprising in 1865. And I paid especial attention to the way in which the political response had the effect of affirming the different jurisdictional track of white settler colonies compared to non-white colonies: the former would progressively enjoy greater independence, while the latter would remain in dependency. In the interwar period, the racialized line that cut through empire was given even greater distinction by the formation of the Commonwealth. Comprising in the main of white-settler colonies, the Commonwealth brought together self-governing polities all of which nonetheless proclaimed fealty to the Crown.

But in 1946 Canada, a Commonwealth member, introduced legislation which effectively reversed political allegiances by making subjecthood to the British Crown secondary to the possession of Canadian citizenship (Hansen 1999: 48). Indirectly, this legislation mooted the prospect that the geographical nature of empire's racial divisions might no longer be informally governed from the metropolitan core (see Waters 1997: 212; K. Paul 1995: 245–7). Arguing that citizenship "must always be equated with some homogeneity and some true community of interest and status", Home Secretary David Maxwell Fyfe responded to Canada by seeking to confer discrete citizenship on every constituency in Britain's empire.

To be fair, Fyfe was only re-amplifying concerns in the interwar and war-time period over the rise of "half-caste" children, caused by the presence of non-white sailors in dockside cities and African-American troops barracked near various towns (see Drake 1955). One might say that the mulatto figure of George William Gordon – white father, enslaved mother – still haunted the corridors of power. For it will be remembered that Gordon's extra-legal execution highlighted the racialized nature of the line that separated the imperial family from its non-white colonial subjects.

Regardless, the contentions over Canada's legislation also held implications for the ongoing attempts to rebuild Britain's postwar economy by drawing upon its "imperial preference" trading zone. Fearing that Britain's imperial power might be under threat of diminution the Colonial Office agitated in far more pragmatic terms against any legislation that might further fracture the empire (Paul 1995: 234). This concern ultimately, if temporarily, won out against the Home Office. Thus, in the same year as the National Assistance Act, the British Nationality Act of 1948 announced a new legal status: "Citizen of the United Kingdom and Colonies". With this act, the racialized distinction between Anglo-Saxon family and non-white colonial subject – the distinction that had heretofore premised the eugenicist innovations in national insurance and welfare – was legally dissolved. All Commonwealth and colonial populations inhabited the same legal status: citizen.

Could not all citizens henceforth share in Britain's new national compact? To address this question, we must turn to the issue of labour power and Britain's lack thereof in terms of the human cost of war and the challenges related to troop demobilization. Towards the end of the war the coalition government appointed a Royal Commission on Population after fears arose that the "race" was in numerical decline (Paul 1995: 255). In 1946 the Labour government set up a foreign labour committee to examine shortages in the industries essential for postwar reconstruction: coal, textiles, steel, construction and agriculture. With the lack of workforce estimated at almost one million, the government turned, necessarily, towards the importation of labour power (Paul 1995: 254–5).

Three sources were immediately available: continental European, Irish, and Commonwealth and dependencies (see McDowell 2008). Race entered into the selection calculus, with the Royal Commission preferring the recruitment of European workers for the manning of essential industries (Paul 1995: 268). Between 1946 and 1949, the Labour government recruited approximately 91,000 European persons displaced by the war (Kay & Miles 1988: 217). Cabinet-level discussions led to their initial delineation as "displaced person" being replaced with "European Volunteer Worker" in order to emphasize the shared heritage of Britons and Europeans (McDowell 2008: 55).

Anglo-Saxon exceptionalism contoured these debates. In 1946, Home Secretary J. Chuter-Ede expressed a preference to the labour committee for an intake from European countries whose populations shared a similar social background (Joshi & Carter 1984). For some pundits, Poles were considered too "Eastern", incapable of undertaking high quality work, partial to "dubious" methods of earning their living, and unable to properly assimilate into British society. The uncleanliness of the "peasant woman type" and her propensity to "drift into undesirable ways of life" was especially commented upon (Kay & Miles 1988: 291). But officialdom at large tended not to attribute such classic undeserving characteristics to Poles who were by-and-large presented as "first-class people", suitable for inter-marriage and breeding, and so of "great benefit to our stock" (Paul 1995: 269; Webster 2010: 154–6).

Labour from Éire was closer to home, albeit still tarred with a sense of degeneracy inherited from nineteenth-century commentaries from the right (Thomas Carlyle) and left (Friedrich Engels). But no ambiguity met the arrival of Black peoples, especially from the Caribbean, even though unlike European volunteer workers and Irish workers they were already British subjects and, from 1948 onwards, fellow citizens. The prospect of a mass movement of Black citizens to the mother country led Labour Prime Minister Clement Attlee, two days after the famous arrival in that year of Caribbean citizens on the *Empire Windrush*, to predict that the Black presence would impair "the harmony, strength and cohesion of our public and social life" (Carter *et al.* 1987: 1).

I want to contextualize Attlee's almost autonomic response to the proximity of Black and English bodies in relation to ongoing debates over colonial development. In the last chapter I argued that colonial policy increasingly equivocated over the possibility that labour's cooperative spirit could sprout from native interiors and subsequently be directed towards an orderly development project. This equivocation was especially directed towards urbanization in the African colonies and the seemingly dangerous and disorderly reactions from primitive natives who experienced the colour bar. Bronislaw Malinowski and other influential social anthropologists investigated these transformative processes throughout the interwar period. But by the 1940s, their investigations of rural to urban migration were steadily complemented by cognate studies of colonial to metropole migration.

Of special importance, in this regard, was the work of social anthropologist, Kenneth Little. In his wartime PhD investigation of the Black community of Tiger Bay, Cardiff, Little self-consciously conceived the study of urbanization in Africa and race relations in Britain as one field joined by the methods and premises of social anthropology (Mills 2010: 135). By the late 1940s, Little had started to curate a research programme in Edinburgh University's social anthropology department. Edinburgh subsequently became the most important academic site for developing "race relations" scholarship in postwar Britain. Little supported and/or supervised a host of academics, including Michael Banton, later to become a pre-eminent figure in the sociology of race, and who undertook an investigation of the "coloured quarter" in that longstanding wild "interior" of London, the docklands (Banton 1955).

In many ways, the work on race relations at Edinburgh was an extension of two existing debates: (1) the means by which to transplant labour's cooperative spirit from the provinces to the urban slums, as well as (2) the utility of the tribal spirit in the pursuit of colonial development. We might say, then, that race relations consolidated as a postwar field of inquiry by addressing a fundamental question: could the tribal spirit be transplanted in an orderly fashion to metropolitan towns and cities?

The work at Edinburgh of Nigerian scholar, Eyo Ndem, was especially pertinent to this line of investigation. Ndem (1957) undertook a study of "coloured communities" in Manchester, the city that had hosted the 1945 Pan-African Congress in which Ndem had taken part as representative for the Calabar Improvement League. Ndem wished to find out whether "natives" could assimilate to English social life by leaving their tribal hinterlands behind. For this purpose, he drew upon a sociological distinction between status gained by ascription – which he associated with the "traditional African system" – and status gained by achievement – associated with the "British social system". Ndem noticed that Africans resident in Britain could side-step the inferiority they might be ascribed within tribal relations by achieving beyond their status in the British system, thereby raising their "class".

Such aspirations for upward mobility were dependent upon whether their white "class" peers would accept the new status of their Black compatriots. Ndem pointed out that acceptance was assessed by white peers not in terms of the achievement itself but by the degree to which the Black citizen had managed to eschew inferior behaviours and norms ascribed to the "native", such as raucous laughter (Ndem 1957: 84–5). In short, the achievement-based British social system was informally ascriptive when it came to race. Effectively, Ndem's study suggested that, while the path to civilization for the Black individual lay in progression out of the colonial-ascriptive world into the metropolitan-achievement world, that path was in practice racialized. Key to this racialization was the "colour bar".

In the colonies, the colour bar was formally institutionalized. But in Britain, as organizations such as the League of Coloured Peoples had long complained, the bar was informal, and all the more pernicious in its effects (see Rush 2002). Recall Malinowski's claim that Europeanized natives had no faculties through which to negotiate the colour bar in an orderly fashion; the same fears of Black disorder also accompanied investigations of Britain's informal colour bar. Take, especially, the early work of Banton. Addressing a similar fear, Banton (1953: 59) claimed that "the slights, rebuffs and discrimination – real and imagined – which [Black citizens] experience [through the informal colour bar] may afterwards cause a reaction of resentment and may lead to a rejection of British cultural values and to political nationalism". Bringing Malinowski and Banton together we could say that, whether in the colony or metropole, the Black citizen was envisioned as caught between worlds, a potential harbinger of disorder and anarchy.

The academic debates regarding "race relations" mirrored concerns expressed in contemporaneous policy debates. In 1950, the Labour government convened a Cabinet committee to review ways in which the immigration of "coloured people from the British colonial territories" could be checked, despite their legal right to move being guaranteed by the 1948 Act. After Labour left office, a confidential meeting of Conservative ministers returned to the issue in 1954. The group recognized that any case for legislation against unrestricted movement required empirical data on the degenerate potential of Black immigration upon British life. As Bob Carter, Clive Harris and Shirley Joshi (1987) have documented, questionnaires were henceforth circulated to labour exchanges asking for commentary upon the industriousness and temperament of Black workers. The working party subsequently reported upon the "lack of stamina" and volatile temperament of Black workers and the "slow mentality" of Black female workers. The working party concluded that Black workers suffered higher rates of unemployment due to their undeserving characteristics and could therefore become a "charge on national assistance" as well as a force for moral degeneration as Black men mixed with "white women of the lowest types".

No legislation was immediately forthcoming. But the pertinence of this episode lies in its suggestion that the deserving/undeserving distinction remained a key organizing principle in policy debates during the era of the national compact. As I will now argue, whilst the 1948 National Assistance Act had outlawed its formal application, the distinction remained active informally, manifested in a colour bar that ranged from the home to the street to the factory. Make no mistake: the colour bar was not simply an element of the English psyche. It actively adjudicated who might be considered more or less deserving of social security and welfare.

The postwar expansion of the British economy, driven by reconstruction and the development of new towns and infrastructure, produced a steady state of labour shortages such that unemployment rates rarely rose above 2 per cent until the mid-1960s (Clegg 1979: 13; Fraser 2009: 208). Consequently, many white male workers experienced an upward mobility as they moved into the skilled manual roles made available by postwar expansion. The social grading of occupations at the time reflected such advances. In general, skilled non-manual roles were most valued, followed by skilled manual roles. Crucially, at least some manual workers valued skilled manual roles specifically in terms of their usefulness to the nation (see Young & Willmott 1956). Postwar expansion thereby allowed more English male workers to capitalize upon the prestige of skilled manual labour which had been promoted by Chartists, affirmed by Disraeli's "one nation" conservatism, and favoured by the 1911 National Insurance Act.

At the same time, the national compact devolved the management of class conflict to the shop steward system of industrial relations. As Satnam Virdee (2000: 549–50) explains, trade unions occupied a strong position in Britain's postwar economy. A high demand for labour allowed competitive collective bargaining for increased pay and better work conditions. Such bargaining, as industrial relations expert Allan Flanders told the Royal Commission on Trade Unions and Employers in 1968, was "largely informal, largely fragmented and largely autonomous" (Clegg 1979: 16). Here, the shop steward occupied a key role, securing local standards in excess of the national average. "Closed shop" negotiations with foremen and managers covered safety, overtime, dismissal, transfers and disciplinary actions (Clegg 1979: 19–25).

In the last chapter I argued that the enfranchisement of skilled and settled working men promoted the need, from the 1860s onwards, to identify in labour cooperation the principle of orderly independence. In the postwar period, marked by a consistent demand for labour, the shop steward exemplified the "self-help" principle of labour's cooperative spirit. The "closed shop" modus operandi usually bypassed national fora – wherein the state would have to expressly intervene in confrontations between capital and labour – for a set of localized and tacit arrangements between stewards and management (Joshi & Carter 1984). In this respect, the shop steward was largely responsible for the depoliticization of the labour/capital relationship. Such depoliticization did not only ensure labour's orderly independence, it was also through the depoliticized nature of this arbitration system that the informal colour bar could coalesce and racialize the postwar division of labour anew.

Trade unionists were amongst the first to protest against the movement of Black and Asian citizens to Britain, arguing that their labour was "cheap" and could be mobilized to undermine collective bargaining (Wrench 1986: 2–3). Numerous examples exist of local unions undertaking protest actions against increases in the employ-ment of Black and Asian labour (Virdee 2000: 551–2; Wrench & Virdee 1995). Shop stewards regularly agitated for a localized quota system that restricted Black and Asian labour to around 5 per cent of the workforce, and established implicit understandings with man-agement that Black and Asian labour would be first to be fired in the case of redundancies. In so far as Black and Asian labour was gener-ally employed in the lower paid and menial positions, the convenient argument could always be made that a specific line of work was being rationalized rather than Black and Asian labour being discriminated against.

Via the informal colour bar, Black and Asian labour was dispro-portionately channelled into either existing low-skill sectors that experienced labour shortages (as white workers upgraded into new sectors) or into deskilled roles created by the introduction of new technology (Joshi & Carter 1984; Ward 1978: 466–7; Sivanandan 2008: 67; Ginsburg 2000: 33). Data from the mid-1970s demonstrates the persistent effects of this racialized division of labour. Black and Asian male workers remained disproportionately represented in semi or unskilled roles compared to white male workers – 42 per cent to 18 per cent respectively. And Black and Asian workers still disproportionately occupied undesirable roles characterized by shift work, unsociable hours, low pay and unpleasant working condition (Phizacklea & Miles 1980: 18–19; see also Ramdin 1986: 262).

The same racialized divisions were applied to occupations that serviced the welfare state, especially in the staffing of the National Health Service. By 1948 local selection committees had been set up in 16 colonies to attract nurses and ancillary workers to the mother country (Ginsburg 2000: 82). Upon arrival, women from the Caribbean were pushed into low-grade work requiring heavy labour, long and anti-social working hours, and providing the poorest pay. This remained the case even if female workers' skills were more advanced and their aspirations higher (Ginsburg 2000: 83; Phizacklea & Miles 1980: 19; Noble 2015). The NHS was partially underwritten by the recruitment of such relatively cheap labour, wherein the cost of training was in good measure outsourced to the peoples and governments of the colonies (Williams 1998: 179–80). Remembering Beveridge's and Moyne's commitments to an imperial patriarchal order, it can be argued that the initial function of Black female labour in the welfare system was to support the cultivation of good white stock.

Alternatively, there was little earnest factoring in of the needs of Black and other non-white Commonwealth when it came to early welfare provision. Take, especially, the case of housing. It is fair to say that, in general, the government regeneration of slums and bombed areas had never caught up with postwar demand in general (Fraser 2009: 209). Still, the majority of Black arrivals and their families were compelled to rent sub-standard and overcrowded accommodation in the private market. When Black citizens sought to claim social housing, they were met with officers who tended to judge their standard of civilization as inadequate to the task of caring for properties. Granted a fairly wide power of discrimination in allocations, officers often saw themselves as protecting public resources against reckless Black clients (Mama 1989: 31). For fear of opening a "floodgate" of Black residents in predominantly white council estates, many officers "dispersed" Black clients to less desirable and less modernized estates (Ginsburg 1992; Henderson & Karn 1990: 3–11).

In sum, the 1948 National Assistance Act formally dissolved the distinction between those deserving and undeserving of social security and welfare as part of the new national compact. Meanwhile, to support Britain's fragile recovery from war, British citizenship became formally homogenized across empire, thus undermining the segregation between an Anglo-Saxon family and non-white colonial subjects. However, Black immigration into Britain, a necessary condition for postwar reconstruction, demonstrated how the racialized distinctions that had, in the past, primarily depended upon geographical distance now had to be remade upon the basis of physical and socio-economic proximity (Ginsburg 2000: 1). The deserving/undeserving distinction became reconstituted principally as an informal colour bar that ran the length of society, and especially through work and welfare. It was this informal bar that materially enabled the "white working class" to gain traction as a constituency.

BLACK SETTLEMENT

In 1951 approximately 74,500 Black citizens were resident in Britain; by 1962 that number had risen to 500,000 (Waters 1997: 209). In the late 1950s a recession in the car industry provoked increased hostility towards Black residents (Joshi & Carter 1984). In 1958 mass attacks by white youths on Black residents in West London and Nottingham were both, in part, instigated as reactions to inter-racial relationships. The "race riots" signalled a shift in articulating the problem of Black presence from one of arrival to permanent settlement and a struggle over resources – economic and sexual. The framing of race concomitantly shifted from that of a multi-coloured empire to a white nation (see in general Schwarz 1996; Hesse 1997).

This circumscription of race from empire to nation was heavily affected by three shifting modalities in Britain's global standing. First, incorporation into the European Economic Community (EEC) was considered necessary to ensure the continuation of Britain's postwar recovery. (By the early 1960s, Britain's attempt to set up an alternative free trade association to the EEC had largely failed.) Second, though, while trade with Europe grew faster than trade with the Commonwealth, the latter remained of crucial economic importance, taking almost three times as many British exports than the six core economies of the EEC (May 2001: 89). Support for retaining Commonwealth ties remained widespread across the political class for this instrumental reason. But third, support for the Commonwealth became fraught due to decolonization turning non-white dependencies (African and Caribbean especially) into inde-pendent members. In other words, the Commonwealth could no longer be said to comprise predominantly of the Anglo-Saxon family.

The postcolonial predicament of the white nation was now defined by the prospect of either European incorporation and/or affiliation with an independent *and* multi-coloured Commonwealth. A poll taken in September 1961 provides a sample of popular opinion on this quandary. When asked which international associ-ation was the most important, a significant majority (48%) identified the Commonwealth, while 19 per cent cleaved to the United States and only 18 per cent to Europe (May 2001: 90). But support for the Commonwealth was qualified by the racialized distinction made between the "old" members – white, Anglo-Saxon settler-colonies – and "new" members – previously non-white colonies and depend-encies (Webster 2010: 174). In the same year, another national poll indicated that 73 per cent of the public supported population controls for, specifically, "coloured colonial immigrants" (Small & Solomos

2006: 243). So much was the expansion of Commonwealth membership an issue that by this point in time Englishness was steadily being defined in opposition to the Commonwealth per se (Webster 2010: 152).

For their part, the ruling Conservative Party chose to cut the Black dependencies free and effectively reinstate the old imperial distinction between the Anglo-Saxon family and its non-white subjects which had been temporarily sutured by the 1948 Nationality Act. This was not without its contradictions; in delivering his "Winds of Change" speech to the South African parliament in 1960, Prime Minister Harold Macmillan signalled his dual intent to facilitate the independence of majority Black colonies and take a more critical stance towards white settler Apartheid. Nonetheless, when Macmillan made clear in 1961 that an application to join the EEC would not be at the prejudice of Commonwealth relations, it was to the Anglo-Saxon members that he was primarily alluding.

The Conservative government pressed on with Commonwealth realignment. The 1962 Commonwealth Immigration Act was a significant recusal of the rights of Commonwealth citizens to move unimpeded across realms. Specifically, the Act permitted entry into Britain only for those Commonwealth citizens with government-issued employment vouchers. In this way, the Act (and subsequent reductions in the number of vouchers issued) further entrenched Britain's racialized division of labour by effectively restricting the amount of skilled Black and Asian labour that could "threaten" the benefits gained by white labour (Sivanandan 2008: 72).

Meanwhile, the simultaneous attraction and reaction to Commonwealth ties placed the Labour Party in a quixotic position. The tradition of socialist internationalism had always partially inoculated Labour against racism. Officially, the Labour Party took a strong internationalist line on racial discrimination to the extent that in 1959, Hugh Gaitskell, then leader of the opposition, pronounced on television that those who wished to accept the colour bar could "go to hell!" (Fielding 2003: 1:141). A class affiliation that exceeded borders and ascriptive identities was, no doubt, a precious sentiment to many in the party. But it must be said that the sentiment was pursued with more fidelity by the Independent Labour Party (ILP). Take, for instance, the address by General Secretary John McNair to the 1945 Pan-African Congress in Manchester. McNair admitted that the "English class, with the British Government behind it" was the "greatest imperialist class of them all". McNair then recalled the opinion of his friend, and ILP supporter, George Padmore, famous Trinidadian Pan-Africanist: "George said it was the duty of white and black workers to remember they were workers and give that mighty heave which would bring down the colossus and break it" (Shilliam 2012).

In any case, despite its internationalism the Labour Party oriented towards old imperial alignments that placed the white British worker at the apex of the Commonwealth's division of labour. Precisely this hierarchy was threatened by Britain's entry into the EEC as merely one member amongst many equals (see in general Davies 1963). In fact, when it came to the party, race forced class politics into stark duplicity. For instance, in 1965 Harold Wilson, as Labour prime minister, affirmed the necessity of Commonwealth immigration restrictions while also announcing legislation that would ensure that Commonwealth residents would be treated as equal citizens. By proxy of a stipulation that the migrant had to have one parent or grandparent born in Britain, the 1968 Commonwealth Immigrants Act effectively limited permanent residence to those who could claim, effectively, the old Anglo-Saxon heredity (see in general Bhambra 2016b). But when it came to welfare provision and employment, the Race Relations Act of the same year made it illegal to discriminate on the basis of race. In effect, Labour endorsed imperial hierarchies and segregations at the same time as advocating for equality and integration on British soil.

This was the political context in which Britain witnessed its most racist election campaign to date. By the late 1950s an explicitly racist rhetoric had started to gain traction in local Conservative parties in the West Midlands (Lindop 2001: 80). Smethwick, on the face of it, seemed a safe seat for Labour, having been occupied for almost two decades by Patrick Gordon Walker, at this point the shadow foreign secretary. As Elizabeth Buettner (2014) documents, in 1962 Gordon Walker published a book lauding Britain's global standing in terms of the common citizenship provided by the multi-racial Commonwealth and bemoaning the imminent eclipse of this polity come the new Immigration Act. The real problem of immigration, Gordon Walker argued, was not the character of the arrivals but rather a lack of "housing, and overcrowding, which produces racial tension" (Buettner 2014: 62).

Opposing Gordon Walker stood Conservative Peter Griffiths, who campaigned on a straightforwardly visceral slogan: "If you want a nigger for a neighbour vote Liberal or Labour" (Buettner 2014: 71). The local newspapers gravitated towards Griffiths' message.

One would expect the "nigger" expletive to reference residents with Caribbean or African heritage. Yet it was Indian Sikhs resident in the West Midlands who were primarily targeted by the election campaign. At this point in time, Commonwealth residents of Asian heritage seemed to engender a special apprehension in terms of introducing to England an un-English – and un-Christian – culture. This cultural subversion was often contrasted to Black peoples of Caribbean heritage who were supposed to have acquired the rudiments of British culture and Christianity through the gift of abolition. But recall that in Chapter 2 we witnessed how poor whites could be blackened via the slave analogy. While in Chapter 3 we witnessed how the Irish could be similarly blackened. The Smethwick election demonstrates how, during the 1960s especially, Asian Commonwealth citizens were rendered a fundamental danger to British society by being blackened as "niggers" (Buettner 2014: 717).

Griffiths provided a major upset in winning the seat, albeit with a small margin. Yet this controversy was soon overtaken by the rise of a fellow West Midlands Conservative MP, Enoch Powell. Overwhelmingly, it was through Powell's rhetoric that Black and Asian Commonwealth settlement was rationalized in public fora as a fundamental threat: not just to the national compact, but to the preservation of the English way of life in a postcolonial era.

Powell initially turned to a political career in order to ensure the retention of India as a part of Britain's empire (Heffer 1998: 99; Nairn 1970: 10). More importantly, Powell initially came to glean the exceptionalism of Englishness from the colonial periphery, specifically, the Egyptian desert where in 1941 he worked for military intelligence (Schofield 2015: 48). In a sense, Powell apprehended Englishness as many a white settler had done so in the late nineteenth century – from abroad, and as an Anglo-Saxon. Indeed, Powell subsequently imagined his generation to be homebound after "years of distant wandering", and on a mission to reclaim an "old England" (Heffer 1998: 337).

However, by the 1960s, Powell sought to impress upon the political class another hard reality. In 1961, he delivered a famous speech to the

Royal Society of St George. The end of empire, Powell argued, "[has] so plainly ended that even the generation born at its zenith, for whom the realization is the hardest, no longer deceives themselves as to the fact" (Heffer 1998: 334–5). Earlier in this chapter I discussed how the 1948 Nationality Act collapsed the late nineteenth-century distinction between the Anglo-Saxon imperial family and non-white colonial subjects. Powell now sought to reclaim this distinction, not by the more discerning methods of the Conservative Party, but by situating the entire Commonwealth edifice (white and non-white) as an un-organic growth upon old England. The "mother country", he audaciously claimed, had "remained unaltered through it all, almost unconscious of the fantastic structure [of empire] built around her" (Heffer 1998: 337).

To be clear, Powell presented this distance in normative terms. Many Commonwealth countries, he reminded his audiences, governed along lines "repugnant to [the English] basic ideas about liberty and democracy" (Powell 1970). Powell measured this distance through racialized coordinates. For instance, the "legal fiction" created by the 1948 Nationality Act bizarrely rendered Britain's nearest European neighbours "aliens" to be "strictly excluded", while the "myriad inhabitants" of Asia, Africa and the Americas were treated in ways "indistinguishable from native-born inhabitants of these islands" (Powell 1970). Therefore, although Powell disavowed the Commonwealth, including its white polities, he never considered their Anglo-Saxon sojourners to be the same fundamental threat as visibly "coloured immigration" (Schofield 2015: 175).

What might be left after empire and Commonwealth? Powell's answer was simple: the true England (Nairn 1970: 5). When Xerxes sacked and destroyed ancient Athens, mused Powell, a sacred olive tree remained standing. So might there also by found "amid the fragments of demolished [imperial] glory" an oak tree, her "sap still rising from her ancient roots to meet the spring, England herself" (Heffer 1998: 336). The kernel that Powell alludes to is consonant with what I have termed the English genus. To retrieve the English genus from amongst the imperial debris, Powell drew upon an interwar aesthetic tradition that had elegiacally turned to the rural idyll. As part of this movement, William Cobbett experienced a small revival from the pens of Fabian historian G. D. H. Cole, whom we briefly encountered in the last chapter, and G. K. Chesterton, a literary critic whom we shall meet in Chapter 7. Powell read Cobbett's *Rural Rides* as a child and was especially taken by the work of Richard Jefferies, a nineteenth-century nature writer known for his attention to the details of English rural life (Heffer 1998: 71).

Powell's mobilization of this aesthetic tradition was indeed redolent of Cobbett's defence of the cottage economy. The vocation of politics, by this understanding, was to safeguard from foreign corruption an English genus that was distinct and exceptional to humanity in so far as it encouraged independence while also supporting the patriarchal order. Yet Powell's project distinguished itself from previous ones. His desire to purify the English genus implicated not only the impact of Commonwealth migration but also that of labour's cooperative spirit and the national compact.

In Chapter 4 we witnessed how reformers celebrated labour's cooperative spirit as part of a reconciliation of skilled and settled working men with the nation and the imperial Anglo-Saxon family. The wellsprings of this spirit were clearly identified in the provincial cooperatives that practised "self-help". But Powell's rhetoric of Englishness ignored labour's cooperative spirit. Instead, he returned the wellsprings of orderly independence to the parliamentary tradition and, more specifically, to parliamentary sovereignty (Whipple 2009: 723; Heffer 1998: 339). In line with Edmund Burke, Powell argued that parliament expressed the genus of "[English] national consciousness" as a gift "transmitted from generation to generation by a process analogous to that of inheritance" (Schofield 2015: 182). Powell's negative valuation of organized labour was resonant with Burke's late eighteenth-century apprehensions of the anarchical influence of Jacobinism. It will be remembered that the Combination Acts of this era had prohibited trade unionism on the grounds that its pursuit of the "self-help" principle was fundamentally disorderly. Put simply, Powell's glossing of England's "little platoons" brooked no labour organization.

For this reason, Powell viewed the national compact to be an un-organic growth upon the English genus akin to empire. Despite universal welfare being a key pillar of the national compact, Powell considered this experiment (except for the NHS) to be an aberration in so far as it degraded the moral character of English people. Welfare was not to be celebrated for abstract universalism but critically assessed by the degree to which its arrangements aligned to the peculiarity of the English tradition (Lewis 1979: 31). We shall come across this argument later when we investigate the contemporary rise of the Blue Labour tradition. For now, it is important to note that Powell attributed the growth of undeserving characteristics to welfare's abrogation of the principle of self-help and orderly independence. For this reason, Powell was a firm proponent of the principle of means testing, which had been central to the venerable poor law distinction between the deserving and the undeserving (Lewis 1979: 33).

1948 was the year not only of the National Assistance Act but also of the Nationality Act. As I argued in Chapter 3, national welfare and colonial development articulated as a defence of empire, and more specifically, of Anglo-Saxon patriarchy. To rebuke any one part meant to rebuke the whole. Similarly, when Powell decided that the English genus had to be purified of empire (race) the logic of purification necessarily required a removal of all mutations (class). In fine, Powell considered the indulgences of empire and "state socialism" to be conjointly responsible for the sullying of the English genus.

Consider, in this respect, Powell's speech to the South West Conservative Association in Wolverhampton, just one year before Smethwick. There, he took issue with the "imperial delusion" that allowed the British people to "consume what we have not produced" as well as the "old superstition of the Labour Party" that "they would be better off if only our existing wealth were differentially distributed" (Powell 1970). These delusions and superstitions, in Powell's opinion, induced undeserving characteristics into the nation's moral compass. They also ran counter to what ordinary people knew "without being lectured", namely, that "on our own ingenuity, effort and husbandry alone depends what this nation, and every class within it, can achieve and enjoy" (Powell 1970). For this project of recovery Powell offered his electorate "neither servitude, nor the safety, ease and irresponsibility of servitude" but "freedom … [and] the responsibilities and the opportunities, which are inseparable from it" (Powell 1970). Servitude to welfare dependency and servitude to empire conjoined; as did freedom from both.

All these logics are present in Powell's infamous "Rivers of Blood" speech, delivered to another Conservative Association meeting in Birmingham in April 1968. Powell (2007) frames his address by quoting correspondence from a "quite ordinary working man". This man (whose "ordinariness" Theresa May would recognize) worries for his children's sake that "in fifteen or twenty years' time the Black man will have the whip hand over the white man". The issue, for Powell, is not the temporary migration of Commonwealth citizens to Britain but their ever-increasing settlement as a British-born "alien element". Invoking fears of miscegenation, Powell singles out the arrival of "unmarried persons". Keen not to undermine the principle of patriarchal order, Powell agitates for the return of individuals to their places of origin so as to reunite with their kith and kin.

Powell then argues for the reasonableness of the ordinary white man's fears by focusing on the pressures that social services are placed under by Commonwealth immigration. To this end, Powell conjures images of "wives unable to get hospital beds in childbirth, children unable to get school places, [and] homes and neighbourhoods changed beyond recognition". One might be reminded, here, of referendum campaigning in 2016 and Vote Leave's arguments against immigration. This said, Powell's comments should not be interpreted as support for universal welfare (another resonance with at least the right-wing of Vote Leave). Rather, Powell makes these comments as a rhetorical strategy designed to dismiss the need for the 1968 Race Relations Bill that has recently been enacted (Lindop 2001: 81). Equalities legislation, for Powell, impinges upon the free will of the citizen and their ability to "discriminate in the management of [their] own affairs" (Schofield 2015: 213). In other words, rather than the welfare state it is principally the moral character of the English that Commonwealth immigration has been undermining.

Once more resonating with contemporary assertions of the "left behind" status of the "white working class", Powell (2007) even presents the "ordinary working man" as the "victim" of equalities legislation. In truth, he argues, the English majority have been minoritized so as to find themselves "made strangers in their own country". Powell is adamant that he and his supporters must not be considered "racialists", just as the United Kingdom Independence Party (UKIP) presently asserts. Alternatively, Powell claims to be making a common sense argument about cultural "fit" and the limits of integrating alien values (Whipple 2009: 721). But Powell's position is wilfully disingenuous in so far as he explicitly racializes those who did not wish to integrate: "their colour marks them out."

Similar to the race politics of the Smethwick election, Powell's principal concern is with the integration of Asian Commonwealth citizens (see Schofield 2015: 219). But his speech is full of racial analogy, blackening the disorderly and disintegrating alien elements in society. By Powell's (2007) own admission, he was moved to imagine the "River Tiber foaming with much blood" after he had looked on "at horror" at the United States. Here, Powell is referencing the tumult that accompanied the assassination of Martin Luther King and the turn towards Black Power. In numerical terms, muses Powell, the social disorder sown by Commonwealth settlement "will be of American proportions long before the end of the century".

Powell increasingly discussed his political conjuncture in a martial register of war and invasion (Waters 1997: 223; Gilroy 2010: 45). Take, for instance, his speech to an election meeting in Birmingham in the summer of 1970. "Britain at this moment", claimed Powell, was "under attack", its future at risk just as much as when imperial Germany had begun to build dreadnoughts or when Hitler began to rearm. There was one difference, mused Powell: the "enemy" intent on "the actual destruction of our nation and society" was now "invisible or disguised". Powell then drew immediate attention to the 1968 student rebellions – a proxy, in his mind, for state socialism – and the urban riots and uprisings by Black peoples across the United States. With regards to the latter, Powell was once again especially concerned to link migration to destruction: "the material for strife provided by the influx of negroes into the northern states, and their increase there, was flung into the furnace of anarchy."

In all these ways, Powell identified Commonwealth immigration as the key process which defiled the English genus. That much is obvious to any discerning mind. But I am making a further argument that, in this identification, Powell necessarily blackened the national compact as well as the means by which conflict between business, labour and state was to be mitigated, that is, the principle of universal welfare.

Surveys indicate that Powell's "rivers of blood" speech resonated with those who benefited from the racialized division of labour that gave the national compact its integrity. It is worthwhile situating this response in the context of a global economic crisis that had eroded the ability of industry to maintain near full employment amongst Britain's working populations. Skilled manual workers, those who benefited the most from the compact and had the most to lose in relative terms from its erosion, were most likely to develop favourable attitudes towards Powell (Whipple 2009: 727 note 45). Amongst trade union members, those in lower-ranked occupations, and, structurally speaking, in closest proximity to Black labour, tended to support Powell the most (King & Wood 1975: 247). This evidence suggests that, in general, downward mobility was associated with a fear of being levelled to the position of Black workers, which in turn influenced support for Powell (see Schofield 2015: 230).

Interestingly, trade union membership did not affect attitudes towards Powell, suggesting that the "brotherhood of man" had not tackled racism amongst its ranks. Indeed, several strikes involving 10,000–12,000 Midlands workers broke out in the aftermath of Powell's speech, in response to his immediate sacking by Ted Heath (at that time leader of the opposition). Strikes by one-third of London dockers especially caught the public mood.

London dockers were somewhat peculiar in the postwar division of labour in so far as they had managed to ensure unskilled workers received the same wages as skilled workers. Furthermore, because employment was only made possible through nomination, the informal colour bar was especially exacting in this sector such that almost all dockers were white. Even if unskilled, dockers nonetheless benefited from the national compact. But job insecurity for dockers was not a major concern at the time of their actions and neither was there any tangible threat of more Black workers joining the docks. For all these reasons, this industrial action was extremely unusual to the extent that it was not called over the standard "economistic" issues of wage and work conditions, but was, precisely, political in its subject matter. As Fred Lindop (2001) argues, in his forensic account of the strike, the source of its politics seemed to be more populist than formal, with most union officials having recused themselves from active involvement.

Of course, the foment of a specifically populist form of nationalism was Powell's aim. He argued that public outrage should be directed not towards "coloured immigrants" but first and foremost towards the politicians who supported or acted upon the logic of national suicide (Barker 1982: 15–17). Crucially, Powell sought and to some extent succeeded in weaponizing what Theresa May would later call the "ordinary working class" into a "popular will" that parliament would have to take notice of. He succeeded in good part because he played to the interests of white workers who wished to defend the racialized division of labour against Commonwealth immigration, interests that were threatened to the extent that race equalities legislation targeted the integrity of informal colour bars.

Does support for Powell demonstrate the fundamental racism of white workers? Let us take stock of the evidence. Powell's defence of the "ordinary working man" was not made through the grammar of class but of national self-respect. In the most salient strike – that of the dockers – we can also identify a populist defence, not instrumentally of the racialized division of labour, but of a racialized nation confronting the settlement of Black and Asian bodies. In the nineteenth century, Disraeli's "one nation" conservatism had incorporated the skilled and settled working man into the Anglo-Saxon family. Powell remixed this conservatism for the end of empire: the "white working class" effectively became the prime national constituency of postcolonial Britain. This is perhaps why Powell's popularity endured even though he overtly sought to disestablish the national compact that the racialized division of labour was embedded within. Powell's populist nationalism demonstrates that, in this postcolonial context, class is race.

As I have argued above, workers racialized as white were disproportionately more likely than workers racialized as Black and Asian to occupy secure, well-paid and desirable jobs. This is not to claim that all workers racialized as white occupied such jobs – of course not. The point, though, is that the racialized division of labour disproportionately favoured whiteness, and that it did so not in a haphazard but *institutionalized* way, albeit informally. Any defence of the extant division of labour necessitated at least a tacit support – or wilful ignorance (Lorde 1984) – of the racialization of those who deserved secure, stable and relatively respectable jobs. To claim deserving status was to claim whiteness, and Powell had reinvented whiteness as the core pillar of national belonging in opposition to the coloured flotsam of empire's past. In other words, the racism that I am attributing to Powell's supporters is one constitutive of class: a defence of the ordinary, deserving working class as the *white* working class.

Tellingly, the resistance to Powell's populist nationalism gathered primarily outside of organized labour. This should come as no surprise considering the fact that since 1955 the Trades Union Congress (TUC) had followed Labour's duplicity by officially opposing "colour prejudice" while still accepting the necessity for curbs on Black and Asian immigration (Fielding 2003: 1:154; Phizacklea & Miles 1992: 34).[1] By the early 1980s, the TUC began to actively campaign against racism in its ranks, and this transformation should not be ignored. Satnam Virdee is right to challenge any interpretation of labour organization at this time – especially militant labour organization – as homogenously racist. Still, racism was so commonplace in the 1960s and 1970s that, in the aftermath of Powell's "rivers of blood" speech, a Black People's Alliance was inaugurated to assist Black and Asian workers make effective representations to their unions (Virdee 2014: 119). By the time that organized labour had begun to attend to its own racism, Black and Asian workers had already begun to undertake an "independent collective resistance" (Virdee 2000: 554).

In 1976 women workers predominantly of Kenyan-Asian background walked out of Grunwick Film Processing Laboratories in protest at exploitative, racist and sexist practices. Upon picketing outside, the women were advised to join a union to represent them. And so they turned to the Association of Professional, Executive, Clerical and Computer Staffs (APEX), which promptly announced the stakes at play to be the right to form a union. While this focus side-lined the actual reasons that caused the workers to walk out (Bryan *et al.* 1985: 36), the strikers persisted for almost two years. During this time, Grunwick attracted a heretofore unseen level of support from white union members across the country.

As it snowballed, the Grunwick strike became emblematic for some of the combined enemy presented by Powell in the form of state socialism – manifest in the form of "totalitarian" trade unions – and the anarchy of Black or blackened Commonwealth immigrants. Keith Joseph, an influential Conservative MP who we shall return to in the next chapter, considered the strike to be a "make-or-break point for British democracy [and] the freedoms of ordinary men and women". Joseph described Labour politicians who supported

---

1. The aborted attempt by Wilson's government in 1974 to produce a "social contract", whereby wages would be national controlled, in principle undermined the power of shop stewards and so in principle disturbed the practical application of colour bars. But this short-lived initiative depended on the support of the TUC, which at this point in time, had shown little capacity to engage with the racism internal to its ranks.

the action as "moderates" behind whom "Red Fascism spreads" (Whitehead 1987: 219).

The point is that, in these years, race invoked a political sensibility that class, strictly speaking, did not. Take, for instance, the first strike in 1971 by agency night-cleaners, wherein Black women featured prominently (Bryan *et al.* 1985: 36). This strike in many ways pre-empted the challenge that non-unionized temporary workers in service sectors currently face in pursuing social justice. Take also the strike in 1972 of largely Black and female ancillary workers who sought to break the old paternalistic and hierarchical labour relations of the NHS. In so doing, these workers began to politicize the management structures of the most beloved of universal welfare services, long before New Labour's managerial revolution (see Bryan *et al.* 1985: 46; Mama 1992: 784–5).

These were emphatically not struggles driven by "identity politics". The "closed shop" system of labour relations disproportionately advantaged those workers who were racialized as white. In so doing, this system quarantined the struggle over capital accumulation, redistribution and labour exploitation from the political sphere. Alternatively, as Joshi and Carter (1984) argue, whenever Black and Asian workers took leadership and/or were numerically prominent their actions challenged the national compact at its weakest points. Black and Asian collective actions had no choice but to politically defend the working class at its most vulnerable points, i.e. in those labour occupations and conditions that lay on the edge or outside of the protections of the national compact. In doing so, Black and Asian struggles made visible the future struggle that waited after the dissolution of the national compact, a future that has subsequently attracted the label of "neoliberalism".

Let us consider one final aspect to this independent collective resistance. Powell had urged his fellow English men to disown empire and Commonwealth. Black and Asian peoples could not. They drew, instead, from living traditions of struggle inherited from the Caribbean, the African continent, South Asia and elsewhere. In doing so, they contextualized their struggles within the legacies of empire, inflected by Cold War realities, and which enflamed the Global South from Vietnam to South Africa to Grenada. Aware of this global context, many British Black and Asian intellectuals charged those white workers who wished to preserve their racialized benefits with complicity in the violence and exploitation of the post-imperial division of labour. As I mooted in the Introduction, this is the political and intellectual genealogy that precedes the "discovery", around 2008, of the indigenous "white working class".

CONCLUSION

When discussing the history of labour organization in the 1970s from the viewpoint of the 1990s it is hard not to presume that all roads inevitably led to Thatcherism. But before we turn to the Iron Lady in the next chapter, I want to conclude by contextualizing her rise to power in struggles over the national compact and its racialized inclusions and exclusions. After all, Thatcher was not a prodigy of Powell, but she did inherit and utilize the populist nationalism that he had engineered.

Just as Powell had blackened the national compact along with its universal welfare system, so too did Thatcher, albeit more tactfully. One year into her leadership of the Conservatives, and immigration dominated Thatcher's postbag. In 1977, she defended the common sense of ordinary (white) citizens who held "genuine fears and concerns" about the subject. In 1978, she famously observed that "people can feel rather swamped" by immigration (Butler & Kavanagh 1980: 78; Schofield 2015: 339–41). At the same time, Thatcher identified the key agent of "state socialism" in the undeserving figure of the loafing, fractious and idle shop steward, along with his irresponsible picketers. In her 1979 manifesto, against a background of winter strikes that affected transport and waste, Thatcher promised to dismantle Labour's "militant's charter". In her estimation, such a compact had "tilted the balance of power in bargaining ... away from responsible management and towards unions, and sometimes towards unofficial groups of workers".

In 1867 Disraeli graciously enfranchised the skilled and settled working class into the Anglo-Saxon family. Thatcher's victory confirmed their return to the conservative fold. Skilled workers swung 11 per cent towards Conservative, which was more than unskilled workers, who nonetheless swung at 9 per cent. Contrast this with a small swing away from Conservative by the managerial class. Tellingly, trade union members swung more towards Conservatives

(8.5%) than non-members (5.5%) (Butler & Kavanagh 1980: 343). Yet Thatcher's victory should not be mistaken as proof that the working classes wished to disestablish the social security and welfare elements of the national compact. True, voters overwhelmingly expressed support for Thatcher's promised tax cuts. But when asked to balance cuts against reduced health, education and pension provision, the majority accepted the present tax burden (Butler & Kavanagh 1980: 340).

The point is that despite the wishes of such electorate, Thatcher's victory lay the groundwork for precisely such a disestablishment to proceed over the course of the rancorous 1980s. Stuart Hall and others famously argued that, as the 1970s wore on, unionism and Black and blackened-Asian communities were increasingly articulated as *the* problem of law and order. Young Black men of the Rastafari faith were particularly singled out as ruthless "muggers" of elderly white English women and as harbingers of anarchy (Solomos *et al.* 1992: 23; Cashmore 1979). As Thatcherism intensified this war against an internal enemy, the protective covering of the national compact for *all* workers and vulnerable peoples was removed. In so far as the Labour Party and the union movement had tacitly or otherwise supported informal colour bars, they, too, eased the path towards the dismantling of social protections against the vagaries of the market.

In this chapter I have detailed how Black and Asian sufferers confronted the deserving/undeserving distinction that had been preserved, postwar, in the shape of informal colour bars. Against the conceit of the national compact, Black and Asian collective action necessarily focused upon non-unionized, unrepresented or casualized workers in lesser valued and/or unskilled roles. Even as they had been disproportionately excluded by the racialized national compact, Black and Asian sufferers nonetheless signalled a global warning over the diminution of public goods and the deepening of marketization. As such, their collective actions logically defended the interests of the white poor who existed on the margins of Britain's racialized division of labour. Some of these struggles even pursued an alternative social – global – compact, wherein no distinction between deserving and undeserving could be allowed to compromise the universal principle of security and welfare for all.

Workers who were racialized as white and who *acted on behalf of a "white working class" constituency* could not but be agents in their own demise. They were complicit in the retention of the distinction between those deserving and undeserving of social security and welfare. Their defence of a racialized division of labour demanded such complicity. Their preference to defend their race over their class unintentionally helped to inaugurate the neoliberal era wherein the deserving/undeserving distinction was wielded by political elites to cut apart this constituency. Even if partially self-authored in this era of British history, the "white working class" lived and died as an artefact of political domination.

CHAPTER 6

SOCIAL CONSERVATISM AND THE WHITE UNDERCLASS

INTRODUCTION

In the last chapter I examined how the deserving/undeserving distinction was formally rescinded in the 1948 National Assistance Act but informally reintroduced through colour bars that moderated the national compact between state, business and labour. At this moment in British history, a short- to medium-term material benefit ensued from membership of a "white working class" constituency. But when Thatcherism destroyed the national compact, this constituency lost its institutionalized – albeit informal – advantage within Britain's racialized division of labour. In this chapter, I examine the ways in which the eugenicist concern for the residuum survived to inform social conservative thinking in the 1970s. Post-Thatcher, social conservatism influenced the reintroduction into social policy of the distinction between those deserving and undeserving of welfare. Concurrently, an obsession rose with a population group who inhabited Britain's council estates, were seemingly immune to character improvement, and were, shockingly, white.

In the first part of the chapter I return to the postwar period and the continued influence of eugenicist interventions into the urban poor. I follow the way in which concerns over parenting and the inter-generational transmission of poverty no longer addressed the "residuum" but rather "problem families". I track these concerns as they gained momentum with the importation from the United States of notions of an "underclass" that lived through a "culture of poverty". Such ideas were drawn upon by Keith Joseph and Margaret Thatcher to inform the social-conservative basis of their economic revolution. In the United States the "culture of poverty" thesis betrayed a racialized subject: the African American mother and absent father. In Britain, this subject appeared as the victim of Thatcher's deindustrialization, that is, a distinctly white underclass.

In the second part of the chapter I turn to New Labour and its incorporation of American "workfare" into British social policy, whereby welfare was once more made formally conditional upon the ability and desire of the claimant to work. I examine how both New Labour and subsequently the Conservatives sought to mend "broken Britain" by returning to a paternalistic politics of improving the character of the undeserving poor. I relate these policy developments to an increased focus in public discourse on residents of council estates, who were disparaged for lacking patriarchal responsibility and industriousness. Within an era also marked by debates over immigration, multicultural values and anti-discrimination legislation, I show how resident problem families became racialized as explicitly white, as a group whose behaviour sullied whiteness. I finish by recounting how this racialization came to a head in the 2011 riots and uprisings that began in Tottenham, London.

In this chapter, some existing concepts take on new life, such as the urban "residuum", which gives way to "problem families" and a "white underclass". I also introduce some new concepts. I examine how New Labour attempted to cultivate a multicultural sense of national belonging in the absence of a national compact and in the presence of long-term white poverty. The concept of "social cohesion" was seminal to such attempts. I differentiate between policies of "national cohesion", seeking to integrate non-white – sometimes immigrant – residents (especially Muslims), and policies addressing "national degeneration", seeking to integrate the white underclass back into the employment market.

PROBLEM FAMILIES AND THATCHERISM

During the interwar depression years, the means testing of welfare provision at the household level created significant public rancour. In fact, William Beveridge's 1942 report was popular in large measure due to its stated aspiration to provide insurance at a subsistence level, thereby making means testing a redundant issue (Deacon 1982: 290, 295). However, Conservatives in the war-time government balked at the loss of means testing and Labour members of the coalition offered no real resistance. Therefore, even as the 1948 National Assistance Act formally abolished the deserving/undeserving poor distinction, the new welfare system was not entirely absent of its normative legacies. Means testing remained under the new system, although it was never entirely arbitrary, being regulated by national statutes (Marshall 1965: 265). Perhaps more importantly, properly "universal" services – for example, education, health and pensions – came to be intrinsically valued more highly than "partial" services – for example, housing and unemployment (Lewis 1996: 110–11). Those who accessed the latter were at risk of being presumed undeserving in so far as they were prone to being "tested".

Meanwhile, eugenics continued to influence debate and policy on the urban residuum (Stone 2001: 403). In the interwar years, an increase of "coloured children" born to white mothers and colonial seamen compounded eugenicist concerns with English "stock" in ways that pre-empted Clement Attlee's postwar response to Black immigration. The Association for the Welfare of Half-Caste Children sponsored the first systematic research on race relations in Britain in 1930, 20 years before Kenneth Little began his initiative at Edinburgh University (Drake 1955: 200). As will be remembered, Baron Moyne's report on colonial development and Beveridge's report on welfare in Britain both sought to put women in their proper place, the latter with a decidedly eugenicist tenor.

Certainly, eugenicists had to step carefully around the horror of the Shoah. But this did not stop the most influential postwar theorist of the "welfare state", T. H. Marshall, from debating the relationship between familial inheritance and universal welfare. Famously, Marshall (1992) argued that the national compact had brought together two egalitarian projects which might never entirely align – an enlargement of citizenry sharing a common culture, and an economic redistribution of wealth. Marshall's suspicion had a eugenic premise. In his Galton Lecture to the Eugenics Society (1953), he admitted that a tension existed between his support of the universal principle that all citizens should be able to perform any role, and his concern that the inheritability of intelligence could not be ignored, even if it could be mitigated. Marshall's argument resonates with Beveridge's concerns, recounted in Chapter 4, that the pursuit of equality of opportunity should not result in the erasure of the family unit.

Perhaps exerting more practical influence than Marshall was a 1943 report, authored by the Hygiene Committee of the Women's Group on Public Welfare, entitled *Our Towns*. The debt the report owed to *fin de siècle* debates on the urban residuum was self-evident, with a quotation from Charles Booth's famous survey appearing in its introduction. The report described the residuum as an "intolerable and degrading burden to decent people forced by poverty to neighbour with it" (Welshman 1999: 793). Eugenicist concerns for the reproductive activities of "feeble-minded" women also reverberated across the pages. One influential term was introduced by the report: "problem families" (see in general Macnicol 1987). Effectively, *Our Towns* repackaged most of the elements that comprised the meaning of the "urban residuum" into the new label of "problem families". Subsequent studies addressed the educational disadvantages suffered by the children of these families (Macnicol 1987: 296). By the 1970s, problem families had become a useful category for the delineation of a new social conservatism.

In the early 1970s, fellow conservatives Margaret Thatcher and Keith Joseph (the more senior politician at the time), co-founded the Centre for Policy Studies (CPS). The CPS advanced Enoch Powell's agenda to break the national compact between state, labour and business, with Joseph utilizing the work of American economist Milton Friedman to develop and communicate an intellectual argument for monetarism and market self-regulation (Desai 1994). In one sense, Joseph's treatises on economic policy were radical for a conservative. In another sense, however, Joseph revealed himself to be a traditional paternalist, demonstrating a sincere desire to break what he termed the "cycle of deprivation" – a purported inter-generational transmission of poverty through problem families (Denham & Garnett 2001).

Joseph developed his argument explicitly in the eugenicist register of late Victorian welfare policy, as demonstrated by his controversial Edgbaston speech in 1974. There, he drew attention to the degenerative effect on "our human stock" caused by adolescent pregnancies and unmarried mothers rearing delinquent youths (Joseph 1974).

Joseph voiced concern over the same moral issues debated by the Charity Organization Society and Fabians at *fin de siècle*. Lacking any impetus to help themselves, argued Joseph, the poor might lose their "traditional morals" by cultivating dependencies that would "ruin" the health of the nation. But Joseph (1974) was far bolder than his predecessors in proposing a market solution. Economics, he argued, was "deeply shaped by values, by the attitude towards work, thrift, ethics, public spirit". By this logic, Joseph anchored the principle of individual freedom, derived from the monetarist/self-regulation position, to a social conservatism that upheld the moral distinction between deserving and undeserving.

The tenor and forthright nature of the Edgbaston speech (rather than its substance) made Joseph's bid for Conservative Party leadership untenable. Powell, who shared similar viewpoints, had already outed himself as far too much of a maverick to run in any such competition. Joseph henceforth supported Thatcher's candidacy. But while Thatcher shared Joseph's instincts when it came to the embedding of free market principles within social conservatism, she notably qualified conservatism's traditional paternalism.

It will be remembered from Chapter 3 that, with the 1867 Reform Act, Disraeli enfranchised settled and skilled working men into the Anglo-Saxon family, a container of nation and empire. As such, familial membership connoted the end of class struggle. In 1950, in her adoption meeting as Conservative candidate for Dartford, Thatcher (née Roberts) announced her concordance with Disraeli's tenet: one nation rather than class struggle. Additionally, she praised Disraeli's "characteristically British" approach to the problems of industrialization and made the argument that the old Tory had always appreciated the "peculiar character" of the English (Evans 2009: 108–9). In other words, Thatcher entered the political arena believing that good small patriarchs would pursue orderly independence.

But Thatcher was also deeply attached to the writings of a non-English (albeit naturalized) Austrian economist, whom she had encountered during her undergraduate years at Oxford. In writing his famous *Road to Serfdom* during the Second World War, Friedrich Hayek sought to make the case that Nazism and socialism shared a totalitarian impulse. Both endeavoured to centrally organize society through the state. In opposition, Hayek argued that social institutions were best shaped organically rather than by top-down ideological fiat.

Thatcher wished to connect what she understood to be Hayek's moral philosophy of individual freedom to Joseph's promotion of monetarism and free-market principles. Thatcher thereby came to identify in the market the mechanisms by which society could be freely shaped. But Thatcher made this connection by dispensing with Disraeli's conception of the "nation" as a filial constituency. The nation, Thatcher believed, had been tainted too much with the ideological design of the national compact. Not only did this compact breed undeserving characteristics amongst its constituents, especially with their reliance upon universal welfare. It was also antithetical to true, British freedoms. In place of the nation per se, Thatcher mooted a "property-owning democracy" (Evans 2009: 108).

It will be remembered that Powell had excised labour's cooperative spirit from the English genus. According to him, the national compact had robbed that spirit of its key deserving characteristic: orderly "self-help". Hence, Powell affiliated the English genus solely with Burke's "little platoons". Similarly, Thatcher rendered filiation to the English genus in terms of property ownership rather than labour cooperation. Interestingly, the originator of the phrase "property-owning democracy", Conservative MP Noel Skelton (1924), had in mind co-ownership of workers in the businesses that employed them. Alternatively, Thatcher returned the term to the eighteenth-century common law understanding of liberty: the liberty to inherit private property.

Rather than assemble the "little platoons" of property owners into a larger patriarchal hierarchy, i.e. a filial nation of Disraeli's "one nation" kind, Thatcher arranged them more horizontally, as equitable units all headed by small patriarchs. This vision was to a large degree compliant with Edmund Burke's, except lacking the broader paternalistic hierarchies that Burke had attached to the nobility and Christianity. Through these subtle measures, Thatcher replaced the traditional conservative deference to one nation with a patriotic defence of property-owning democracy.

Thatcher's most infamous speech directly espoused this new constituency. In an interview for *Woman's Own* in 1987, just after her third election victory, the prime minister berated those who depended upon the welfare state. "They are casting their problems on society", she opined, "and who is society? There is no such thing!" (Thatcher 1987). The quote has usually been interpreted as a promotion of radical individualism – indeed, a disbelief in society per se. Yet in her original interview Thatcher immediately continued:

> There are individual men and women and there are families and no government can do anything except through people and people look to themselves first. It is our duty to look after ourselves and then also to help look after our neighbour and life is a reciprocal business and people have got the entitlements too much in mind without the obligations.
>
> (Thatcher 1987)

Thatcher's point, as she later expressed in Hayekian fashion, was that society was not an abstraction, but a "living structure of individuals, families, neighbours and voluntary associations" (Thatcher 1993: 626).

Thus, in Thatcher's estimation the market was moral in so far as it checked the un-organic and totalitarian designs of the national compact, its corporatist compromise between government, business and labour, as well as its universal welfare system. Everything about the compact, for Thatcher, not only promoted unfreedom but, crucially, also bred undeserving characteristics amongst its constituents. Instead, Thatcher praised the market in so far as its mechanisms redeemed the deserving characteristics that had traditionally underwritten the orderly independence of England's small patriarchs, and which had been debased by the enforcement of universal welfare. In disowning the national compact and its welfare system for a property-owning democracy, Thatcher reintroduced the deserving/undeserving distinction back into the centre ground of social policy. To begin with, the reintroduction was rhetorical. But over the course of the 1980s, legislation followed.

Thatcher conceived of the political revolution that we now know as neoliberalism in an era where the derserving/undeserving distinction had been principally institutionalized through informal colour bars. That much is evident from the last chapter. As I also argued, Thatcher drew upon Powellite rhetoric in her election strategy, suggesting that a white nation was being undermined by Commonwealth "aliens". But while Powell had turned race into fate,

Thatcher pointed out that Black and Asian residents could aspire to assimilate, that is, to develop the deserving characteristics that were fundamental to the English genus. Take, for instance, the speech to her Finchley constituency in the 1979 general election:

> It does not matter what your background is, where you come from. If you want to use your own talents, be responsible for our own families, work jolly hard and be prepared to help your neighbour, we are the party for you.
> (Evans 2009: 110)

Consider also the Conservative campaign in the 1983 election which featured one poster of a young Black man, wearing a slightly ill-fitting suit, accompanied by the strapline: "Labour says he's Black. Tories say he's British." As Paul Gilroy (2010) notes, the image gives the sense of a somewhat awkward attempt by a young man to claim social respectability, in other words, to affiliate with England's "little platoons".

It would be fair to argue, then, that Thatcher's neoliberal revolution was ambivalent when it came to race. On the one hand, her electoral success was in good part dependent upon channelling Powell's racialized populist nationalism. On the other hand, her and Joseph's project of marketization required the destruction of the national compact and its colour bars that benefited white workers in the division of labour. Thatcher in no way sought to structurally redress the racialized inequalities, exclusions and violences historically suffered by Commonwealth citizens in Britain. Nonetheless, her revolution had the effect of delinking the deserving/undeserving distinction from informal colour bars and returning it to the general economy as a test of moral character. To explore this shift and its racial implications I now want to turn to the influence of American social conservatism.

In 1966 Oscar Lewis wrote an influential anthropological treatise on the slums of America's de facto Caribbean colony, Puerto Rico. In this work, and drawing upon his previous research in Mexico City, Lewis (1966) identified a "culture of poverty", its key characteristics being short-term calculations, a fatalistic attitude, sensual decadence and poor family planning. Lewis was keen to point out that these classically undeserving traits were not the product of traditional culture nor of racial affiliation. They were, instead, an effect of a Western-imposed economic system. Lewis's was a careful and considered thesis. But it would not remain so on the North American mainland. There, the idea of a "culture of poverty" became embroiled in controversies over the pathologies of the urban Black family (see Wilson 2009).

In 1965 Daniel Patrick Moynihan reported to the US Department of Labor on entrenched urban poverty. One of the key findings that Moynihan presented came via a comparison of the habits of relatively affluent white families and those of poor African Americans. The report claimed that in the families of the latter comparatively more marriages dissolved, more births were illegitimate, and more households were female-headed and trapped in welfare dependency (US Department of Labor: Office of Policy Planning and Research 1965: 6). The racialization of the culture of poverty, represented by reports such as Moynihan's, was subsequently popularized through commentaries in magazines such as *Time* (Aponte 1990: 120). By the 1980s, the cultural pathologies of what had come to be known as the "underclass" were firmly associated with the absent Black father and the single-headed Black female household (Aponte 1990: 132–3).

The postwar tradition of studying "problem families" in Britain was buoyed by the work of Moynihan and others. For instance, in his time as secretary of state for social services in Ted Heath's government, Joseph sought to bring the cultural pathology approach to bear on the issue of poverty alleviation (Deacon 2003: 130–1). In this regard, the American influence contributed to a movement of British policy making rightward. The "culture of poverty" thesis buoyed the existing socially conservative emphasis on malformed character and the inter-generational transmission of classical undeserving traits such as idleness and dishonesty (Welshman 2005: 315). It was hardly difficult for the racialization of these traits to be considered common sense in colour-bar Britain. Or so it seemed.

In 1989 social scientist Charles Murray visited London. Murray had gained notoriety in the United States by making arguments regarding the relationship between race, environment and intelligence, which in many ways would have been common sense to Beveridge *et al*. Like Joseph, Murray mobilized these arguments to make the case, very influentially, that welfare only exacerbated the social pathologies that produced poverty. It should be noted that the book wherein Murray made these claims, *Losing Ground*, was written under the aegis of America's arch social-conservative, Irving Kristol. While in London, Murray publicly promoted his argument that the "civilizing force of marriage" was the only way to check the "spreading disease" of "underclass" single mothers having babies with absent fathers, a practice he termed "essentially barbarianism" (Slater 2014: 962).

Writing in *The Times*, though, Murray disputed a presumption that he heard "everywhere, from political clubs in Westminster to some quite sophisticated demographers in the statistical research offices", namely, that the underclass was a "Black problem" (Murray 1996: 30). Such was the view, for example, of politician, sociologist and one-time director of the LSE, Ralph Dahrendorf (later to become Lord). In 1987 Dahrendorf had written an article for the *New Statesman* in which he argued that the underclass posed a critical challenge to the "moral hygiene" of British society and should be understood as a "phenomenon of race", just as it was in the United States (Lister 1996: 10). Yes, Murray responded, with a critique that Baron Moyne would have made back in 1938, "Blacks born in the West Indies have much higher illegitimacy ratios … than all whites". But, Murray pointed out, such "Blacks" formed a negligible percentage of the UK population.

Murray's demographic qualification of the association between "Black" and "underclass" must be contextualized within the social and economic upheavals of the early years of Thatcherism. By mid-1984, the employment base had contracted by 1.7 million. Manufacturing was especially hit by the economic downturn, with output declining 20 per cent and fixed investment by 23 per cent (Yeandle 2003: 8–10). Such decline affected not only Wales and the North but also relatively prosperous manufacturing regions such as the West Midlands. Male unemployment decreased drastically in this sector, only to be partially offset by new – often part-time – employment in services, heretofore a less prestigious and feminized sector. So, while part-time jobs taken by women increased dramatically, the same period witnessed a growing phenomenon of long-term unemployed older men. Younger men would have to navigate a precarious, mercurial, less-prestigious and low-wage job market.

While these economic contractions were part of a global recession, it was clear that the imposition of monetarist policy severely exacerbated the fallout in Britain and was responsible for approximately half of all jobs lost during the period. For its part, the Conservative government claimed that, although painful, the loss of employment was necessary to shed the unproductive overmanning that had plagued the previous decades (Martin 1991: 240–2, 258). Certainly, Thatcher's intentional programme of deindustrialization was designed to break the national compact, whose strategic site was the local union and factory-based "closed shop" that mainly represented skilled manual labour. But because the compact dispro-portionately advantaged white male workers through its informal colour bars, Thatcherism had the effect of introducing a down-wardly levelling trajectory for working conditions between labourers racialized as white, Black and Asian.

In many ways, then, as Murray wrote on the British underclass, the conditions, wages and prospects of white male workers had progres-sively worsened to take on similar characteristics to those suffered disproportionately by Black and Asian workers. The latter, after all, had been regularly excluded by informal colour bars from occupying relatively stable and well-paying jobs that garnered social status.

The line of argument that I am taking here is delicate and can be easily misconstrued. It is entirely the case that, despite Thatcher's reassurances, fear of and disdain for Black and South Asian Commonwealth citizens and their progeny never subsided during the 1980s and 1990s. Racialized discrimination remained vitriolic in the criminal justice system and in welfare provision. Yet while the job market remained discriminatory, this discrimin-ation became more individualized and fractured in its application. My precise point is that the racialized division of labour was no longer given integrity through a *national* compact that impelled colour lines to be informally yet systematically defended. After Thatcher, that constituency co-authored by various political elites as well as trade unions – the "white working class" – became of rhetorical value only. Moreover, as Thatcherism ran its course, the racialized nature of the deserving/undeserving distinction shifted from a generic concern for "problem families" towards a specific reference point: a white underclass.

WORKFARE AND COUNCIL ESTATES

Tony Blair and Gordon Brown's renovation of the Labour Party owes much to their infatuation with Bill Clinton's winning strategy

119

in 1994, which folded the social-conservative critique of the "culture of poverty" into an ostensibly liberal-left politics (King & Wickham-Jones 1999: 62–3). The Democrat's embrace of the conservative critique, with its infamous depiction of the Black "welfare queen", was arguably more crudely racist and misogynistic than the rhetoric of the republican right. Regardless, the New Labour position owes much to two normative tenets that underlay Clinton's electoral success: a promise to "end welfare as we know it" (Vobejda 1996) by subscribing to a policy of "welfare to work", and an attenuated but pronounced defence of the principle of redistribution.

Blair and Brown were especially infatuated by the Clintonite distinction between an "active" and "passive" welfare system. The former, unlike the latter, made receipt of insurance and welfare conditional on the claimant participating in work-related and work-promoting activities (Daguerre 2004; Lister 1998: 219). This "welfare to work" or "workfare" model resonated with attempts by previous Conservative governments to introduce more conditionalities into welfare provision, beginning with "restart" interviews for benefit claimants in 1986. Upon unveiling the Welfare Reform Bill in 1999, Alastair Darling, then social security secretary, explained that there was "no automatic right to benefit" and that peoples' minds had to be "focused on work rather than benefit" (BBC News 1999). The principle underlining the Bill was one of "work for those who can and security for those who cannot". After a set time period, claimants would have to choose between job placements, voluntary work, environmental work or full-time education or training, else risk being sanctioned and lose benefits.

The punitive nature of welfare reform only increased over New Labour's tenure, with the 2009 Welfare Reform Act effectively extending workfare conditionalities and sanctions to encompass the disabled and mentally ill. The weight given to conditionality in turn focused policy making far more keenly upon the behaviour of benefit recipients. The policy aspiration was for undeserving behaviour to be socially engineered into deserving behaviour through the instruments of welfare. New Labour even found inspiration in early twentieth-century attempts to reform the character of the urban residuum. Take, for instance, their Fabian-influenced preference to dispense benefits in kind (which could affect behaviour) rather than in cash (which would not) (Lund 1999: 456). And, just like nineteenth-century charity organizations, eugenicists and twentieth-century social conservatives, New Labour also focused its behavioural engineering on low-income and single-parent families. Opening such families up to a world of work was believed to be both economically advantageous and morally corrective. This was the thinking behind initiatives to improve childcare provision as well as tax credits to boost income (see in general McDowell 2005).

New Labour accepted the fact that Thatcher had destroyed the old national compact and that the corporatist arrangement could not return. With this ground (enthusiastically) conceded, New Labour shifted the socialist commitment to redistribution from "equality of outcome" to "equality of opportunity". During the 1997 election campaign, Brown, future Chancellor of the Exchequer, promised that a New Labour government would not seek to raise taxation for redistribution through welfare and social services, but would rather seek to expand opportunities for social advancement through education, training and access to employment (Lister 1998: 216–17). It cannot be denied that Blair's government actively sought to address the social inequalities suffered by those who had once been Labour's traditional constituency. But this was not guided by the language or politics of class. Crucially, the chosen language of "exclusion" reflected New Labour's definition of redistribution as "equality of opportunity". The return of class after Thatcherism would have to wait until a global financial crisis threatened New Labour's electoral viability.

In sum, New Labour abandoned any socialist commitment to the national compact and its mediation, through universal welfare, of class struggle. In socially conservative fashion they re-inscribed the deserving/undeserving distinction upon the heart of social policy. Deserving characteristics would be encouraged – and rewarded – through an expanded equality of opportunity. Alternatively, undeserving characteristics would be penalized through conditionalities and sanctions related to workfare.

However, the New Labour strategy of reinvention was dependent upon economic growth, especially a successful reorientation of Britain's location in the global economy. It was in this respect that the deserving/undeserving distinction took on even more political weight through the contentious movement towards a multi-cultural national identity.

As part of New Labour's economic reorientation, immigration became a fundamental element of macroeconomic policy. But as immigration increased, so did emigration, leading to a significant and steady rise in "foreign born" residents and citizens. With an increasingly global division of labour, and in the (often muted) tradition of internationalism, a set of landmark anti-discrimination and equalities legislation came to mark New Labour's first term: the Human Rights Act of 1998, the Macpherson Report of 1999, and the subsequent Race Relations (Amendment) Act of 2000. These instruments sought to address the historical legacies of racism against Commonwealth citizens and migrants, thereby legislating for Britain's present and future "multicultural" population.

To be clear, a concern for Black inner-city youth and their propensity for "mugging" had never vanished under Thatcherism. Furthermore, under the New Labour governments, Black and South Asian women were over-represented in an increase of incarceration rates caused by various newly authored crime and disorder acts (Fisher 2006: 54). Still, early on in New Labour's tenure, Brown announced a New Britain wherein the proud internationalism of the country's past would be retrieved, consigning the Tory "mistrust of foreigners" to history (Richards 1999). That this retrieval was deemed harmonious to the demands of the global economy is demonstrated by Brown's comments at the 2004 Labour Party conference. There, he aligned internationalism to an "enterprising" culture that nonetheless renewed the British tradition of civic values, a sense of duty and fair play (Wright 2004).

As New Labour entered office, the Runnymede Trust commissioned a report on the "future of multi-ethnic Britain", chaired by Bhikhu Parekh. Although not officially sanctioned, the report was ultimately launched by Jack Straw, Blair's first home secretary, at the Royal Commonwealth Society in 2000. Parekh's conception of British citizenship radically displaced Powell's attempt to purify the English genus of empire by presenting devolution within the Union as part of a postcolonial forging of a "community of communities". In this respect, Parekh argued for a recognition that England, Scotland and Wales were "multi-ethnic, multi-faith, multi-cultural, multi-community societies" (Parekh *et al.* 2010: 2). The significance of Parekh's report was to reinvent a category of belonging, Britishness, that de-racialized the filiation to an English genus.

Despite these promising signs, New Labour's celebration of multicultural diversity soon turned (back) to the racialized management of those "outsider" peoples who threatened Britain's "cohesion" (Squire 2005: 55–6). Already in 1999, the Immigration and Asylum Act had repealed the provisions of the 1948 National Assistance Act for persons "subject to immigration control", i.e. asylum seekers. This was the first piece of legislation that made postwar welfare provision conditional rather than universal. 9/11 and the Global War on Terror are obvious reference points for a turn away from Parekh's multi-ethnic embrace of Britishness. Nevertheless, the proximate coordinates were a set of riots and uprisings earlier in 2001 which occurred less than two weeks before Blair's second electoral victory.

At one point in time, Oldham, Burnley and Bradford had been served well by the textiles industry. But by 2001, in the aftermath of Thatcher's contrived deindustrialization, these northern towns possessed some of the most deprived boroughs in the country. Areas in the boroughs where people of South Asian heritage lived suffered disproportionately from poor and insufficient housing stock, unemployment and low-wage labour markets. Following a march organized by the far right through some of these localities, riots and uprisings broke out over a weekend in May 2001. In the aftermath, Blair's government commissioned a report, chaired by John Denham. Despite coming soon after the Macpherson report, Denham's report focused less on institutional racism and much more on the problem of "community cohesion" (Rhodes 2009). One year after the disturbances, the Home Office set up a Community Cohesion Unit as well as a Community Cohesion Pathfinder Programme for utilization by local authorities.

Claire Worley (2005: 485–6) has perceptively noted how the discussion of "community cohesion" by New Labour politicians often slipped into a concern for "national cohesion". This concern betrays a subterranean commitment, in the minds of policy makers, to retain a singular, racialized filiation to the English genus. Put otherwise, from an initial impulse to reframe Britain's constituencies within a post-imperial constellation, New Labour soon fell back onto familiar postwar framings of national belonging. In the counter-terrorism strategies that grew in intensity after the London bombings of 2005, a Powellite vision once more took hold. Non-white immigrants – especially Muslims and refugees – were painted as threats to Britain's

idyllic landscape. Assimilative rather than truly multicultural direct-
ives informed cohesion policies. Citizenship ceremonies demanded
a knowledge of Britain that not even the native-born possessed.
And the promotion of "British values" through the PREVENT
counter-terrorism agenda even made schools a front-line of national
defence (see in general Back *et al.* 2002; Wolton 2006; NUS Black
Students 2015).

Community cohesion, though, was Janus-faced. The English
genus faced an outward problem of national *cohesion* exemplified by
non-white migrant religion and culture; but it also faced an internal
problem of national *degeneration* exemplified by problem families.
In 1997, Blair claimed Thatcher's long-term legacy was the creation
of families with three generations of unemployed. That no study
had (or has since) found substantive evidence of such acute inter-
generational unemployment did not deter Blair from identifying a
new dysgenic site associated with this legacy (see Macmillan 2011;
Macdonald *et al.* 2014). If the urban residuum of the nineteenth century occupied the East End slums, the degenerate "underclass" of the
twenty-first century inhabited the council estate.

In pursuit of a "nation of property owners" the Conservative Party
had introduced the right to buy social housing for its residents in
1979. But not all residents could afford to take advantage of this offer.
Consequently, two-thirds of social housing came to be occupied by
the poorest two quintiles of the British population (Valentine & Harris
2014: 86). This progressive concentration of poverty into council
estates was by and large left unaddressed during the Conservative
governments (excepting the New Life for Urban Scotland initiative).
However, in June 1997, Blair appeared in front of the Aylesbury estate
in South London, one of Britain's largest and most impoverished
agglomerations of social housing (Johnstone & Mooney 2005).

Blair's appreciation of neighbourhood was remarkably similar to
Thatcher's and resonant with Edmund Burke's depiction of "little
platoons". The neighbourhood was a site where, for Blair, "bonds of
civil society" could salve "rootless morality", and where "rights and
duties" might be balanced (Johnstone & Mooney 2005). In effect, it
was the "resident's association" rather than labour cooperatives that
for the Labour leader exemplified the spirit of orderly self-help. By
contrast, Blair viewed council estates as seedbeds of idleness, delin-
quency and broken families. Addressing the residents of Aylesbury,

whom he considered to be the "forgotten people" of Thatcherism, Blair targeted the culture of "fatalism" that, in his understanding, was partly responsible for long-term unemployment and other ills.

Henceforth, the council estate became the quintessential site in which the deserving/undeserving distinction would be mobilized by New Labour to inform social policies. After Blair's visit to Aylesbury, Harriet Harman, New Labour's first secretary of state for social security, announced an attack upon the causes of "social exclusion" and made the case that employment was central to the struggle (Lister 1998: 219). The new Social Exclusion Unit was promptly set up to tackle truancy, school exclusions, sleeping rough and the "worst estates" (Lister 1998: 221). The resident youth of such estates suffered especially from overwhelming surveillance and sanctions (Johnstone & Mooney 2005).

Still, as Murray had already intonated, poverty in post-Thatcher Britain was by no means predominantly Black. Furthermore, this was an era wherein Britain's population was more and more "foreign born" (Haylett 2001: 351). In this confluence, the predominant whiteness of the council estate demographic became visible in a way that signalled national degeneration. As had been the case in the late nineteenth century, the idea of degeneration strongly implicated motherhood. Yet now, while counter-terrorism strategies placed the onus on immigrant families abiding by – what would sardonically come to be known as – "British values", Muslim women, even if "oppressed", were seen to at least occupy their station with decorum. Contrast this orientalist image with the regular "reality TV" portrayals of white female benefit recipients as unhealthy, unruly and immoral (Skeggs 2005). I would also connect these racialized and gendered apprehensions to the way in which the return of the grammar of class to mainstream politics post-2008 fixated upon the educational failures of "white working class" *boys.*

As journalists and reporters turned to investigate this white underclass, they self-consciously inhabited the persona of late nineteenth-century explorers of the urban residuum. Take, for instance, *Dark Heart*, the journalistic exposé by Nick Davies of council estates. Davies (1998: vii–viii) considered himself to be akin to "some Victorian explorer penetrating a distant jungle", there to visit sprawling collections of battered old housing estates, crack houses and "shebeens". Terms such as jungle and shebeen (an Irish term for an illicit drinking establishment popularized in South Africa and Zimbabwe) demonstrate the application, once more, of anthropological language now mobilized to render the avowedly white poor as savages.

One term especially provided the cognitive space for which to deposit the anxiety surrounding the whiteness of Britain's underclass. The "chav" emerged in 1990s' north-east England as a term that denoted a person ensconced in a culture of low-level criminality. Probably deriving from the Romany word for a small child, the chav was associated with market places populated by travellers and South Asian hawkers, etc. Through these linguistic and spatial associations, the residual non-whiteness of the term was applied to white people whose behaviour had degenerated to match the same non-white anti-social and sub-normal groups. Being "chaved" even came to refer to being robbed at home, and in this respect the term also echoed older contrived fears of being "mugged" by Black youth (Garner 2015: 4–5; Nayak 2009).

To what degree was all this a novel racialization of the British poor? In eighteenth-century debates over their undeserving nature, the rural poor had been blackened via the slave analogy. These poor had yet to be accepted into the Anglo-Saxon family; their racial affiliation was therefore ambivalent. Crucially, this was not the case for those who most keenly experienced the downwardly levelling effects of Thatcher's deindustrialization. Under New Labour, the underclass became racialized as white, precisely by being attributed the degenerative characteristics of the "blackened" poor. This expression of whiteness no longer signalled an enfranchisement into the Anglo-Saxon family or national compact; it marked an alienation from it.

The Conservative Party struggled for some time to regroup in the face of New Labour's repeated electoral success. After his resignation as leader of the Conservative Party in 2003, Iain Duncan Smith turned his energies towards the creation of a Centre for Social Justice (CSJ), a think-tank that sought to develop "effective solutions to the poverty that blights part of Britain". In 2006 the party's new leader, David Cameron, asked the CSJ to write a report that might serve as a policy platform for the next election. One year prior, during the leadership contest, Conservative MP Liam Fox had spoken of a "broken Britain". The CSJ report popularized this pithy term as part of a strategy to make New Labour accountable for the degenerative effect visited upon the nation by the existence of a white underclass. That the breaking point clearly had a geographic epicentre was affirmed by visits from both Duncan Smith and Cameron during a 2008 by-election to the estates of Glasgow East. *The Times* considered these territories to be ruled by "the law of the jungle, not Westminster". Mirroring Blair's speech at Aylesbury, Duncan Smith painted the quintessential picture of a white underclass:

> This individual has low life expectancy. He lives in social housing, drug and alcohol abuse play an important part in his life and he is always out of work. His white blood cell count is killing him directly as a result of his lifestyle and its lack of purpose. (Gray & Mooney 2011: 13–15; see also Hancock & Mooney 2013: 57)

In the same year as the CSJ released its report, Jesse Norman (future Conservative MP) and journalist Janan Ganesh co-wrote another report for another think-tank – the centre-right Policy Exchange. Also designed to guide Cameron's future election strategy, the report noted the dissolution of social ties evidenced by the popular images of "crack use" and "hoodies" on "blighted" estates (Norman & Ganesh 2006: 22–3). The task that only a "compassionate" conservatism could perform was to renew trust in social bonds and civic mutualism. Similar to the CSJ, the Policy Exchange report proposed local government and voluntary organizations as the solution to the problem of national degeneration (Norman & Ganesh 2006: 66–7). In an effort to rid the Conservatives of their popular identification as the "nasty party", Cameron presented himself as the compassionate force that would mend "broken Britain" (see Corbett & Walker 2013).

At the Hugo Young Lecture in 2009, Cameron laid out his plan to alleviate social exclusion through the inclusivity of a "big society". His address signalled a partial reorientation of the party's moral compass away from individual freedom towards the normative ground of New Labour with its emphasis on redistribution and equality of opportunity. The state, argued Cameron, needed repurposing as a catalyst of "social renewal". The Conservative leader even praised the record of the welfare system during the era of the national compact. Not only was this system "well-intentioned and compassionate", but "generally successful" in tackling poverty and expanding opportunities. Harking back to this era, Cameron spoke of an "ethos, a culture to our country – of self-improvement, of mutuality, of responsibility".

Cameron's key criticism targeted New Labour's perversion of the self-improvement principle. At present, he claimed, Britain's so-called meritocratic system kept "millions of people at the bottom locked out of the success enjoyed by the mainstream". Cameron argued that New Labour had embraced the worst of Fabianism and its "mechanistic view of the state", thereby ignoring the "social consequences" of economic reforms. By "undermining personal and social responsibility", New Labour's policies had ended up "perpetuating poverty instead of solving it". In short, "state control" had become substituted for "moral choice". Alternatively, Cameron advocated both a focus on equality of opportunity, especially in the area of education, and on a "stronger, more responsible society", one that was "aggressively pro-family, pro-commitment, pro-responsibility".

Cameron's "big society" initiative committed to a rebirth of moral agency along social conservative lines. To this effect, Cameron proposed significant decentralization of the provision of (and responsibility for providing) public services as well as the opening up of service delivery to local private (for profit) and third sector organizations – the small platoons of Thatcher's (and to some extent Blair's) imaginative landscape (North 2011: 818). Against the overbearing hand of big government, which took away the impetus of self-help and responsibility, Cameron turned towards a "libertarian" paternalism drawn from behavioural economics. In this new dispensation, policy makers would act as "choice architects", "nudging" the local publics towards those decisions that would have been taken in accordance with deserving characteristics (Corbett & Walker 2013).

It is fair to say that most of the principles behind the "big society" resonated with those espoused by New Labour: social conservatism bound both parties in myriad ways. But in the event, Cameron's conservatism during the life of the 2010 coalition government was neither compassionate nor even paternalist; it was, in fact, more punitive than the Fabianism of New Labour. This was certainly the case for those communities who threatened national cohesion. In 2011, at the Munich Conference on Security, Cameron announced a turn towards "muscular liberalism". Facing "Islamist extremism", government, argued Cameron, could no longer passively support

SOCIAL CONSERVATISM AND THE WHITE UNDERCLASS

multicultural policies. In fact, when it came to Muslim communities who did not "fully endorse" liberal values, the big society still required the strong hand of state. And just as heavy-handed was the coalition government's response to the problem of national degeneration.

Along with the Chancellor of the Exchequer, George Osborne, Cameron ideologically embraced austerity measures as a response to the global financial crisis that had begun in the last years of New Labour. As the new secretary of state for work and pensions, Duncan Smith embarked upon a welfare reform driven primarily by a demand for unprecedented cost-cutting rather than any concern to support the deserving poor. The reforms viciously targeted those household demographics that ideologically represented the undeserving – single-parent, council-housed, long-term unemployed. Moreover, by encouraging devolution to local authorities the coalition reforms increasingly mapped the uneven geography of wealth carved out by previous Conservative governments onto social service provision.

But as Cameron, Osborne and Duncan Smith intensified punitive measures against the undeserving poor so did the whiteness of the underclass intensify the moral panic over national degradation. To understand this process in more detail, I need to briefly document the political apprehensions of blackness in the years following the break-up of the postwar national compact.

Recall the 1983 Conservative election poster that presented a young aspiring man accompanied with a stark choice between identifying him as either Black or British. Such a choice inferred that to become deserving of Britishness one would have to disavow one's blackness. The choice is a quintessentially abolitionist one. The term "Black British" would from here on encompass both an acceptance of the possibility of assimilation as well as an abiding fear of national degeneration. Take also, in this respect, the Macpherson report of 1999, which inquired into the murder of a young Black man, Stephen Lawrence, by racist white youth in April 1993. Stephen's terrible case eventually attracted surprising support from some quarters. The usually right-wing, xenophobic *Daily Mail* committed itself to supporting the Lawrence campaign, some say due to the "respectable" nature of the family and their upwardly aspiring trajectory (Kundnani 2000: 8). Regardless, the Metropolitan police still orchestrated a long-term campaign to harass, discredit and defame Stephen's parents as they pursued justice for their son (Wright 2014).

Thus, in the Thatcher era and beyond, Black British families who demonstrated identifiably deserving characteristics could be considered worthy of assimilation. But no matter how aspirational, their Black presence always prompted a suspicion of disorder that legitimated extraordinary treatment.

Let us now revisit the CSJ's 2006 report on "Breakdown Britain", specifically its central chapter, which focused upon "family breakdown" and "dad-lessness" (Social Justice Poverty Group 2006: 28). Picking up on the social conservative concern for "problem families", the report noted that the trends towards "single mother households" and "youthful pregnancy" were more pronounced in the UK in comparison to other European societies. The report also found it necessary to consider "ethnic variation" in levels of family breakdown in Britain, noting a high incidence of marriage in Indian families compared to much lower levels of male commitment in Black families. While the report did not dwell on Black families specifically, two out of three illustrative pictures in the chapter featured them. In these ways, the report – albeit subtly – blackened broken families in a manner that has its origins in the slave analogies of the abolition era.

This blackening process reached a high point in the aftermath of the riots and uprisings that shook urban England in the summer of 2011. There is a specific history of racism, criminal justice and the Black community which informs the local reaction to the police killing, in August 2011, of Mark Duggan, a young Black man from the Broadwater Farm estates in Tottenham. In October 1985, another young Black man, Floy Jarrett, was arrested and charged with theft and assault (and later acquitted on both counts). Floy's arrest occasioned a search of his mother's Broadwater residence. The violent nature of the search led to Cynthia Jarrett dying on the spot from heart failure. The next day, crowds descended on the police station in protest, and were met with baton charges. Come night-time, rioting broke out in response to the police presence around the estates. In the disorder, PC Keith Blakelock was killed. This first killing in the twentieth century of a British police officer during a civil disturbance was met with racist diatribes in the media.

In response the police undertook an extremely hostile investigation, arresting hundreds of Black residents, usually with little due process. Three were eventually charged with Blakelock's murder but were subsequently acquitted. Over the years the police have consistently reopened the inquiry. Nicholas Jacobs was the latest person to be tried (and acquitted) over the murder in 2014. Some community organizers, who were present in 1985, argue that this recent trial was a reaction to the community's holding the police to account for Mark Duggan's death.

The 2011 riots and uprisings were met by a political response that directly attributed their causes to anti-social behaviour emanating from "broken" families. Cameron's reaction yearned for the order of the traditional patriarchal family:

> Irresponsibility. Selfishness. Behaving as if your choices have no consequences. Children without fathers. Schools without discipline. Reward without effort. Crime without punishment. Rights without responsibilities. Communities without control.
> (North 2011, 818; see also Hancock & Mooney 2013: 47)

In a further speech to parliament, Cameron claimed that the riots were not caused by structural issues concerning poverty, but rather by a "culture that glorifies violence, shows disrespect to authority". Cameron blamed parents for neglecting to discipline their children (as did Labour MP for Tottenham David Lammy) and implied that a benefit system which did not incentivize claimants to work was also irresponsible (*Telegraph* 2011). The gentle nudge of policy architects would, once again, need to give way to the strong hand of the state.

In these ways, Cameron conjured the spectre of violent council estate youth to quicken support for Duncan Smith's welfare reforms that were, at that time, making their way through parliament. Cameron even suggested that welfare sanctions be made against those who were caught up in the disturbances. For instance, he argued for the eviction of households whose members had received a conviction, and this measure was taken up by a few local authorities and housing associations (Hancock & Mooney 2013: 50). By late 2011, the government produced an initiative that directly responded to the riots and uprising. Identifying 120,000 most "troubled families" in Britain, Cameron promised to modify the undeserving behaviour of their members, just as the Fabians and the Charity Organization Society had promised with regards to the underclass's forebears, the urban residuum.

For his part, Duncan Smith reflected on the riots and uprisings thus: "we had ghettoised many of these problems, keeping them out of sights of the middle-class majority … but last month the inner city finally came to call" (Hancock & Mooney 2013: 49). Duncan Smith's comments imply a kind of social contagion. Others made the point more explicitly, identifying the riots with national-racial degeneration. This was the case presented by David Starkey, a television personality and popular historian of English constitutionalism. In the immediate aftermath of the summer uprisings and riots, Starkey gave comment on *Newsnight* about, what seemed to him to be, the shocking inclusion of white youth in the riots.

Ever since the moral panic over "mugging" in the 1970s, politicians and pundits had been unsurprised when Black youth apparently revealed themselves to be harbingers of social disorder. Consider, for example, Oliver Letwin, an advisor to Thatcher's Downing Street policy unit, who responded to the 1985 Broadwater Farm riots and uprisings by differentiating white and Black residents of poor estates along deserving and undeserving lines. For Letwin, "lower-class unemployed white people had lived for years in appalling slums without a breakdown of public order on anything like the present scale". In contrast, the rioting amongst Black residents was due to "bad moral attitudes". Thereafter, Letwin dismissed funding initiatives for poor Black youth in the aftermath as simply enabling "new entrepreneurs [to set up] in the disco and drug trade" (Travis 2015).

But what of the fact that many rioters in 2011 had been white? Explicitly referencing Powell's fear of cultural genocide brought about by the Black presence, and referencing longstanding eugenicist concerns over miscegenation, Starkey bemoaned the fact that the "whites have become the new Blacks" ("David Starkey on *Newsnight*" 2011). Utilizing a racialization of the riotous Tottenham poor similar to Letwin, Starkey blamed the actions of white youth on the transmission of a "nihilist" Black culture to England's own. In a follow-up newspaper article, Starkey dug-down on this point: "it is the white lumpen proletarian, cruelly known as the 'chavs' who have integrated into the pervasive Black 'gangsta' culture … [to become] … as disaffected and riotous" (Rhodes 2013: 50).

Starkey's comments resonate with Powell's desire to unsully the English genus. We can, in fact, situate the historian's diatribe within a longstanding apprehension of blackness, leading us back to Edmund Burke's analogizing of Jacobins as maroons from Haiti intent upon breaking the English patriarchal order with their Black anarchy. But we must also recognize that his comments implicitly signalled a redemptive possibility for the white underclass. Let me clarify. Blackening is an adjective, not a noun. Those who become blackened are not apprehended as essentially Black. They are rather believed to have degenerated. For Letwin in the 1980s and Starkey in the 2010s, Black is undeserving in and of itself; while the white undeserving might still be rescued, regenerated.

CONCLUSION

Thatcher broke the material grounds upon which the "white working class" had been patched together by various elites and trade unions as a meaningful constituency. Thereafter, a politically significant amount of this constituency's small patriarchs became the detritus of deindustrialization. As New Labour celebrated a financialized, multicultural and globally connected society, the remnant socialities of the national compact – racism, sexism, provincialism, small-mindedness – were rhetorically deposited into those long-term white male unemployed as embarrassing and unredeemable characteristics (Haylett 2001: 359).

Despite involvement by trade unions, the making and breaking of the "white working class" as a constituency was predominantly an elite affair. Specifically, the granting and rescinding of the constituency's "deserving" status was at all times an act of political domination. But in the years following the 2011 riots and uprisings, a remarkable turnaround in elite affections seemed to occur, expressed more often than not in the question "what about the *white* working class?". The duty to redeem the white victims of deindustrialization was amplified as the furore over EU migration reached its high-point in the EU referendum of June 2016. This is the point at which this book began.

However, the path by which political elites could return the "white working class" to deserving constituency status was not just a Conservative construction but inadvertently laid by New Labour. The Parekh report had mooted a postcolonial settlement to post-Thatcherite Britain: a society of multi-ethnic, multi-faith, multi-cultural, multi-community societies. Failing to engender such a change, New Labour instead carved out two distinct policy niches: anti-discrimination legislation and social exclusion policies. Anti-discrimination was necessitated by the embrace of multi-ethnic Britain as part of a post-imperial repositioning within the global economy, which in turn, at least partly, produced the problem of national cohesion. Social exclusion policies were necessitated by an embrace of redistributive justice in the attenuated form of "equality of opportunity", which in turn produced the problem of national degeneration.

National cohesion was apprehended as a political problem, a case of security. National degeneration was apprehended as a problem of social exclusion, a case of redistribution. National cohesion was espoused principally as a problem of order; national degeneration as a problem of social justice, albeit a weak one. National cohesion was a problem populated by foreigners, Muslims especially; national degeneration was a problem populated by the white underclass. And that the whites could be blackened in the aftermath of the 2011 riots and uprisings was also testimony of the need for their salvation. That class could return so quickly to the public and political diet was due to the already racialized grammar of social exclusion. There was never a time when whiteness and class articulated except as an arte-fact of political domination.

CHAPTER 7

BREXIT AND THE RETURN OF THE WHITE WORKING CLASS

INTRODUCTION

In the last two chapters I paid attention to how Enoch Powell and the social conservatives that followed him expunged organized labour from their narrations of the English genus. For Powell and others, labour's cooperative spirit had proved corrupt when it had lodged itself in the national compact and compromised its self-help principle to the lure of welfare dependency. Margaret Thatcher identified Edmund Burke's "little platoons" in property owners; and Tony Blair largely accorded to this vision, adding responsible residential associations. But by the end of New Labour's tenure, the "white working class" had returned to elite discourse in the form of a maligned constituency deserving of some kind of social justice. This present chapter makes three passes through the philosophies, party politics and rhetorics which provided for their return. In doing so, the chapter seeks to make the case that the politics of the 2016 EU referendum were deeply entangled in the historical rise and fall – and rise again – of the "white working class" as a deserving constituency.

In the first part of the chapter I explore the emergence of Red Tory and Blue Labour, both philosophical responses to the perceived failures of New Labour. The Red Tory position sought to reaffiliate labour's cooperative spirit to conservative understandings of orderly independence. The Blue Labour position sought to reaffiliate the conservative character with labour's cooperative spirit. In doing so, however, both political philosophies made claims to an English genus that distinguished itself through its tradition of orderly independence. Accordingly, within the logic of both philosophies is an identification of non-white immigration as a destabilizing and divisive influence on the relationship between indigenous working and governing classes. The first part of the chapter therefore examines how the deserving working class returned, in political philosophy, but as a re-racialized constituency.

In the second part of the chapter I turn to Labour and Conservative genealogies of Euroscepticism. Consolidating in the 1960s, Labour's Eurosceptical tradition mounted a defence of the working class, but in a wider political context where such a defence supported the integrity of the national compact and its informal colour bars. In effect, I argue that Labour's Eurosceptic tradition was congenitally racialized. Crucially, it was through this tradition that the first challenge to parliamentary sovereignty was mounted by a so-called "popular will" in the form of the 1975 referendum on EEC membership. Alternatively, the kernel of Conservative Euroscepticism has more often than not been English nationalism. Beginning with G. K. Chesterton, moving to Powell and then to the Bruges Group, I track how the working class disappeared from this nationalism such that Euroscepticism ends up as a racialized defence of national sovereignty. ↳ criticism of the EU

The lines of inquiry taken in the first two parts of the chapter demonstrate that, historically, Labour never eschewed its racialization of the working class based on the putative threat of immigration; while, historically, Conservatives predicated their Euroscepticism on a racialized nationalism. Hence, why UKIP could take the political centre-ground so effectively from both Labour and Conservative through its anti-immigration rhetoric and delineate the contours of the EU debate so influentially. In the third part of the chapter I show how the historical rise and fall of the "white working class" frames the demographics of the Brexit vote. It is this movement that ultimately coheres the "left behind" into an electoral constituency.

I do not introduce any new concepts in this chapter, but work with ones explored previously. The key conceptual concern of this chapter is the contested and problematic retrieval of labour's cooperative spirit as an expression of the English genus and in the rhetorical form of the "left behind" and "white working class".

RED TORY/BLUE LABOUR

In the aftermath of Margaret Thatcher's removal from power, David Willetts, former director of her Centre for Policy Studies, sought to refashion the Tory image by restating a conservative vision of "community" (Hickson 2013: 411). Rather than a singular obsession with marketization, Willetts (1998) argued that the conservative tradition was based on a "creative tension" between the belief in individual freedom and property ownership, and the commitment to "maintain the institutions which hold our nation together". The Conservatives, Willetts claimed, understood the "tribal drumbeat" of British national identity in the countryside and metropolis. Returning explicitly to Burke's image of the "little platoons", Willetts attributed the distinctiveness of this identity to the orderly independence provided by the country's constitutional arrangements.

In crafting his model of compassionate conservatism in the mid-2000s, Jesse Norman was indebted to Willett's work on civic conservatism. Norman's conservatism, like Willetts, pays homage to Burke. He celebrates the intermediary institutions that have historically lain between the individual and state – the family, church and guild. These institutions have always helped to generate "a tribal feeling of belonging", i.e. an associative spirit based on affection and friendship (Norman & Ganesh 2006: 42, 46). Formed through practice, those institutions embody "the collective experience of previous generations". This experience, suggests Norman (Norman & Ganesh 2006: 47), has often outstripped "the wisdom of those who would reform them".

But Norman departs from Willetts in one key respect. In exampling the wisdom of tradition, Norman recalls the nineteenth-century Friendly Societies that in his estimation provided for a "spirit of self-reliance and mutual support … [and] discouraged reliance on charity and on state provision". Norman also claims that these societies were "relegated to the margins", especially with the rise of the welfare state (Norman & Ganesh 2006: 47–8). His critique resonates with the ideological positions of Powell and Thatcher: universal welfare has been responsible for a decline in the principle of "self-help". Yet unlike Powell and Thatcher, Norman narrates labour's cooperative spirit as that which animates the English genus and has contributed to its best traditions of orderly independence.

The conservative embrace of labour's cooperative spirit is also evident in Philip Blond's espousal of the "Red Tory". Although originally coined in Canadian political debates during the 1960s (see Preece 1977), Blond's usage of the term owes much more to theological debates led by John Milbank, a proponent of Radical Orthodoxy. Milbank's work seeks to redress the nihilism and individualism of a social world that no longer considers community as sacred. Searching for a re-enchantment of social bonds has led Milbank and others to prefer a Christian socialist tradition, predicated on moral critique and character improvement over the scientific socialism of Marx *et al.* with its secular prophesy of class conflict. Blond, a theologian himself, has utilized these currents of Radical Orthodoxy to direct the "red" into the Tory (see Coombs 2011).

In outlining the disposition of the Red Tory, Blond (2010: 9–11) is at pains to present the working class as a moral force and an indispensable element of Britain's "organic culture". Echoing William Cobbett's warnings, Blond (2010: 13) links the land enclosures of the late eighteenth and early nineteenth century to the collapse of a working-class civic culture. The contemporary legacies of this collapse are, for Blond, most evident in "working-class sink estates that surround our cities". In Blond's estimation, then, the pathologies of working-class culture are not innate; rather, it is exploitation and marginalization that has historically hollowed out the culture. Alternatively, Blond (2010: 13–14) narrates a grand tradition of working-class organization, springing from personal and provincial associations, running through the London Corresponding Society, to the Chartists, and to the Friendly Societies and Cooperatives.

Similar to Norman's narrative, Blond (2010: 15) also identifies the "welfare state" as the instrument that has produced a "supplicant citizenry dependent on the state". According to Blond, universal welfare destroyed the "indigenous traditions of working-class self-help, mutuality and social insurance". This part of Blond's argument echoes early twentieth-century debates over national welfare, which questioned the degree to which labour's cooperative spirit might be transplanted into the urban milieu. Specifically, Blond's concerns over the nationalization and universalization of welfare resonate with those raised by the Charity Organization Society against the impersonalized designs of the Fabians.

THE RETURN OF THE WHITE WORKING CLASS

What can we draw out from these political philosophies? Norman and (especially) Blond dared to suggest that it was not enough, as a conservative, to be pro-market and anti-dependency; one also had to be pro-labour. What is more, the Red Tory critique resonated with some conservatives who were seeking ways to resituate their party in an electoral landscape dominated by New Labour. As new party leader, David Cameron brought Red Tory sensibilities to the front line.

In 2007, Cameron launched Norman's Conservative Co-operative Movement in Manchester. In his speech, Cameron paid homage neither to the capitalist nor socialist heritages of the city but rather to the Rochdale Society of Equitable Pioneers, "the first successful cooperative in the world" (Cameron 2007). The cooperative principle, Cameron suggested, was an inspiration for the localist reforms to public services that he planned in so far as the history of cooperatives vindicated the role of "strong independent institutions, run by and for local people". Two years later, and Blond was being introduced as the "Conservative Party guru" (Coombs 2011: 81). In his 2009 Hugo Young Lecture, Cameron explicitly endorsed Blond's Red Tory philosophy while introducing the notion of a "big society" that might counter the overwhelming interventionism of the state. In this regard, Cameron looked favourably towards the tradition of "self-improvement, of mutuality, of responsibility" promoted by "the co-operatives, the friendly societies, the building societies, the guilds".

Inevitably, as the Blair/Brown era ended, it was also time for the Labour Party to undertake a soul-searching of its roots. Of special importance was Maurice Glasman, a political theorist, and long-time Labour member who had risen to prominence through his work with the community-organizing charity, London Citizens. Just as Norman and Blond had injected red into their Toryism, so, in the aftermath of New Labour's defeat, did Glasman (2011: 23) suggest the need to inject "blue" into Labour.

Glasman's philosophy expands around a core premise: that "distinctive labour values" are "rooted in relationships" and in practices that strengthen "an ethical life". He argues that the Labour Party's tradition features a strong conservative concern with the "preservation of status" and "an attachment to place". When it comes to exemplars of such tradition, Glasman presents "the co-operatives and the unions" (2011: 14–15). For Glasman, as for Norman and Blond,

139

labour's cooperative spirit must be considered a traditional part of the orderly independence that lies at the heart of the English genus.

In the preceding chapters I have demonstrated that the English genus is fundamentally patriarchal in its transmission. Although Glasman does not use such discrete terminology, it is telling that he relies upon the metaphor of a patriarchal family to demonstrate Labour's mix of conservatism and radicalism. Glasman proposes that the Labour Party was the child of a "cross-class marriage between a decent working-class Dad and an educated middle-class Mum". The Dad represents "the trade unions, the co-operative movement, and the building societies and mutuals"; the Mum represents the Fabian Society and all the "ruling-class" public servants connected to the labour movement with "ambitious plans for government". In the past, narrates Glasman (2011: 21–2), Dad was a traditional pre-server of the "common good"; Mum, a progressive idealist.

Glasman claims that this balanced relationship was disrupted by the rise of the postwar welfare system. "Universal benefit", he claims, replaced "mutual responsibility" and "managerial preroga-tive [became] the fundamental principle of organization" (Glasman 2011: 29). Glasman makes the same critique as his Red Tory colleagues of the national compact between government, business and labour. Glasman expresses it metaphorically: the postwar settle-ment consolidated Dad's loss of power at work, while power in the home was ceded to Mum as the Labour Party became dominated by "middle-class policy technocrats". In order to develop a "good society" rather than just a "big society", Glasman argues that Labour has to give power back to Dad. Only by such rebalancing might relationships of "reciprocity, mutuality and solidarity [be built] all the way up and all the way down, in politics and within the economy" (Glasman 2011: 27). Through this logic, Glasman effectively endorses the small patriarch as the key carrier of labour's cooperative spirit in terms not too far removed from the Conservative's "one nation" tradition.

Glasman's philosophical provocations resonated with the inclinations of a section of Labour Party MPs, most prominently Frank Field. Just months before the 2010 election that finished New Labour's run, Field claimed that "the major reason why Britain is rougher and more uncivilized than it was in the early postwar period has been the collapse of the politics of character" (Mooney & Neal

2009: 146). In the same year, Field suggested that young men who consistently refused jobs should lose benefits, while bemoaning the breakdown of the patriarchal family (Edemariam 2010). Indeed, David Cameron felt comfortable enough with Field's socially conservative disposition to invite him to chair the review on poverty and life chances under the new coalition government.

In fine, while Norman and Blond were keen to give room for labour self-organization (Red) within the Conservative focus on character, Glasman was keen to give room to the conservative character (Blue) within labour cooperation. But whether Conservative or Labour, in all cases labour's cooperative spirit was baptized in claims as to the distinctiveness of the English genus. Enunciated in a firmly multicultural era, these claims were not just of a national provenance. They also – subtly or otherwise – racialized the wellsprings of labour's cooperative spirit as white.

Norman's racialization is relatively straightforward. His compassionate conservatism essentializes the "British experience" into an "island story" with all its indigenizing connotations including, even, the erasure of Ireland (Norman & Ganesh 2006: 53–4). Blond's racialization of labour's cooperative spirit is more convoluted. Through a peculiar turn of causality, Blond (2010: 16) argues that the welfare state bequeathed a "legacy of racism and inner-city fragmentation", which "shattered the vivid communal life of the urbanised white working class". In Blond's writing, it is almost as if the national compact's informal colour bars destroyed the working class rather than helped to sculpt the "white working class" into a constituency.

More importantly, Blond believes that New Labour's management of national and community cohesion replaced an "old paternalism" with "identity politics", thus disengaging the new left from "the needs of working-class people". Here, Blond parses a Powellite logic, namely, a valorization of the sensibilities of the "ordinary" working man over and above the obfuscating discourses of politicians. Parsed through this logic, New Labour's anti-discrimination legislation appears almost as a wedge that separates government from its most deserving (white) constituency.

By these peculiar turns of argument, Blond effectively places race outside of the mechanisms by which the national compact was consolidated and shattered, while wedding the detrimental consequences of Thatcherism to the presence of non-white

141

immigrants and citizens. Such argumentation allows Blond to clarify the task of the Red Tory: to resurrect a distinctly indigenous working-class tradition of collective self-help to mitigate against long-term economic neglect and political disengagement. Effectively, the Red Tory's fundamental constituency is presented as a redeemed "white working class".

Even Blond's intellectual genealogy betrays such a racialization. In coming to his philosophical position, Blond explicitly recounts how he found "the noble history of conservatism" exemplified in the work of Cobbett, Thomas Carlyle (whom Cameron had also name-checked in his 2007 speech for Norman) and John Ruskin. All these luminaries, Blond (2010: 28) notes, "decried the loss of a settled and happy economy of the self-sufficient – and despised the slavish dependency now forced upon the poor". The adjective pertaining to slavery is telling. For all of these luminaries, as we have seen, contrasted the deserving English poor to the damned of the empire – especially the anarchical, undeserving Black. Carlyle and Ruskin, it will be remembered, even took Edward John Eyre's side in the fallout over the Morant Bay uprising, normalizing the execution of a British subject, William Gordon, whose father was white. Similar to his intellectual forebears, Blond draws upon a racialized image of the English genus and all those who could be expected to compe-tently discharge its tradition of orderly independence.

What of Blue Labour? I argued in Chapter 5 that, when it came to racism, the Labour Party was historically duplicitous – paradoxical, even – in terms of claiming an internationalist ethos while at the same time pursuing and even enacting anti-immigration legislation. The tract of this duplicity cuts into Blue Labour's philosophy. Frank Field, for instance, has repeatedly embraced the conservative tradition of labour while arguing that immigration has detrimentally affected the traditional – read, white – working class (Edemariam 2010).

Immigration – and anti-immigration sentiment – is more subtly mobilized in Glasman's philosophical defence of this tradition. On the one hand, Glasman (2011: 18) positively embraces immi-gration from Europe to Britain, albeit in so far as it constitutes the "grandparents" of the labour movement with the arrival of non-established churches. Notably, in recounting his work on the Living Wage campaign with London Citizens, Glasman does acknowledge the impact of Muslim as well as non-conformist faith groups in the

THE RETURN OF THE WHITE WORKING CLASS

scoping out of the project. But on the other hand, as I shall now demonstrate, immigration is negatively implicated in Glasman's criticism of New Labour's ability to communicate to the traditional working class.

While deriding New Labour's attenuation of the redistributive ethic to mere "equality of opportunity", Glasman (2011: 14) bemoans the abstract and implicitly out-of-touch nature of values linked to this ethic, such as "freedom" and "equality". At the same time, Glasman (2011: 24) claims that New Labour embraced abstract concepts that were integral to globalization, for instance, moving from a valuing of "specific vocational skills" to "general transferable skills". Reflecting on these shifts in register, Glasman (2011: 24) claims that New Labour replaced the "specific language from within the political traditions of our own country" with generic notions of "justice" and "fairness" that would resonate in any country. The substance of "tradition", for Glasman, is best supported by the integrity of family life and the upholding of the common good. And tradition is precisely what is undermined when abstract, rootless principles of plurality and diversity are promoted in the service of economic globalization (Glasman 2011: 26–7).

Glasman's argument implies that New Labour's refusal to provide a meaningful politics of redistribution also denied the party an ability to communicate with its core constituency, the "traditional" working class. So, it is not unfair to say that within Blue Labour's appeal to tradition can also be gleaned a Powellite argument, one shared with Red Tories: the language of parliamentary politics is one that no longer speaks directly to the indigenous population.

But what, we might ask, of the bearers of these so-called abstract values – immigrant workers, the majority of whom at the time Glasman was writing in 2011 were non-white? The logic of Glasman's argument, unless specifically corrected otherwise, infers that non-white immigrants undermine English tradition. For instance, he makes a strong plea for the labour movement to return from managerialism and neoliberalism back to the value system of the grandparents – that is, to a faith base (Glasman 2011: 23). Only with this return might love and reciprocity be rekindled between Mum and Dad. But despite Glasman's practical knowledge to the contrary, the faiths of non-white immigrants – especially Islam – are excessive to this English/European faith-based lineage of labour tradition.

The racialized anti-immigrant sentiment that can be identified in Blue Labour's philosophy is best exemplified in the writing of David Goodhart, a self-describing post-leftist "post-liberal" who has in part been influenced by Glasman. In 2004, drawing upon arguments made previously by Willetts, Goodhart presented a "progressive dilemma" that had come to light through New Labour's tenure. In his estimation, progressives wished for both solidarity – social cohesion and a generous welfare system – and diversity – respect for a wide range of people, values and ways of life (Goodhart 2004). Solidarity and diversity, asserted Goodhart, tended to contradict each other.

More recently, Goodhart has divided society along the lines of two "value clusters" that, in fact, map closely onto those provided by Glasman. Goodhart (2017) takes his own tribe as emblematic of the "anywheres" – well educated, socially and economically mobile, and "who value autonomy and fluidity". Standing aside from this tribe are the "somewheres" – the "more rooted", less well-educated who prioritize group attachments and security. Goodhart demands that the mobile "anywheres" not look with derision upon the rooted identities of the "somewheres". In this way, Goodhart valorizes the "ethnic attachments" of Britain's "white majorities" over their uprooting by non-white immigration.

In Goodhart's schema, and despite his many protestations to the contrary, race fundamentally informs the logic that he uses to resolve the immigration problem presented by the "progressive dilemma". For instance, there is no logical place for immigrant peoples and their progeny who are not from Goodhart's own "tribe" yet whom nonetheless value achievement as a way of integrating into British society. Nor is there any logical place for considering how, in principle, the ascriptive identities of immigrant peoples and their progeny cannot be utilized for rooting into British society. The gaps in and twists of logic in Goodhart's work demonstrates that the racialization of "somewhere" is not incidental to the argument but fundamental.

I do not charge Norman, Blond, Glasman or even Goodhart with visceral racism or with an aversion to immigrants' rights. But I am arguing that the "red" in Tory and the "blue" in Labour reference a small-c conservative working-class tradition of orderly independence, a cooperative spirit of labour that intrinsically affiliates to the English genus, thereby racializing the ordinary/traditional working class as white. This racialization is fundamental to the way in which

Red Tory and Blue Labour fantasize the working class as a "moral agent" deserving of redemption from the ravages of the global market, including its coloured avatars in the form of immigrants (see Gilbert 2017).

The fantasies of political philosophers are all-too-often rudely confronted by political practice. This was exactly what transpired during the coalition government of 2010–2015. Red Toryism was quickly side-lined by Cameron and Osborne's austerity pro-gramme. Ironically, their decimation of much local council funding undermined the capacity for any local wellsprings of cooperative spirit to develop. Meanwhile, Blue Labour could muster no convin-cing response to the surge of anti-immigration rhetoric provided by UKIP, which, despite its visceral nature, resonated deeply with Glasman and Goodhart's logics. That Labour's northern bases of support could be captured so relatively easily by the right in the 2015 general election was worrying testimony as to the in-distinctiveness of Blue Labour's message.

Most importantly, Euroscepticism came to frame debates over Britishness and immigration such that on the eve of the 2016 ref-erendum it was almost impossible to disaggregate the political case against the EU from the moral case for Britain's indigenous "left behinds". So, in what now follows, I examine the political history of Euroscepticism, a history that runs before and besides the Red Tory/ Blue Labour debates.

EUROSCEPTICISM: LEFT AND RIGHT

When it came to the first unsuccessful attempt at British accession to the EEC in 1963, the Labour Party's position was clear. If accession damaged the economic interests of the Commonwealth then it would be opposed because Britain, according to the Party's National Executive Committee, was the "centre and founder member of [this] much larger and still more important group" (Grob-Fitzgibbon 2016: 290–2). Although Labour depicted the Commonwealth in internationalist terms as a "multiracial association of 700 million people", often that association was conceived as a racialized hier-archy. For instance, one year before the accession attempt, Hugh Gaitskell, Labour leader, proclaimed that "we at least do not intend to forget Vimy Ridge and Gallipoli" (Wellings 2014: 101). In popular memory, white Canadian and Australasian troops had made the blood sacrifice in both battles (although it is forgotten that not all their soldiers were white). In other words, in defending the Commonwealth, Gaitskell was primarily thinking of his Anglo-Saxon kith and kin.

Still, economic considerations relentlessly tilted the political calculus towards EEC membership. By the mid-1960s, Britain was faced with an enormous balance of payments deficit. The relative importance of Commonwealth trade was steadily decreasing, while one after another of Britain's non-white dependencies were gaining independence. Becoming prime minister in 1964, Harold Wilson, although sharing Anglo-Saxon sentiments with the prior Labour leader, had no choice but to launch another unsuccessful bid for accession. European integration was therefore increasingly considered by Labour in instrumental terms as a way to restore the global standing of Britain in lieu of empire's end.

At this point, a committee of Labour members began to agitate for the Five Safeguards on the Common Market, as laid out by Gaitskell in 1962. These safeguards included protection of Commonwealth trade and the socialist principle of economic planning (see Forster 2002). The "anti-marketeer" position gained the support of the TUC in 1972, which in part led to a radical programme being approved at the 1973 Labour Party conference (see Rosamond 1993: 422). There, nationalization of industry once more took central place in policy considerations. Pressure was put upon Harold Wilson by this grouping, which made the likes of Tony Benn a strange bedfellow to Enoch Powell.

In the meantime, Britain had finally joined the EEC under Ted Heath's Conservative government. For the sake of party unity, Wilson, who was returned to prime minister in 1974, provided a referendum in 1975 on Britain's continued membership of the EEC. Referendums were not unheard of in Britain's political history, but most had previously addressed local issues (Wellings & Vines 2016: 313). Wilson's referendum was exceptional in that it required, for the first time, a popular decision to be made on an issue of fundamental national importance (Wellings 2010: 492). It is instructive, then, to clarify the conjuncture which produced such an interruption of the popular will into the practice of parliamentary sovereignty.

The anti-marketeer position was endorsed by the TUC during an era of marked public agitation over Black and Asian Commonwealth immigration, with the dockland strikes over the censure of Powell's racist speech occurring just a few years prior. As I argued in Chapter 5, those strikes could be conceived as an expression of populist nationalism. Moreover, at this point in time, the TUC had yet to seriously address informal colour bars, which were an integral part of the national compact between state, business and labour. Now, remember that union involvement in the anti-marketeer movement provided its initial populist element (Lazer 1976: 260), and that this populism made possible a re-radicalization of the Labour position on nationalization. In short, populist nationalism, racist trade unionism and anti-marketeering co-implicated each other. I am suggesting that, regardless of the intentions of anti-marketeers, their opposition to the EEC on behalf of a national working-class constituency unavoidably carried with it a populist racialization of that national class as white.

I began this book by noting how many commentators on Brexit claimed that through the 2016 referendum a "popular will" had challenged the sovereignty of parliament. What is clear at this point in the argument is that the interruption of parliamentary sovereignty by the popular will was first orchestrated in modern political history from within the Labour Party. It is possible to further argue that this interruption was in good part driven by an attempt to preserve a racialized compact between the state, business and white labour against dilution by membership into the European community.

After 1997, New Labour used EU membership as part of its strategy for managing Britain's position in the global economy (Gifford 2014: 517). By this point in time, the anti-marketeer project had been firmly minoritized within the party. Even the TUC had shifted its position in the late 1980s (parallel to its anti-racism work), building cross-European trade union solidarity against Thatcher's incisions, and signing up to the "social protections" promised in the run up to the 1992 Maastricht Treaty (Rosamond 1993: 420–3). Nevertheless, Euroscepticism remained a background sentiment in Labour, to be triggered again when David Cameron announced a 2016 referendum on EU membership. Subsequently, John Mills founded Leave Labour, an informal group that campaigned for a left-leaning Brexit. Mills, a business man and Labour affiliate from the 1970s, was also secretary of the Labour Euro-Safeguards Campaign – the body that had taken over from the 1967 committee.

In making the case for a left-leaning Brexit, Glasman (2016) argued that New Labour's embrace of EU membership had been a deflection strategy that left Thatcher's domestic legacy unaddressed. In Glasman's estimation, by embracing a neoliberal common market New Labour had also privileged the "more general, abstract and administrative" language of EU politics over the traditional language of the British working class. Such an embrace mitigated against a "serious politics of national transformation, of building the coalitions necessary to constrain capital and strengthen democracy". But in making their case, Blue Labour and others who called for a "left exit" never critically addressed Labour's record before Thatcher. Specifically, they did not reflect upon or confront the racialized aspects of the party's historical oppositions to European integration.

Before moving to an examination of the 2016 vote I first need to explain how populist Eurosceptic sentiment came to be driven from the right rather than the left. For this purpose, I want to track a nationalist commitment to the defence of the English genus that runs through Powell to Thatcher and to UKIP. The departure point for this genealogy is G. K. Chesterton, early twentieth-century writer and literary critic who laid out much of the groundwork that later accompanied conservative Euroscepticism, especially the angst over a lost or betrayed Englishness. Engaging with Chesterton also allows us to connect Euroscepticism back to some of the early nineteenth-century concerns over the English poor, which we have engaged with in previous chapters.

Chesterton committed much of his work to rescuing the dignity of the English majority from the damning aloofness and pretensions of Fabian socialists and aristocratic intellectuals. Famously, Chesterton introduced his constituency in poetic style: "smile at us, pay us, pass us; but do not quite forget. For we are the people of England that never have spoken yet" (Wright 2004). This passage has been regularly reproduced by those who worry about England's diminution via devolution within the Union and Europeanization from without.

In his writings, Chesterton sought to retrieve an even older sensibility towards the English poor that had been cast aside in the late Victorian era. For this purpose, he wrote a defining biography of William Cobbett who, in Chesterton's estimation, had advocated for "liberty, England, the family, the honour of the yeoman, and so on" (Chesterton 1910: 5). In rehearsing Cobbett's critique of agricultural marketization and its degradation of the "English power of self-support", Chesterton (1910: 27) identified in Cobbett a contemporary cause. Chesterton was not afraid to exemplify the English majority as the working and deserving poor, represented by "innumerable millions of cabmen, navvies, dustmen, and crossing-sweepers" (cited in Stapleton 2006).

The reader might remember that Cobbett charged middle-class abolitionists with ignoring the plight of their own charges in England as they pursued moral righteousness abroad. In cognate fashion, Chesterton identified the bureaucrat and racialized alien (especially the Jew) as those agents set upon undermining the deserving nature of common English people (Wright 2004). It is possible, then, to identify in Cobbett and Chesterton a sense of elite betrayal of England's little people, a tradition that Goodhart and others reproduce. Furthermore, like Cobbett's, Chesterton's English majority was racialized.

The reader might recall how Cobbett's politics depended on the slave analogy: poor law reforms driven by mendacious elites would reduce the deserving rural poor to Black slaves. Writing in the early twentieth century, Chesterton drew upon the *fin de siècle* racialization of the English genus as an Anglo-Saxon family (see Stapleton 2006). But he was also clear that the English genus had to be apprehended in distinction to British empire. For instance, Chesterton took issue with the way in which Rudyard Kipling had addressed the question "what do they know of England who only England know" by distributing the repositories of such knowledge across the colonies and dominions. Alternatively, Chesterton refuted the idea that the English condition could be understood better via the study of "Wagga-Wagga [New South Wales, Australia] and Timbuctoo" (Chesterton 2011: 17). If there was any immediate geocultural context to take account of, for Chesterton (as for Glasman) it would have to be European Christendom.

Mourning for the rural idyll cast aside by industrial urbanization, Chesterton waxed lyrical on an English genus that had been betrayed by internal forces and sullied by imperial influence. Thus, his position was also powerfully resonant with Powell's subsequent intervention against empire, Commonwealth immigration and the national compact. In many ways, Chesterton's interpretation of the

149

English genus forms the intellectual link between Cobbett's and Powell's —moralized, traditionalized and racialized There is, though, a crucial change in delineation between Cobbett, Chesterton and Powell's elegiac England. In the case of Cobbett and Chesterton, the deserving working poor had to be affiliated to the English genus. In contrast, Powell's sensibility was distinctly Burkean. Eschewing labour's cooperative spirit, Powell situated Englishness only in patriarchal character and parliamentary tradition. It was through this sensibility that Powell developed his incredibly influential critique of European integration.

By the 1960s Powell was railing against what he determined to be a prevalent but disabling myth of national decline. Specifically, he took issue with the measurement of national decline which used the economic and political capabilities garnered from empire as a reference point. But Powell saw the present shift in Britain's global position less as decline and more as a resetting of its optimal position: Britain was finally becoming independent of the unnecessary appendices of empire and commonwealth. Especially important for Powell was his belief that precisely the rush to mitigate imperial "decline" had led to an unwise embrace of the EEC project. Powell had no problem engaging with Europe on an economic footing; Britain was, after all, a commercial nation. But the process of European integration would lead to a new political dependency, a replacement of its imperial handicap, and with that, parliamentary sovereignty would be fatally compromised (see Powell 1967, 1969).

Hence, what was at stake in EEC membership was never, straightforwardly, British sovereignty. Powell's Euroscepticism was part of a project set upon redeeming the English genus from imperial and other geopolitical contaminants and dependencies. In this respect, resistance to the EEC was organically part of Powell's broader populist nationalism. The "silent" English majority were once more under threat of being minoritized not only by Commonwealth immigration but by EEC accession and, astoundingly, with the complicity of their own governing classes. The mendacity of political elites was a central topic in Powell's diatribes against EEC membership during the early 1970s. He consistently criticized all parliamentary parties for their unwillingness to engender debate with the "ordinary" people of their constituencies.

Powell thereby bequeathed to Euroscepticism a racialized populist nationalism, condensed into a defence of Englishness that no longer referenced the deserving poor as its prime constituency, which had been the case with Cobbett and even, partly, with Chesterton. True, Powell was side-lined – and side-lined himself – because of his Euroscepticism. But ideologically, his position remained extremely influential within Conservative debates.

The contemporary departure point for Conservative Euroscepticism lies in Thatcher's 1988 Bruges speech. Previously supportive of the European project in so far as it could benefit the project of marketization, the Iron Lady now rang the alarm at the erosion of British sovereignty. This, at a moment when the Conservatives had only just begun to disassemble the fetters that the national compact had placed upon the market. Issues came to a head with the Maastricht Treaty of 1992, which proposed even deeper European integration and the implementation of a "social chapter". This instrument extended qualified majority voting for equal opportunities issues, working conditions and the integration of those excluded from the labour market. Conservative Prime Minister John Major "opted-out" of the chapter due to the prospect of being unable to unanimously block all legislative developments in these policy areas. New Labour quickly "opted-in".

The Bruges Group was established by conservatives to take forward Thatcher's critique. By the time that Blair and Brown came to power, this grouping as well as other bodies of right-wing sceptics had begun a campaign that purposefully extended beyond the Conservative Party into business, academia and publishing. Concomitantly, extra-parliamentary Eurosceptic groups began to proliferate, while hard-core Eurosceptics also radicalized rules of parliamentary conduct by resisting legislation every step along the way (Forster 2002: 304).

LSE academic Alan Sked was a founding member of the Bruges Group. In a book that served as a manifesto for the Group – consisting of a forward by Thatcher and a chapter by Powell – Sked argued in quite traditionally conservative terms that any political process of European Union had to be consistent with "individual freedom, national integrity and parliamentary accountability" (Sked 1992: 6). Powell was a clear inspiration for Sked's evolving political position. In 1993 Sked inaugurated UKIP. One year later, accompanied by future party leader Nigel Farage, Sked sought to recruit the now retired firebrand to stand as a candidate in the European elections (Amara 2014).

Powell's ideological influences are clearly identifiable in UKIP's 1997 manifesto, which linked a set of issues deemed threatening not just to national sovereignty but to the English genus. For instance, Sked linked EU bureaucracy not only to inefficiency but also to immorality in terms of promoting idleness and dependency through its "gravy train". Sked argued that only by defending "national sovereignty" and removing regulations could Britain trade freely. And only free trade could create employment. By this logic, Sked's manifesto also described the welfare system in terms consonant with EU bureaucracy – i.e. as a producer of dependency and an abrogation of the hallowed principle of self-help.

While Sked was in many ways a straightforward conservative, his party unavoidably attracted the far right, who had been occupying the terrain of English nationalism since the days of Oswald Mosley's fascist party. A. K. Chesterton, G. K.'s cousin, was one of Mosley's troops and later established the League of Empire Loyalists which, in the 1950s, attracted ex-colonial administrators and Tories opposed to the ending of empire. John Tyndall was a young recruit to the Loyalists and subsequently founded the British National Party (BNP). In an attempt to differentiate his party from that of the BNP, Sked protested with the same spurious rhetoric as Powell that his English nationalism was not racist. To be fair, soon after the 1997 manifesto, Sked resigned in protest that UKIP had been infiltrated by the far right. Yet, as I will now explain, the issue was less to do with visceral racism and more to do with the fact that the English nationalism that UKIP ascribed to was unavoidably racialized.

Just as Cobbett and especially Chesterton and Powell concerned themselves with the specifically English genus of Great Britain's exceptionalism, so was UKIP's populist nationalism predicated on a defence of England's political supremacy from both devolution and Europeanization (see also Kenny 2015: 42–3). Indeed, despite Sked's absence, UKIP's association with Powell – the architect of populist nationalism – remained strong. As new party leader, Farage named Powell his political hero (Absolute Radio 2015; Dale 2008). In 2014, Farage defended his concordance with Powell's 1968 argument that the English had become cultural strangers in their own country and were unable to access public services due to Black and Asian immigration (Mason 2014). That Powell's political presence contoured UKIP's membership is demonstrated by a 2013 Ashcroft poll, which revealed that 90 per cent of UKIP voters knew what he stood for, compared to 58 per cent of the general population (Ashcroft 2013).

In his 1997 manifesto, Sked had at least identified "the friendly societies" as a source of "mutual help" that exemplified the British character. Farage's "people's army", however, referenced no historical working class as its core constituency. Just as Powell had not been an MP of or for the "working class", neither was UKIP a party of or for the "working class". Tellingly, the demographics of UKIP's support base during the 2015 general election was more middle than working class (Seymour 2016: 33). Farage's "people" were delineated in populist nationalist rather than class terms: an army of England's "little platoons" betrayed to Scotland, Wales, Northern Ireland, Europe and the coloured Commonwealth by the mendacious Westminster elite.

In an era marked by financial crisis and austerity, UKIP rapidly moved to the centre-stage of politics by channelling its defence of England into a critique of EU immigration. UKIP first enjoyed a surge in national support after the 2009 Treaty of Lisbon, signed at the height of the global financial crisis, and which also provided a formal process for leaving the EU. UKIP took advantage of this conjuncture by unapologetically aligning conservative Euroscepticism with a longstanding populist nationalism that held immigration responsible for a diminution of welfare provision and wages experienced by England's "indigenous" workers.

UKIP's populist manoeuvrings eclipsed the political philosophies of Red Tory and Blue Labour. Both, it will be remembered, sought to philosophically rehabilitate the working class as part of a distinctly English tradition of orderly independence. Both racialized this tradition in distinction to empire's non-white multitudes. Such racialization proposed a normative division of labour: white workers deserved social security and welfare; non-white workers were undeserving of both, or at least, were significantly less deserving. Was this not precisely – and viscerally – the message of UKIP's populist nationalism?

Electorally, UKIP's Euroscepticism put the Conservative Party on the back foot in so far as Farage had effectively taken over the public space occupied previously by Thatcher's epigones. In the years leading up to the referendum, some in the party tried almost desperately to win that space back. Consider, for instance, one-time director of the Eurosceptic European Research Group, Daniel Hannan. Shortly after it was revealed in late 2014 that Sked and Farage had courted Powell in the early days of UKIP, Hannan (2014) rushed to rehabilitate Powell's conservatism from its racist image. In tandem, UKIP outmanoeuvred the Labour Party, whose Eurosceptic tradition was grounded in a defence of the "white working class". UKIP, unrestrained by any lingering internationalism, spoke directly to this sentiment. The populism originally injected into the issue of European integration by the anti-marketeers in the early 1970s was easily capitalized upon by UKIP in the 2015 elections.

BREXIT AND THE "LEFT BEHIND"

Even though Powell despised the national compact, most of his working-class supporters were not mistaken in identifying their immediate material interests vicariously reflected in his anti-immigration populist nationalism. Thatcher channelled Powell's rhetoric to help secure a marginal victory in 1979. She then proceeded to destroy the national compact, and with it, the securities afforded especially to white manual skilled labour by informal colour bars. I have made the argument in previous chapters that the "white working class" has never been a self-authored constituency but, at least in good part, an artefact of political domination. A question then arises: what comprises "white privilege" when that "privilege" no longer systematically maps onto a national – and imperial – division of labour?

The question is germane to the politics of Brexit. For UKIP impacted upon the 2016 EU referendum principally by drawing upon a racialized melancholia that harked back to a time when the racialized division of labour could be said to defend "England for the English". UKIP was not a worker's party, but for those who looked backwards it was their party in so far as it articulated a racialized – rather than purely classed – grievance.

When, after 2008, the political and media commentary increasingly took on the deserving case of the "white working class", their plight was often characterized as being "left behind". We have encountered this term already, in *fin de siècle* debates over urban poverty. Back then, the meaning of "residuum" referenced (part of) a race left behind by civilizational advance. By the 2010s, the sense of being left behind was gauged by comparing the economic position of the "white working class" to the political advances unfairly made on behalf of Britain's minority ethnic groups. This, for example, was the claim made by John Denman, in his capacity as Labour's communities secretary (*Telegraph* 2009).

In 2014 political scientists Rob Ford and Matthew Goodwin introduced a framework through which to better understand the meteoric rise of UKIP and its attraction for the "left behinds". Ford and Goodwin assayed the significant socio-economic and cultural shift that had occurred between the era of the national compact and the end of New Labour's rule. In the early 1960s almost half of the labour force was employed in manual work and over 40 per cent belonged to trade unions; by 2010, manual labour had shrunk to 30 per cent of the workforce and union membership had shrunk to 20 per cent. In the early 1960s, 70 per cent of voters had no education qualifications, 30 per cent of voters depended upon state housing, and 98 per cent were white; by 2010, 33 per cent of voters were university educated, only 10 per cent of voters occupied state housing, and minority ethnic peoples constituted approximately 13 per cent of the UK population. Reflecting on these differences, Ford and Goodwin (2014) identified the "left behind" as "older, working-class, white voters", lacking the educational qualifications, incomes and skills required for the "modern post-industrial economy".

Ford and Goodwin's schema usefully identifies the remnant of white, manual skilled labour whose sectors have significantly declined since Thatcherism. While this contextualization is helpful, Ford and Goodwin's analytical framework mitigates against an adequate reflection of the "whiteness" of this class of voters. Effectively, they replicate New Labour's distinction between national cohesion (race) and national degeneration (class). That is, "race and immigration" is categorized as a problem of shifting "values" and not one of socio-economic substance, i.e. "exclusion". Conforming to this analytical distinction effectively presents whiteness as a recently garnered perception of being left behind instead of an abiding feature of the post-war British economy.

Yet such perceptions are not as new as might be presumed. Let us return for a moment to the late 1960s and the furore that erupted over Powell's speech against Commonwealth immigration. One survey in 1969 found that those respondents who most strongly perceived their socio-economic position to have declined since their childhood were most prone to support Powell (Schofield 2015: 230). From additional data gathered in 1970, one correlation stood out: the lesser the time in formal education the greater the support for Powell (King & Wood 1975: 243). From this evidence it appears that, rather than being predicated on post-industrial decline, anxieties over a perceived economic and cultural diminution of status – i.e. being "left behind" – had already accompanied discussions in the late 1960s over Commonwealth immigrations.

Therefore, it is more historically accurate to place the sentiment of being "left behind" within a defence of the national compact that at one point granted white workers an institutionally advantaged position, with some still today enjoying its legacy benefits, for example, occupational pensions. Contextualized thus, being left behind connotes a racialized socio-economic distance, that is, an advantage attached to whiteness that has relatively diminished rather than zero-sum declined (see Bhambra 2016a). To put it another way, the contemporary "left behind" are not incidentally white; the diminution of the benefits that whiteness once afforded is what makes them feel left behind. The vote for Brexit must be placed within the rise and fall of the "white working class", a trajectory managed predominantly by political elites.

With this in mind, I want to recall the regional unevenness introduced by Thatcher's intentional process of deindustrialization. This is especially important considering that throughout the referendum campaign the "left behind" were popularly characterized as the traditional northern-English working class. That the northern voting base had already shifted significantly to the right in the 2015 general election only heightened this geographical sensitivity. For instance, in the weeks before the vote, Labour MP Andy Burnham, shadow home secretary at the time, raised alarm that the Remain campaign had so far placed the emphasis "far too much on Hampstead and not enough on Hull" (*Guardian* 2016).

So, let us consider the North. As part of her new economic strategy Thatcher significantly rolled back regional aid, and her government initially retained a regional industrial policy only because it would continue to receive assistance from the European Regional Development Fund (see Martin 1991). Under New Labour, and despite various aspirations, workfare initiatives remained beholden to national priorities, and employment strategies were never devolved to local offices (Finn 2015). New Labour's stimulation of regional economies devastated by deindustrialization resolved, in good part, to increased public spending on services (many of them being linked to welfare), especially in the North West and North East (Hazeldine 2017: 58). After the 2008 financial crisis, northern regions that had depended upon resources of this kind suffered job losses in the public sector at a rate relatively greater than in the South East. And these self-same regions experienced some of the worst impacts of austerity, especially *vis-à-vis* welfare and social services (Beatty & Fothergill 2014; Hazeldine 2017: 66).

At this point I want to consider an argument mooted by John Holmwood (see 2017; see also Orrenius & Zavodny 2008). It is quite possible that the lower-wage economy set in place during Thatcherism effectively excluded those with dependents from participating in the job market. Subsequently, rather than redress low wages, New Labour replenished public services via private finance initiatives while expanding the pool of low-wage labour via immigration from Britain's old colonial circuits and, more and more, from the EU. In 2004, New Labour allowed immediate free access to the British labour market for workers from the EU's new member states. By all measures, the migration from lower-income central and east European states was sustained and significant, comprising almost half of the EU residential total in the 2011 UK census (Geddes 2014: 290). In 2007 the government granted a limited amount of A2 (Bulgaria and Romania) visas, primarily for access to low-skilled work schemes that had previously been filled by non-EU workers, predominantly from non-white Commonwealth countries (McDowell 2008: 59; Fox *et al.* 2012).

What effect did this migration have on voters' decision making during the 2016 EU referendum? It would certainly be disingenuous to ignore the extent to which EU migration served as a cause for grievance. Take, for instance, the Ashcroft polls (2016), the best array of data that is available on the vote, and collected as voters exited polling stations. The polls suggest that those issues considered most *relevant* to the vote – i.e. quality of life, opportunities for children, economic security, the economy as a whole, and job prospects – were less likely to be those issues that polarized voters *vis-à-vis* EU membership – primarily, the ability to control laws, the immigration system and border controls. What is more, the white vote to leave was stronger in those areas that had seen a recent and relative (but not absolute) increase in "outsiders".

Nevertheless, that immigration was only a vicarious and not immediate cause for grievance is suggested by an Ipsos MORI poll conducted shortly before the referendum. The poll revealed that only 39 per cent of potential leave voters believed European immigration had negatively impacted upon the area where they lived, and only 36 per cent believed that such immigration had personally impacted them in a negative fashion (Ipsos MORI 2016). What is more, negative changes in earnings over the last 15 years did not strongly correlate to a vote to leave, and this was the period of sustained expansion of EU immigration. Alternatively, historically entrenched geographical differences in earnings correlated far more closely to a leave vote (Bell 2016). These differences are better explained by Thatcher's deindustrialization, especially since the leave vote was more predominant in areas of decline, which happened to be old manufacturing centres.

From the evidence presented so far it can be argued that EU migration did not create regional inequalities within England. Rather, increased EU migration was, in good part, caused by the existing low-wage employment base, a result of Thatcher's deindustrialization project. Various sedimentations of inequality accumulated on this base, through New Labour's fragile redistribution and globalization policies, and especially by the coalition government's disastrous austerity measures. The Brexit vote bears the traces of these sedimentations.

We can follow these traces by paying attention to a peculiar feature of the Ipsos MORI poll on European immigration referenced above. When asked about the *national* impact of such migration, 65 per cent of leave voters concurred that it had been negative. The difference in moral significance imputed into the personal/local and national impact of immigration is suggestive. I would argue that it demonstrates how anti-immigration sentiment, seemingly directed at EU immigration, was not only a response to prior deindustrialization, but also bound to a desire to retrieve the racialized securities of the postwar national compact.

To substantiate this claim, I will now account, as much as is possible from available evidence, for perceptions amongst the white (working) poor as to the relationship between sovereignty, immigration and deserving/undeserving distinctions. First, consider the fact that, according to the Ashcroft polls, the abstract issue of sovereignty prevailed as the first choice amongst all social grades of leave voters, while the more concrete issue of immigration came a close second. A survey undertaken by NatCen Social Research just after the referendum also found that 88 per cent of those who identified immigration as the most important issue voted leave, as did 90 per cent who identified sovereignty (Swales 2016). The Ashcroft polls further reveal that approximately 51 per cent of ABC1 voters (that is, approximately lower middle class and higher) identified sovereignty as of prime importance to their voting decision compared to approximately 44 per cent of C2DE (working class and poor) voters, and that approximately 30 per cent of ABC1s deemed immigration to be of prime importance to their decision compared to approximately 37 per cent of C2DEs.

It is entirely plausible to understand the preference for sovereignty displayed by ABC1s as, in fact, a proxy critique of immigration. As Steve Garner has shown, middle classes tend to engage with race and immigration on a more abstracted register, and I would associate this with the concept of "sovereignty". The white (working) poor, however, tend to be focused upon tangible local conditions such that immigration becomes an issue directly imputed into, for example, housing issues (Garner 2012). Interestingly, the Ashcroft polls report that across all tenure types the highest percentage of leave voters were those who occupied council housing. And as I have suggested in Chapter 5, of all welfare provisions, housing was historically most open to the racialized distinction between deserving and undeserving. So, the first point I wish to make is that immigration was far more apprehended by C2DE voters as a tangible problem, and one perhaps connected directly to welfare and public services.

Second, in the lead up to the EU referendum, the category of "immigrant" took on an expansiveness that exceeded its prior racialization as predominantly Black and Asian. Polish residents were vitriolically targeted, with one national being killed in a hate crime. But were not

Poles white? To pose such a question reveals a lack of historical fluency on racialization. Recall the ambiguity by which Poles were assessed in the aftermath of the Second World War. Then, their deserving nature was adjudicated according to the degree that they were racialized as compatible or incompatible with the English genus – in terms of their characteristics and genes. Similar adjudications have been made since 2004 with the increase of central and east European migration. Currently, the benefits of whiteness to these recent migrants are real, but circumscribed to their occupation of lower-skilled positions in the division of labour (see Samaluk 2014).

We can better explain the logics of such racialized adjudications by turning to some recent investigations of the perceptions of the deserving/undeserving distinction held by predominantly white, lower-income communities from old industrial towns such as Nottingham and Birmingham, as well as London. These studies demonstrate the importance of "respectability", a value mobilized by community members to dis-identify with the label "poverty" and quite possibly the "white underclass". Community members tend to describe their economic condition otherwise, as for example "managing" (Flaherty 2008) – a term that Theresa May has latched on to. Understandably, then, community members tend to claim for themselves and their families deserving characteristics such as "solidarity, community-mindedness, work ethic, cleanliness, strong parenting and respect for others" (Garner 2012). Undeserving characteristics are associated with laziness, welfare dependency and benefit fraud (Flaherty 2008: 194).

In general, community members often use the deserving/ undeserving distinction to explain inequality (see Hoggett *et al.* 2013; Fenton 2012). The distinction, however, is not only evaluative but moral. The undeserving who live amongst the deserving are variously classified as criminals, unmarried mothers, disabled, chavs, Poles, immigrants and asylum seekers (Hoggett *et al.* 2013: 10; Valentine & Harris 2014: 86; Flaherty 2008: 206). It is interesting to note from this data that the "undeserving" category still draws together elements of eugenics, respectability and patriarchy.

But additionally, it seems that a line runs through this articulation, sorting the undeserving according to their proximity to whiteness and to Englishness. While the white English undeserving poor might be perceived by fellow community members to be dragging down the respectability of their locality, these undeserving might at least be begrudgingly tolerated by their "own" deserving poor (Garner 2012). In other words, a racialized (white) and nationalized (English) line sorts who might be tolerated or salvaged from those who remain more intractably undeserving. Such sensibilities resonate with David Starkey's comments on the white youth of council estates, blackened by their riotous behaviour, but in need of salvation, even if by a rod of correction.

Drawing together these two points it can be argued that for community members of poor, predominately white areas, the racialized distinction between deserving and undeserving is only fully activated when it comes to the issue of welfare provision. For instance, when asked a direct question about nationality, i.e. being English, community members usually respond with silence or indifference. But if the national question pertains to welfare entitlement, especially housing, they are much more likely to express their resentment regarding "special treatment" through a claim to Englishness (Garner 2012; see also Hoggett *et al.* 2013). Attributing the moral significance of welfare specifically to the national level suggestively corelates with the Ipsos MORI poll discussed above, which reported that immigration was only perceived as strongly negative when it came to its national impact.

It is here that the racialized anxieties over the worth of Englishness – prevalent in both UKIP and conservative quarters – find a broader public resonance. Tellingly, data from a 2013 survey indicates that of those who identified as exclusively English, 63 per cent regarded EU membership in negative terms, and that these sentiments were over-represented in UKIP supporters, compared to 28 per cent of those who identified exclusively as British (Hayton 2016). Similarly, the Ashcroft polls suggest that the more a voter in the EU referendum identified themselves as English the more (68%) they would see immigration as a force for ill in distinction to voters who identified themselves as British (30%). Finally, a study of recent data from the UK Household Longitudinal Survey suggests that "imagined communities" delineated by national and ethnic belonging were more influential to referendum voters than tangible connections to local communities (Surridge *et al.* 2017). In other words, those who might be considered part of a "white working class" constituency did not vote Brexit (if they did) from a class interest but to defend a melancholic racialized nationalism (see Gilroy 2006).

CONCLUSION

By the end of New Labour's rule, ideologues aligned to both Conservative and Labour parties constructed arguments by which to recover labour's cooperative spirit and its propensity to promote an orderly independence consonant with the English genus. However, both Red Tory and Blue Labour racialized the deserving/undeserving distinction in so far as they attributed to non-white immigration a destabilizing effect on the English labour movement's relationship to its own governing class. These attempts at ideological renewal were in many ways disarmed at birth by both Labour and Conservative traditions of Euroscepticism. If one favoured the working class it did so to preserve the white benefits granted through the national compact and its racialized division of labour; while the other discarded labour's cooperative spirit in favour of English nationalism. UKIP took control of the Eurosceptic tradition by drawing from Powell's populist nationalism its rhetorical force with none of its philosophical depth.

When it came to the EU referendum, immigration was primarily held responsible for the loss of social security and welfare provision which had given the "white working class" constituency an ostensibly "class" interest. Remember that Thatcherism devastated old industrial towns; and recall that New Labour replaced the racialized benefits of the national compact with investment into public services. Through all these twists and turns of social and economic policy, the interest of the "white working class" became detached from the labour market to run vicariously through public service and welfare provision, albeit through a reintroduction of the distinction between the "managing" poor and the white underclass. Those of the poor who cleaved to respectability sanctioned the behaviour of their own white English undeserving. They also charged immigrants with unfairly taking precious housing and other means-tested forms of social assistance. Such perceived injustices were only intensified as the coalition government decimated public services through its austerity policies.

Farage confidently claimed that the Westminster elite, who were busy sacrificing public provisions on the altar of austerity, were also betraying the forgotten people of England by encouraging even more immigration. It did not so much matter that these migrants were increasingly "white". What mattered was that central eastern Europeans were not white-English. In any case, as Farage bravely intonated, behind every Pole was a Muslim and/or African waiting to invade the heartlands (see also Aughey 2010; Virdee & McGeever 2017).

The vote to leave cannot be considered a rational choice made by a working class, if by rational we mean a forward-looking cost–benefit analysis. Except that the calculation was not made on personal or "class" interest. Rather, it was a melancholic racialized nationalism that in large part carried the Brexit vote. So, perhaps we should not dismiss the populist resentment of the "left behind" too hastily. Instead of an irrationality, I would argue it is the logic of class as race. And to clarify the political stakes at play in this logic, I will now conclude by considering Brexit from the perspective afforded by Grenfell Tower.

Discussion outline:

- left behind ✓
- white english working class ↑ nationalism ✓
- Brexit nostalgia

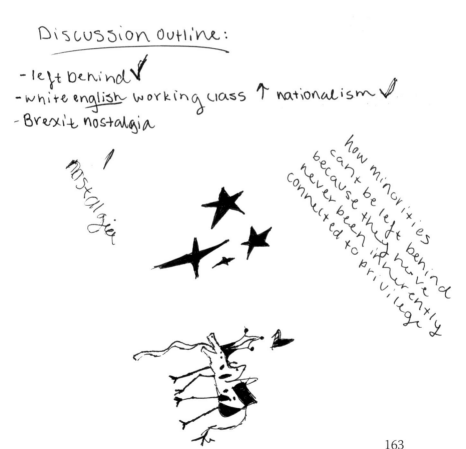

nostalgia

how can't minorities be left behind because they've never been in the privilege/connected to it

CHAPTER 8

CONCLUSION: BREXIT, VIEWED FROM GRENFELL TOWER

On 14 June 2017, a fire took hold of Grenfell Tower, a 24-storey high-rise in the Lancaster West Estate in North Kensington, London. At times approximating the temperature of an incinerator, the building smouldered for days afterwards. The tower comprised 129 flats, most of which were social housing managed by the Kensington and Chelsea Tenant Management Organisation (KCTMO). The official death toll of 71 residents remains hotly disputed by many witnesses and community members. But even this number still makes the event Britain's deadliest structural fire since the beginning of the twentieth century. So appallingly inept and callous was the local government response to the fire and its aftermath that within five days the Royal Borough of Kensington and Chelsea (RBKC), one of the richest local councils in the country, had been side-lined at the highest level of government in favour of a "gold command", which then coordinated the response.

The intensity and spread of the fire, seemingly starting in one fourth floor flat, is widely attributed to the flammability of the cladding that was attached to the exterior of the building as part of an insulation upgrade between 2015 and 2016. An original contractor had been dropped by the Tenant Management Organisation (KCTMO) in favour of a cheaper competitor. Building experts warned in 2014 that the material scheduled for Grenfell Tower had to be used in tandem with non-combustible cladding (Prescod & Renwick 2017). Nonetheless, a cladding that featured superior fire resistance was ruled out due to cost, and a sub-standard type fitted instead. Ultimately, RBKC's building control team certified that work complied with "relevant provisions" (Prescod & Renwick 2017).

Many community members, leaders and activists have criticized the proposed terms of the public inquiry into Grenfell Tower, which focuses on the immediate causes of the fire, the responsibilities of the local authority, and the local and national response. They argue that the wider context of gentrification must frame any investigation. Taking this prompt, I want to connect Grenfell to the racialization of the undeserving poor that I have presented in this book.

It will be remembered that as far back as the second half of the nineteenth century, middle-class philanthropists and policy makers had become obsessed with the dysgenic effects of urban slums and poor housing. Fast-forward to the postwar national compact, and housing had become the prime element through which the provision of social assistance was politicized and racialized, with Black Commonwealth citizens considered incompetent to look after public stock. By the end of the Thatcher era, the council estate had become synonymous with the white underclass and in more general terms with the undeserving poor. Tony Blair subsequently chose to launch his war against "social exclusion" from the Aylesbury estate in South London. While Philip Blond's high-minded Red Tory philosophy identified in estates the civic collapse of indigenous working-class culture. In the aftermath of the 2011 uprisings and riots, Cameron intonated that estates bred cultures that glorified in violence.

Originally, social housing was intended to be occupied by a cross-section of society. But Thatcher's introduction of a right for residents to buy social housing in 1979 induced a trend whereby the poorest who could not afford to buy have remained in occupation whilst at the same time expenditure on social housing has consistently declined. This trend has only intensified in the years of austerity that have accompanied the global financial crisis. Between 2009 and 2015, capital commitment by government towards building homes has decreased from 0.7 per cent (£11.4 billion) to 0.2 per cent (£5.3 billion) of GDP (National Housing Federation n.d.). Nevertheless, local councils still retain a duty to find accommodation for vulnerable residents. Housing benefit paid to private landlords for this purpose has risen dramatically despite costs to local councils being approximately 23 per cent greater.

Not only the physical stock but the very principles of managing social housing have transformed. When New Labour introduced the decent homes standard, leading the way to the refurbishment of most social housing between 2000 and 2010, they introduced a condition-ality. In order to fund their upgrade, residents would need to agree to the management function being transferred from the direct control of their local authority to a housing association or registered social landlord who could then access private funding (Hanley 2017). More recently, the Localism Act of 2011 has enabled local government to set its own guidelines as to how to manage waiting lists. Some of the new innovations at local level have included workfare elements, such as making volunteering a criterion for registry (Koksal 2014). Meanwhile, the government has pushed to fix tenancies between two and five years, making provisions far more mutable and much less certain (Stephens *et al.* 2016). Additionally, the government has recently introduced a new "affordable rent" category that offers housing associations lower grants but permits them to raise rents to up to 80 per cent of market levels.

These changes have empowered/compelled social housing man-agement organizations to make resident selection more contingent on deserving/undeserving distinctions at the same time as shortening tenancies and increasing rents. I would argue, then, that the social housing sector can be considered exemplary of the wider shifts in welfare provision authored by New Labour and Conservatives and described in Chapter 6.

Grenfell Tower's management organization must be assessed as part of this broader context marked by increased contingency and moral adjudication of public provisions alongside their steady marketization. KCTMO was formed in 1996 with the transfer of the borough's entire social housing stock – approximately 9,700 homes at the time. Although KCTMO is non-profit, as an arm's-length management organization it has absorbed millions of pounds a year in management fees and interest charges, leaving approximately just one pound in three collected from rent for maintenance and repairs (Ebrahimi 2017). What is more, in an extremely unequal borough such as Kensington and Chelsea, KCTMO helps to functionally separate provision for the poor (social housing) from resources for the affluent. Indeed, Grenfell residents report that KCTMO usually treated them with contempt, even going so far as to issue cease and desist orders against the most persistent critics of its management practices (Prescod & Renwick 2017). Of especial importance is the Grenfell Action Group, which for many years called attention to the problems that ultimately led to the catastrophic fire (Grenfell Action Group 2017).

In all these ways, KCTMO provides an extreme example of the way in which public accountability between tenant/citizen, local authority and national government has been significantly compromised by the long-term decline of and more recent management transformations in social housing.

The fatal mal-management of Grenfell Tower must also be contextualized within longer-term processes of gentrification and social cleansing. This is no conspiracy theory. A freedom of information request revealed that in 2010 RBKC put together a redevelopment plan that proposed bulldozing the entire Lancaster West estate on which Grenfell sits (Prescod & Renwick 2017). More recently, the council leased North Kensington library to a private school, and has planned to demolish the building which houses the Kensington and Chelsea College of Further Education in order to build a private housing development (Gentleman 2017).

All these issues – managerial, governmental, economic, etc. – have led to a deterioration in accountability for the provision of public goods. And such accountability has especially been eroded by national government's desire to cut regulation. Since the creation of Tony Blair's Better Regulation Task Force, "better" has meant "less" (Cobham 2017). The most recent Conservative Manifesto in 2017 affirmed a continued commitment to the same project. The One-in-Two-Out rule endorsed by the manifesto espouses the principle that for every new piece of regulation introduced, two existing pieces should be rescinded. The manifesto also supported the Red Tape Challenge, which effectively claims that excess regulation has eroded the self-help principle practised by responsible citizens. The Challenge encourages individuals and organizations to proactively inform government of any red-tape that stands in their way ("About Red Tape Challenge" 2015).

Prior to the 14 June fire, the Grenfell Action Group had become concerned with the findings of the Lakanal House fire in 2009, where six people (including three children) died in a 14-storey South London social housing block. The inquest found that a number of renovations had removed fire-stopping material and that safety inspections by Southwark council had not identified the problem (Wainwright & Walker 2017). At the time, the coroner of the Lakanal House case called for a review of part B of the Building Regulations, which covers fire safety. This part was last reviewed in 2006 even though the intervening years have seen constant innovations in building technology and materials. Housing Minister Gavin Barwell reported to the House of Commons in October 2016 that the government would indeed be reviewing Part B (Barnes 2017). But no review was forthcoming up until the events of 14 June.

Once partially comprised of slum housing, North Kensington now includes some of the most valuable real estate in Britain. The network of community activists and organizations in the local area who have resisted mal-management, gentrification, social cleansing and deregulation are part of an historical struggle over meaningful community control of the area's redevelopment. They consider the Grenfell fire to be a seminal and galvanizing moment in this struggle. Take, for instance, the Westway: an elevated motorway originally built in the late 1960s which cuts through the borough just north of Grenfell Tower. During its construction, community members agitated against the pollution that accompanied the project and were compensated with use rights of the 23 acres that lay underneath the motorway. Amenities and resources for local lower-income residents initially predominated in the use of the land including, until recently, stables where horse riding lessons were provided for children, especially those with disabilities. But while commercial operations were initially in the minority, they have over time come to dominate usage under the Westway.

In 2015 the Trust which now holds the land released "Destination Westway", a plan that seeks further commercial redevelopment. In response, Westway23, an organization chaired by Niles Hailstone (Ras Asheber), a noted Rastafari elder, and administered by Emzee Haywoode, a performing artist and tutor, disputed the Trust's plans. They even occupied part of Acklam Village, a food and entertainment area under the motorway. The Village subsequently became a key logistical and planning node for the local effort to support the survivors of Grenfell Tower. Its large hall was filled three times over with donations in the weeks that followed the fire.

The point is that neither KCTMO, nor RBKC, nor national third sector and charity organizations can be said to have driven the local cooperative spirit fantasized by Thatcher, Blair or Cameron. When it comes to Grenfell Tower, this spirit has been driven first and foremost by the predominantly low-income community. What is more, this "little platoon" is neither pure white nor purely indigenous.

Provision of social housing in Britain continues to be racialized. Black and minority ethnic residents are still more likely than white counterparts to suffer from overcrowding and poor-quality housing. One geographer, Danny Dorling, has recently argued that Black and minority ethnic social housing tenants are disproportionately housed in flats such that "the majority of children who live above the fourth floor of tower blocks, in England, are Black or Asian" (Hanley 2017; Gulliver 2017). These racialized inequalities are pertinent to Grenfell Tower. According to 2011 census data, just over half of residents in the Grenfell postcode were born outside of England. White residents were in the minority – albeit the biggest minority – with the majority comprised mostly of Black African and Caribbean, "other Asian" and "other". As far as can be presently ascertained, a significant amount of those killed in the fire on 14 June were Muslims with North African backgrounds, especially Moroccan (Prescod & Renwick 2017; Horton 2017).

Just as important as race is occupation. A majority of residents in Grenfell Tower's postcode were either semi-skilled or unskilled workers. Half of residents were employed, with one-quarter in full-time employment and a small percentage being unemployed; the rest were retired, carers, students or sick and disabled. The area was in the UK's top quintile of deprivation when it came to income, barriers to housing and services, and in the top two quintiles of deprivation when it came to employment. In contrast, the postcode was halfway in the deprivation index when it came to education, skills and training (Snowdon *et al.* 2017). From this statistical disjuncture between high deprivation in income and jobs, and medium deprivation in education, skills and training, it is reasonable to suppose that a notable percentage of the postcode's working population occupied positions below what they technically deserved. Plenty of data suggests that racism is still a major factor in the job interviewing process (Runnymede 2017).

By most measures, then, and taken collectively, the residents of Grenfell Tower were deserving poor – industrious, aspirational, orderly. Regardless, being associated with a council estate, these residents were first and foremost assumed to display all the characteristics of an underclass – lazy, dishonest, parentally irresponsible. Now, compound this association with the fact that Grenfell Tower did not stand in a predominantly white suburban sink estate, in need of salvation, but in a multicultural inner-city one, accompanied by expectations of terminal disorder. It was not hard, for instance, to catch the muted surprise amongst many media pundits when it was revealed that an up-and-coming artist such as Khadija Saye lived – and died – in Grenfell Tower. It has been even harder for many liberals and leftists to appreciate that the area shared in a North Kensington tradition of informed, articulate and critical citizenship (Goodfellow 2017).

There is a profound learning moment tragically afforded by the Grenfell Tower fire. The distinction that renders some deserving of social security and welfare and others not is racialized so as to classify collectives in order to judge individuals. This classification is made before and despite the facts being known or even required. To repeat, even if we accept the appropriateness of such classifications (I do not) then we would still have to admit that by most measures the residents of Grenfell Tower, as a collective, were deserving poor.

And ... they were multi-faith, multi-national, Black, Asian, Arab, "other" as well as white, with nuclear, extended as well as single-parent families. Grenfell's working class, a metropolitan-stone's throw from the seat of government, was not the white northern working class of Brexit lore. Yet Grenfell Tower, more than any other event in recent history, revealed the plight of the "left behind", which had been so comprehensively appealed to in media and parliament. Grenfell Tower singularly demonstrated the callous abandoning of Britain's working poor by mendacious elites who have pursued marketization over redistribution, gentrification over social security, and contracting-out over public accountability.

Infamously, Theresa May, a home secretary and subsequently prime minister obsessed with immigration numbers, could not even meet the motley crew of Grenfell residents during her first visit in the aftermath of the fire. She preferred, instead, to stand at a distance with emergency services and local government. May is also a firm proponent of PREVENT, a counter-terrorism programme which has disproportionately targeted Muslim residents in its surveillance measures. Could May conceive that if it was not for Muslims, up late at night observing Ramadan and immediately raising the alarm, that many more might have perished in the fire (Horton 2017)? Is it of any surprise that according to BMELawyers4Grenfell not one individual took up the government's initial paltry offer of a one-year immigration amnesty for undocumented residents inhabiting the tower (Snowdon 2017)?

In his ode to Grenfell, award-winning Nigerian author Ben Okri writes: "sometimes it takes an image to wake up a nation". It was the charred tower, blackened in the immediate aftermath of a general election, that spoke directly to the renewed focus on social justice and redistribution that gained remarkable national traction through Jeremy Corbyn's Labour campaign, and which finished just weeks before the fire. For all its merits, the Labour campaign was strategically silent upon Brexit and as such side-stepped the issue of immigration. Unlike May, Corbyn did meet with the people of Grenfell face-to-face, and with obvious empathy and sincerity. Still, just over one month later he appeared on the popular Andrew Marr television show arguing against the "wholesale importation of underpaid workers from central Europe in order to destroy conditions in the construction industry". Instead, Corbyn advocated advertising "jobs in the locality first" (BBC News 2017).

Corbyn has never comfortably occupied the Blue Labour camp. But this does not change the fact that he took on leadership of a party that had yet to adequately reckon with its historical complicity in upholding the racialized deserving/undeserving distinction. Indeed, members of his party were responsible for entangling populist nationalism and its racialized sentiments with the first referendum on EEC membership in 1975. Corbyn should have known that his comments could easily be translated into an admittance that immigration detrimentally affects the living standards of England's indigenous/ordinary/white working class.

How might we think differently about Brexit after Grenfell Tower and beyond conventional left and right?

This book has catalogued some of the key moments through which the distinction between those deserving and undeserving of social security and welfare has been racialized and re-racialized. Initially directed towards the parish poor, the distinction quickly expanded to include working classes, colonial natives, and even whole nationalities. As the chapters demonstrate, it was never primarily the poor who created these distinctions or modified them. Even if elements of the working classes sometimes oriented their interests *vis-à-vis* this racialized distinction, it was state functionaries, politicians, power brokers, pundits and intellectuals who ultimately decided on the degree and direction of enfranchisement – political, socioeconomic, cultural and otherwise – into the imperial order and its postcolonial afterlife. "Deservedness" is a racialized discourse and rhetoric that works to consistently offset the disorders necessarily engendered in the pursuit of empire's capital. Put another way, political domination in (post)colonial commercial society leaves its trace in the racialization of the undeserving poor.

In documenting the racialization of the deserving/undeserving distinction I have focused on one crucial thread – the Black thread – for a substantive historical reason. The morality of the poor was racialized through the single-most important economic enterprise of the late eighteenth century – African enslavement. Moral sanction was embedded in the difference between free and unfree labour, a fundamental grammar in the tradition of political economy. Soon, this sanction exceeded a technical concern for poor relief. For on this sanction depended the precarious maintenance of political order in what was called, at the time, commercial society, but which we have since labelled capitalism. Of course, the Black subjects of empire were part of a much broader kaleidoscope of peoples violently integrated into empire's order and sharing its fate in distinct ways. In this respect, I have also recounted how Irish, South Asian and even white subjects have at times been "blackened" as they were made to collectively bear undeserving characteristics and the stain of disorder.

If there is an ethos to be derived from this book, then, it is one that cannot accept a simple reversing of the terms so that Black and minority ethnic working classes are considered deserving in distinction to the undeserving "white working class". It is the categorical and collective distinction itself which must be destroyed. Finally, then, we must turn to the present-day architects of this distinction.

Nigel Farage, alongside a host of others ranging from blue left to red right, all wielded the Brexit vote as proof of a populist will cast

by the unfairly excluded and forgotten. Most importantly, they identified the wellspring of this will in the northern "white working class".
But it was not this deserving class who authored the Brexit vote. Yes,
the Ashcroft polls (2016) clearly demonstrate that the "lower" the
social grade (C2DE) – the standard proxy, albeit problematic, for
"working class" – the more likely one was to vote leave. Nevertheless,
as would be expected, turnout amongst the "upper" social grades
(ABC1) remained higher than for C2DE. Roughly 68 per cent of the
C2DE population eligible to take part in the referendum did not, for
whatever reason, vote to leave (Flood 2016), and this was despite the
participation of 2.8 million usually disengaged citizens who overwhelmingly buoyed the leave vote (Singh 2016). In fact, 59 per cent
of the leave vote was cast by ABC1 social grades and 41 per cent by
C2DE (Dorling 2016).[2]

Furthermore, because of differential turnout, approximately 52
per cent of respondents to the Ashcroft polls who voted leave were
from southern constituencies and not from the North (Dorling
2016). The leave vote did not even map neatly onto topographies
of poverty, and at local authority level, indices of deprivation did
not strongly correlate with a Brexit disposition (Rae 2016). To these
considerations we must add differences within the urban environment (Rosenbaum 2017). Peripheral, predominantly white urban
housing estates tended to vote leave; inner-city areas with significant percentages of Black and minority ethnic peoples tended to vote
remain. With Grenfell Tower this point has gained poignancy. Note
also that Black voters overwhelmingly cast a ballot to remain, and
Britain's Black citizens are twice as likely to live in poverty than their
white counterparts (Institute of Race Relations 2017).

---

2. One Ipsos MORI poll suggests that C2DE voters provided a slim majority of
   leave votes. www.ipsos.com/ipsos-mori/en-uk/how-britain-voted-2016-eu-ref
   erendum (accessed 5 February 2018). This poll is far less reliable than Ashcroft's
   for two reasons. First, respondents to Ipsos MORI were polled by phone during
   the campaign, while Ashcroft pollsters spoke directly to respondents who had
   just voted; second, the numerate base of the Ipsos MORI poll was significantly
   smaller than that of Ashcroft's. But even if one chose to prefer the inferior Ipsos
   MORI poll to that of Ashcroft, it is still the case that the majority it attributes
   to C2DE voters is very slim, such that any claim that Brexit was a "working
   class" vote must be significantly qualified. My thanks to Danny Dorling for these
   considerations.

The vote to leave cannot, therefore, be characterized in straight-forward terms as a revolt by the working class and certainly not of the traditional "white working class". But if not an authentic popular will drawn from the "little people"/the "left behind"/the "silent majority" of England, which interest predominantly drove Brexit? To address this question, I want to briefly return to the Eurosceptic tradition.

Conservative Eurosceptics broke with one cardinal principle of Powell's populist nationalism: the imperative *not* to resurrect empire. A retired Margaret Thatcher proposed in 1999 an alternative to the EU, drawing upon an idea by historian Robert Conquest of an "Anglo-Oceanic" association (Bell 2017). Likewise, many conservative Eurosceptics who supported Brexit believed that "global Britain" needed to be released from the fetters of EU bureaucracy so as to resurrect the Commonwealth. This geopolitical melancholia was especially notable amongst UKIP politicians (Tournier-Sol 2015: 144; Hayton 2016). Indeed, the notion of an Anglosphere, a collection of English-speaking polities predominantly composed of Anglo-Saxon ex-settler colonies (with India occupying an uncomfortable place on the margins), gained much traction in Brexit circles among figures such as Nigel Farage, David Davis, Michael Gove, Daniel Hannan and Boris Johnson. Through the Anglosphere, they imagined, Britain might retake the imperial heights (Wellings 2014: 93–4; see also Vucetic 2011).

Of course, the prospect of reforming the Anglo-Saxon family in the era of Chinese globalization is impractical, to put it politely. But it is nonetheless a delusion that has served the ideological purpose of carrying forward a far more practical project. And that is to forge an ever-closer relationship between UK and North American social conservatism.

In Chapter 6 I examined how the predicates of social conservatism speak to the morality of marketization in so far as the market mechanism alone encourages the deserving characteristics of industriousness and self-help. With respect to social upheavals that might accompany marketization, conservatives depend upon the sacrosanct principle of inherited private property that would provide an orderly – and patriarchal – independence. Throughout the book I have argued that the patriarchal root of the English genus has been variously racialized since abolition via slave analogies, Anglo-Saxonism, eugenics, populist nationalism and Euroscepticism.

Those on the right who promote a geopolitical realignment away from the EU primarily wish to utilize the deserving/undeserving distinction to drive through an intense marketization of heretofore sacrosanct public goods. Key architects of the Conservative leave campaign were Thatcherites (see Worth 2017). Prominent leave campaigners were also prominent "Atlanticists", such as Liam Fox, head of the Atlantic Bridge charity, now defunct, but whose president when it was founded in 1997 was Thatcher. Many prominent welfare "reformers", such as Iain Duncan Smith, were also key leave advocates. In sum, the movement for Brexit amongst political elites is in large part defined by its combination of social conservatism, welfare reform and market-friendly Atlanticism.

It is here that the question of regulation, raised in the Grenfell Tower atrocity, returns to the fore. Consider the following pieces of evidence. Thatcher's 1988 Bruges speech framed the issue of British sovereignty by reference to a historical conjuncture. After having rolled back the over-regulations embedded in the postwar compact between government, business and labour, Thatcher implored that now was not the time to return the British state to another compromising compact at the European level. Boris Johnson, the predominant personality of Vote Leave, was largely responsible for popularizing Thatcher's position in the early 1990s through his journalistic lampooning of European over-regulation in the pages of the *Telegraph* (Helm 1995). The same newspaper made the same Thatcherite argument in the aftermath of Brexit as it launched its "Cut EU Red Tape" initiative (Rayner & Hope 2017).

Despite having been a soft remainer, Theresa May shared with leavers from her Home Office days a visceral disdain of the European Court of Justice (ECJ), ultimate arbiter of EU regulations. UKIP, the *Daily Mail* and other right-wing voices presented the Supreme Court as traitors of the "people" when it ruled that parliament had to legislate on Article 50, the instrument for withdrawing from the EU. The Court's legal reasoning, however, revolved around the fact that the recusal of people's rights in domestic law – i.e. those provided by the 1972 European Communities Act – could not be enacted by the government's prerogative powers. Such rights and regulations covering labour, environment and consumer protection, many of which were buoyed by the EU's social chapter, all intersect through the ECJ.

I would argue, then, that at the heart of right-wing Euroscepticism there lies less an abstract concern for sovereignty and far more a practical concern for social and economic deregulation. Any combination of quotes can confirm this fact. Take Liam Fox (2012), currently secretary of state for international trade, who wrote back in 2012 that "to restore Britain's competitiveness we must begin by deregulating the labour market [because] [i]t is too difficult to hire and fire and too expensive to take on new employees". Writing for *Forbes* magazine just after the referendum, Tim Worstall (2016), economic journalist and UKIP supporter, enthusiastically looked forward to a deregulated City of London that could restore large bonuses for bankers. Jacob Rees-Mogg, a Conservative backbencher and hard-Brexiteer who in 2017 experienced a surge in popularity, projected a growth in Britain's economy, once freed from the "single market". He did, however, note that such a positive outcome of Brexit would only be possible if regulations were reduced and taxes lowered, especially corporation tax (Walker 2017). I should add that many of these imperatives can be found in Alan Sked's 1997 UKIP manifeso.

Deregulation is the mechanism by which the aims of social-conservativism, welfare reform and Atlanticism are pursued. They have been pushed forward through a moralizing rhetoric that identifies in marketization the rejuvenation of the English genus and its exceptional propensity for orderly independence. This rhetoric has instrumentally promoted a "popular will" that deeply racializes that genus, reforming once more the distinction between those deserving and undeserving of adequate social security and welfare. Undoubtedly, the "white working class" is an artefact of political domination and the racialization of the deserving/undeserving distinction has deadly implications, as suggested by the following story.

In April 2017, mild Eurosceptic Oliver Letwin launched the Red Tape Initiative. Letwin (who, it will be remembered, responded to the Broadwater riots and uprisings in 1985 by claiming that poor whites – unlike poor Blacks – didn't riot) had previously been Cameron's short-lived Director for Exiting the European Union until being culled by Theresa May. The purpose of Letwin's Red Tape Initiative was to help to "forge a consensus on regulatory changes that could benefit businesses and boost jobs in a post-Brexit Britain". Although an independent organization, Business Secretary Greg Clark offered the Initiative the cooperation of his officials. In May 2017, one month the Grenfell Tower fire, the Initiative received a report it had issioned from Hanbury Strategy, which suggested dismantling EU regulations on fire safety of cladding and related construction materials. Hanbury Strategy was set up by Paul Stephenson, communications director for Vote Leave (Laville 2017).

What, then, of the reinvigoration of a public ethos post-Brexit, post-Grenfell? The message of this book is that, no matter how painful, a double-critique of progressive politics is required. Criticism of marketization, deregulation and austerity is not adequate without a critique of the racialization of these processes. Moreover, the racialization of those deserving and undeserving of social security and welfare precedes and structures neoliberal times. It has structured abolition, imperialism, eugenics, colonial development, even the welfare state and its national compact, as well as Thatcherism, workfare and our austerity era. There is no golden age of "public goods" to return to that was not already racialized and because of this fact contained the seed of its own destruction.

We must face the fact that the "white working class" is not – and has never been – a category indigenous to Britain, least of all England. We must acknowledge that the working class was constitutionalized through empire and its aftermaths; and in this respect, class is race. So long as that remains the case, the popular will can never be a progressive alternative to the sovereign will of parliament. Both implicate each other in the pursuit of postcolonial capital accumulation. I finish with two provocations to this effect, as well as two related recommendations, which I address primarily to organizations and activists who consider themselves in some way to be socialists.

First, Britain's division of labour has never been national in constitution or scope. This trite historical fact holds significant consequences for the openings of social justice that some hope might accompany Brexit (for a general critique see Holmwood 2017: 31–40). The parliament of Great Britain was formed in 1707 by the union of England and Scotland, two polities that possessed colonies and colonial ambitions. In the succeeding centuries, parliament governed over not just a national economy but a vast and shifting imperial hinterland of land, labour, raw materials, markets and influence. Later this hinterland became a Commonwealth that effectively saved the sterling economy in the reconstruction period immediately following the Second World War.

Pre-empting the effective loss of this hinterland, Prime Minister Edward Heath finally engineered the successful accession of the British economy to the EEC in 1973. The EU has since functioned for the British economy as a kind of substitute to the hinterlands of empire, especially in the post-Thatcher era in terms of regional funding. The significance of Brexit is that the British economy has partly depended upon hinterlands to provide social security and welfare to its general populace. At the very least, those considered deserving of adequate security and welfare have usually been considered beneficial to empire's integrity. Brexit marks the ultimate loss of empire's protective hinterlands: for the first time ever, the geo-political coordinates of Britain's economy will be primarily national. It is thus entirely reasonable to suppose that post-Brexit deregulation will cut into the national economy in ways that significantly deepen and widen the disparities and exclusions previously entrenched by deindustrialization, marketization and austerity.

To take this history seriously is to realize that race cannot be apprehended as a "minority" issue. True, in Britain, as in many other polities of the Global North, the majority population is racialized as white. But this blunt demographic "fact" in no way infers that a broad-based left politics should play to the lowest-common denominator and be led by the concerns and conditions of a "white working class". There is a question beyond demography, which pertains to the operation of power: where do policies detrimental to the living standards and securities of the majority first make their cut into the social fabric?

This book provides one answer: at its weakest seam, in the racialization of the undeserving poor. For example, the first legislation to reintroduce conditionality into welfare provision concerned asylum seekers; and nowadays, welfare is conditionally granted to all. Hence, the socialist left must recognize that it is in the micro-sites – usually coloured as "ethnic" or "immigrant" – that the battles for tomorrow are first won or lost. The suffering of Grenfell Tower residents should, in principle, be apprehended as the post-Brexit fate that awaits the "just about managing" in the North as well as the inner-city South. Justice for Grenfell is justice for all.

Second, public debate since the EU referendum has almost entirely obscured the imperial and postcolonial constituencies of working peoples. Grenfell Tower placed this quotidian reality in sharp and painful relief. In the current political lexicon, Black citizens appear only in terms of victims of or aggressors in the criminal justice system and Muslim citizens only as victims of Islamophobia or suspects of terrorism. It is almost as if it does not matter that Black and minority ethnic communities – especially their women – have in relative terms been most detrimentally impacted by austerity measures over the last ten years (Bassel & Emejulu 2016).

The histories that I have woven into this book reveal that race is fundamental to political economy. But ever since New Labour, race is only supposed to make sense as political discrimination; while economic inequality is a class issue proper, to which race is safely derivative of. Remember: the popular will for Brexit has been enunciated as a moral compulsion primarily in the language of inequality (class) rather than – in fact explicitly over and above – discrimination (race). Those deserving of social security and welfare are currently racialized as white. But does it not matter that Black voters overwhelmingly cast a ballot to remain; and that Britain's Black citizens are disproportionately more likely to live in poverty than their white counterparts? Is this not, at least, a compelling correlation?

There is a tendency for socialists to disparage as "identity politics" social movements that foreground race (as well as gender and sexuality). This tendency derives from conjoint premises: the objective structure of class gives its politics a universal reach, hence enabling a solidarity that matches the global reach of capital; alternatively, race is a particular identity arising from ruling class ideologies, hence the pursuit of justice along race lines will always subvert the cultivation of wider and deeper solidarities. Throughout this book I have made the claim that class is race. What I mean by this pithy phrase is that there is no politics of class that is not already racialized. This reality must be confronted rather than avoided for fantastical definitions of class purified of racial contamination.

Presently, socialism seems to have been rejuvenated in mainstream politics. In different ways, both Bernie Sanders in the United States (2016) and Jeremy Corbyn in the UK (2017) gained electoral traction – albeit not success – through an unapologetic grammar of social justice, public goods and meaningful redistributive policies. But the fragility of this comeback is remarkable, especially in the UK. It rests upon a tactical deferral of confronting racialized nationalisms and anti-immigration sentiment in favour of a putatively neutral focus on class injustice. I have demonstrated that this cognitive arrangement is nothing new and has historically facilitated the rise of the socially conservative right.

The justice pursued by socialists is premised on a universal commitment to overcome inequality, exploitation and oppression suffered by the working class. Yet once again, tacitly or otherwise, this project is currently being pursued through and on behalf of a racialized nation whose own justice demands partiality. This partiality gains traction in the deserving/undeserving distinction, even though the undeserving should just as much be considered a part of the resident working class. An internationalism adequate for our postcolonial era therefore requires a first order analytical and ethical engagement with class as race.

Those are my closing provocations and recommendations. I write them in December 2017, at a moment in time when nothing of certainty has yet to eventuate from the Brexit negotiations. This seems to be a pivotal moment: when things that were not supposed to happen have happened, and where history's needle vacillates between total eclipse and a horizon of possibility. Despite the uncertainty, might we orient the progressive compass towards the racialized classification of the undeserving, of the unsalvageable? Less a romantic moralizing of the poor, I am pointing towards the violence of empire's commercial society, a violence that will remain after Brexit, after Grenfell; a violence that runs through New Labour, Thatcherism, universal welfare and the national compact, colonial development, eugenics, inter-imperial rivalry, Anglo-Saxonism and abolition.

Besides this violence lies a thread of resistance handed down by all those collectively punished as undeserving but who have refused such a system of classification. I have alluded to them over the course of this book: the Haitian revolutionaries, the abolitionist movements amongst British workers, the Black Baptists of Morant Bay, Black Power in Britain, Grunwick, Westway, and there are many more. This detritus of empire has rarely been considered the material from which to build new publics, and certainly not in the metropolitan core. But the stone which the builders rejected shall become the chief cornerstone.

REFERENCES

"About Red Tape Challenge" 2015. National Archives. http://webarchive.
nationalarchives.gov.uk/20150507103822/http://www.redtapechallenge.
cabinetoffice.gov.uk/about/ (accessed 20 December 2017).

Absolute Radio 2015. "Nigel Farage on Absolute Interview". www.youtube.com/
watch?v=ZcmIHT6J0wc (accessed 20 December 2017).

Alborn, T. 2001. "Senses of Belonging: The Politics of Working-Class Insurance
in Britain, 1880–1914". *Journal of Modern History* 73 (3): 561–602.

Allen, J. 1938. *Negro Liberation*. New York: International Pamphlets.

Allen, S. & C. Smith 1974. "Race and Ethnicity in Class Formation: A
Comparison of Asian and West Indian Workers". In *The Social Analysis of
Class Structure*, F. Parkin (ed.), 39–53. London: Tavistock.

Amara, P. 2014. "UKIP Founder Alan Sked and Nigel Farage 'Begged Enoch Powell
to Stand as a Candidate'". *Independent*, 12 December. www.independent.
co.uk/news/uk/politics/ukip-founder-alan-sked-begged-enoch-powell-to-
stand-as-a-candidate-9922502.html (accessed 20 December 2017).

Aponte, R. 1990. "Definitions of the Underclass: A Critical Analysis". In *Sociology
in America*, H. Gans (ed.), 117–37. Westbury Park, CA: Sage.

Ashcroft, M. 2013. "45 Years On, Do Ethnic Minorities Remember 'Rivers
of Blood'?" http://thinkethnic.com/wp-content/uploads/2012/02/Multicul
tural%20Britain%20Research.pdf (accessed 20 December 2017).

Ashcroft, M. 2016. "EU Referendum 'How Did You Vote' Poll". http://
lordashcroftpolls.com/wp-content/uploads/2016/06/How-the-UK-voted-
Full-tables-1.pdf (accessed 20 December 2017).

Aughey, A. 2010. "Anxiety and Injustice: The Anatomy of Contemporary English
Nationalism". *Nations and Nationalism* 16 (3): 506–24.

Back, L., M. Keith, A. Khan, *et al.* 2002. "New Labour's White Heart: Politics,
Multiculturalism and the Return of Assimilation". *Political Quarterly* 73
(4): 445–54.

Bailey, D. 1973. "Defence Committee for STC". *Red Weekly*, 31 August.

Bakshi, P., M. Goodwin, J. Painter & A. Southern 1995. "Gender, Race, and Class in the Local Welfare State: Moving beyond Regulation Theory in Analysing the Transition from Fordism". *Environment and Planning A* 27 (10): 1539–54.

Banton, M. 1953. "The Economic and Social Position of Negro Immigrants in Britain". *Sociological Review* 1 (2): 43–62.

Banton, M. 1955. *The Coloured Quarter: Negro Immigrants in an English City*. London: Cape.

Barker, M. 1982. *The New Racism: Conservatives and the Ideology of the Tribe*. Frederick, MD: Aletheia Books.

Barnes, S. 2017. "Government Delay in Reviewing Fire Safety Regulations 'Putting Tower Blocks at Risk'". Inside Housing. www.insidehousing.co.uk/home/home/government-delay-in-reviewing-fire-safety-regulations-putting-tower-blocks-at-risk-50024 (accessed 20 December 2017).

Bassel, L. & A. Emejulu 2016. "Minority Women and Austerity". www.minority womenandausterity.com/ (accessed 20 December 2017).

BBC News 1999. "Welfare Set for Reform", 10 February. http://news.bbc.co.uk/1/hi/uk_politics/276598.stm (accessed 20 December 2017).

BBC News 2010. "Harriet Harman: Class Holds You Back More than Gender", 21 January. http://news.bbc.co.uk/1/hi/uk_politics/8472904.stm (accessed 20 December 2017).

BBC News 2017. "Andrew Marr Interviews Labour Leader Jeremy Corbyn", 23 July. www.youtube.com/watch?v=hxb0z_YhO1Q (accessed 20 December 2017).

Beatty, C. & S. Fothergill 2014. "The Local and Regional Impact of the UK's Welfare Reforms". *Cambridge Journal of Regions, Economy and Society* 7 (1): 63–79.

Bell, D. 2007. *The Idea of Greater Britain: Empire and the Future of World Order, 1860–1900*. Princeton, NJ: Princeton University Press.

Bell, D. 2017. "The Anglosphere: New Enthusiasm for an Old Dream". *Prospect Magazine*, 19 January. www.prospectmagazine.co.uk/magazine/anglosphere-old-dream-brexit-role-in-the-world (accessed 20 December 2017).

Bell, T. 2016. "The Referendum, Living Standards and Inequality". Resolution Foundation blog, 24 June. www.resolutionfoundation.org/media/blog/the-referendum-living-standards-and-inequality/ (accessed 20 December 2017).

Beveridge, W. 1942. "Social Insurances and Allied Service". DO 35/993/11. National Archives UK.

Beveridge, W. 1943. *The Pillars of Security, and Other War-Time Essays and Addresses*. London: Allen & Unwin.

Beveridge, W. 1944. *Beveridge on Beveridge: Recent Speeches of Sir William Beveridge*, J. Clarke (ed.), London: Social Security League.

Beveridge, W. 1948. *Voluntary Action: A Report on Methods of Social Advance*. London: Allen & Unwin.

Bhambra, G. 2016a. "Class Analysis in the Age of Trump (and Brexit): The Pernicious New Politics of Identity". *The Sociological Review* blog. www.thesociologicalreview.com/blog/class-analysis-in-the-age-of-trump-and-brexit-the-pernicious-new-politics-of-identity.html (accessed 20 December 2017).

Bhambra, G. 2016b. "Brexit, the Commonwealth, and Exclusionary Citizenship". Open Democracy, 8 December. www.opendemocracy.net/ gurminder-k-bhambra/brexit-commonwealth-and-exclusionary-citizen ship (accessed 20 December 2017).

Blackstone, W. 1766. *Commentaries on the Laws of England. Book the First*. Dublin: John Exshaw, Henry Saunders, Samuel Watson & James Williams.

Blond, P. 2010. *Red Tory: How the Left and Right Have Broken Britain and How We Can Fix It*. London: Faber & Faber.

Bolt, C. 1971. *Victorian Attitudes to Race*. London: Routledge & Kegan Paul.

Bonnett, A. 1998. "How the British Working Class Became White: The Symbolic (Re)Formation of Racialized Capitalism". *Journal of Historical Sociology* 11 (3): 316–40.

Booth, C. 1897. *Life and Labour of the People in London. Vol. IX*. London: Macmillan.

Booth, W. 1890. *In Darkest England and the Way Out*. London: Funk & Wagnal.

Bosanquet, B. 1910. "Charity Organization and the Majority Report". *International Journal of Ethics* 20 (4): 395–408.

Bosanquet, B. & H. Dendy (eds) 1895. "The Industrial Residuum". In *Aspects of the Social Problem*, 82–102. London: Macmillan.

Bosanquet, H. 1902. *The Strength of the People: A Study in Social Economics*. London: Macmillan.

Brougham, H. 1803. *An Inquiry into the Colonial Policy of the European Powers*. Edinburgh: E. Balfour, Manners & Miller.

Brown, C. 1999. "Empire without Slaves: British Concepts of Emancipation in the Age of the American Revolution". *William and Mary Quarterly* 56 (2): 273–306.

Brown, J. 1968. "Charles Booth and Labour Colonies, 1889–1905". *Economic History Review* 21 (2): 349–60.

Bryan, B., S. Dadzie & S. Scafe 1985. *The Heart of the Race: Black Women's Lives in Britain*. London: Virago.

Buettner, E. 2014. "'This Is Staffordshire Not Alabama': Racial Geographies of Commonwealth Immigration in Early 1960s Britain". *Journal of Imperial and Commonwealth History* 42 (4): 710–40.

Burke, E. 1796. *Two Letters Addressed to the Present Parliament, on the Proposals for Peace with the Regicide Directory of France*. Dublin: P. Wogan *et al.*

Burke, E. 1910. *Reflections on the French Revolution*. London: Dent.

Burke, W. 1760. *An Account of the European Settlements in America, 6 Vols*. London: R. & J. Dodsley.

Bush, J. 1993. "Free to Enslave: The Foundations of Colonial American Slave Law". *Yale Journal of Law & the Humanities* 5 (2): 417–70.

Butler, D. & D. Kavanagh 1980. *The British General Election of 1979*. London: Macmillan.

Cameron, D. 2007. "Cameron's Co-Op Speech", 8 November. http://news.bbc. co.uk/1/hi/uk_politics/7084865.stm (accessed 20 December 2017).

Carlyle, T. 1867. *Shooting Niagara: And After?* London: Chapman & Hall.

Carlyle, T. 1899. "The Nigger Question". In *Critical And Miscellaneous Essays in Five Volumes, IV*, 348–83. London: Chapman & Hall.

Carswell, D. 2016. "Labour's Heartlands Will Turn to Ukip, and We Will Not Fail Them". *Guardian*, 28 November. www.theguardian.com/commentis free/2016/nov/28/ukip-labour-paul-nuttall-douglas-carswell (accessed 20 December 2017).

Carter, B., C. Harris & S. Joshi 1987. "The 1951–55 Conservative Government and the Racialisation of Black Immigration". Policy Papers in Ethnic Relations, University of Warwick.

Cashmore, E. 1979. *Rastaman: The Rastafarian Movement in England*. London: Allen & Unwin.

Chamberlain, M. 2002. "Small Worlds: Childhood and Empire". *Journal of Family History* 27 (2): 186–200.

Charlotte Street Partners 2016. "15 Minutes with Liam Fox". www. charlottestpartners.co.uk/insights/15-minutes-with-liam-fox/ (accessed 20 December 2017).

Chase, M. 2017. "The Popular Movement for Parliamentary Reform in Provincial Britain During the 1860s". *Parliamentary History* 36 (1): 14–30.

Chesterton, G. 1910. *William Cobbett*. London: Hodder & Stoughton.

Chesterton, G. 2011. *A Short History of England*. Auckland: Floating Press.

Clark, A. 1997. *The Struggle for the Breeches: Gender and the Making of the British Working Class*. Berkeley, CA: University of California Press.

Clegg, H. 1979. *The Changing System of Industrial Relations in Great Britain*. Oxford: Basil Blackwell.

Cobbett, W. 1829. *Advice to Young Men, and (Incidentally) to Young Women*. London: Mills, Jowett & Mills.

Cobbett, W. 1872. *A Legacy to Labourers*. London: Charles Griffin.

Cobbett, W. 1912. *Rural Rides. Vol. 2*. London: Dent.

Cobham, A. 2017. "If You're Wondering How and Why 'Cutting Red Tape' Could Have Led to the Grenfell Tower Fire, Here's Your Answer". *Independent*, 16 July. www.independent.co.uk/voices/london-fire-grenfell-tower-how-why-did-it-happen-cladding-health-safety-theresa-may-government-a7793921. html (accessed 20 December 2017).

Cole, G. 1924. *The Life of William Cobbett*. London: Collins.

Colonial Labour Advisory Committee 1955a. "Draft Mintues of Meeting 10 November". ACT 1/717. National Archives UK.

Colonial Labour Advisory Committee 1955b. "Draft Mintues of Meeting 29 September". ACT 1/717. National Archives UK.

Coombs, N. 2011. "The Political Theology of Red Toryism". *Journal of Political Ideologies* 16 (1): 79–96.

Cooperative Union, Manchester 1900. "Letter to Colonial Office". CO 318/300. National Archives UK.

Corbett, S. & A. Walker 2013. "The Big Society: Rediscovery of 'the Social' or Rhetorical Fig-Leaf for Neo-Liberalism?" *Critical Social Policy* 33 (3): 451–72.

Cowen, M. & R. Shenton 1991. "The Origin and Course of Fabian Colonialism in Africa". *Journal of Historical Sociology* 4 (2): 143–74.

Creech Jones, A. 1945. "Some Considerations of Social Policy and Its Costs". In *Fabian Colonial Essays*, H. Brailsford & R. Hinden (eds), 67–84. London: Allen & Unwin.

Daguerre, A. 2004. "Importing Workfare: Policy Transfer of Social and Labour Market Policies from the USA to Britain under New Labour". *Social Policy & Administration* 38 (1): 41–56.

Dale, I. 2008. "In Conversation with Nigel Farage". *Total Politics*. www.totalpolitics.com/articles/interview/conversation-nigel-farage (accessed 20 December 2017).

"David Starkey on *Newsnight*" 2011. www.youtube.com/watch?v=OVq2bs8M9 HM&t=48s (accessed 20 December 2017).

Davies, C. 1966. "Slavery and Protector Somerset: The Vagrancy Act of 1547". *Economic History Review* 19 (3): 533–49.

Davies, I. 1963. "The Labour Commonwealth". *New Left Review* 22: 75–94.

Davies, N. 1998. *Dark Heart: The Shocking Truth About Hidden Britain*. London: Vintage.

Davis, D. 1975. *The Problem of Slavery in the Age of Revolution*. Ithaca, NY: Cornell University Press.

Davis, M. 2010. "Labour, Race and Empire: The Trades Union Congress and Colonial Policy, 1945–51". In *The British Labour Movement and Imperialism*, B. Frank, C. Horner & D. Stewart (eds), 89–106. Newcastle upon Tyne: Cambridge Scholars.

Deacon, A. 1982. "An End to the Means Test? Social Security and the Attlee Government". *Journal of Social Policy* 11 (3): 289–306.

Deacon, A. 2003. "'Levelling the Playing Field, Activating the Players': New Labour and 'the Cycle of Disadvantage'". *Policy & Politics* 31 (2): 123–37.

Denham, A. & M. Garnett 2001. "From 'Guru' to 'Godfather': Keith Joseph, 'New' Labour and the British Conservative Tradition". *Political Quarterly* 72 (1): 97–106.

Desai, R. 1994. "Second-Hand Dealers in Ideas: Think-Tanks and Thatcherite Hegemony". *New Left Review* 203: 27–64.

Dicey, A. 1889. *Introduction to the Study of the Law of the Constitution*. London: Macmillan.

Dilke, C. 1869. *Greater Britain: A Record of Travel in English-Speaking Countries During 1866–7*. Philadelphia, PA: Lippincott.

"Disraeli's Speech on the Reform Bill: 15 July 1867". www.historyhome.co.uk/polspeech/reform.htm (accessed 20 December 2017).

Dorling, D. 2016. "Brexit: The Decision of a Divided Country". *BMJ* 354. www.bmj.com/content/354/bmj.i3697 (accessed 20 December 2017).

Drake, S. 1955. "The 'Colour Problem' in Britain: A Study in Social Definitions". *Sociological Review* 3 (2): 197–217.

Drescher, S. 1981. "Cart Whip and Billy Roller: Antislavery and Reform Symbolism in Industrializing Britain". *Journal of Social History* 15 (1): 3–24.

Drescher, S. 1987. *Capitalism and Antislavery: British Mobilization in Comparative Perspective*. New York: Oxford University Press.

Drescher, S. 1999. *From Slavery to Freedom: Comparative Studies in the Rise and Fall of Atlantic Slavery*. New York: New York University Press.

Dugger, J. 2006. "Black Ireland's Race: Thomas Carlyle and the Young Ireland Movement". *Victorian Studies* 48 (3): 461–85.

Dyck, I. 1993. "William Cobbett and the Rural Radical Platform". *Social History* 18 (2): 185–204.

Ebrahimi, H. 2017. "Grenfell: TMO Spent Millions on Management Fees Rather than Refurbishment". Channel 4 News, 25 July. www.channel4.com/news/grenfell-tmo-spent-millions-on-management-fees-rather-than-refurbishment (accessed 20 December 2017).

Edemariam, A. 2010. "Frank Field: 'Labour Has Always Been Conservative'". *Guardian*, 2 July. www.theguardian.com/politics/2010/jul/03/frank-field-interview-labour (accessed 20 December 2017).

Eldridge, C. 1973. *England's Mission: The Imperial Idea in The Age of Gladstone and Disraeli 1868–1880*. London: Macmillan.

"Empire – A Bi Monthly Record of the Fabian Colonial Bureau 4 (1)" 1941. CO 875/11/11. National Archives UK.

Epps, G. 1943. "To George Gater, Colonial Office". ACT 1/717. National Archives UK.

Erickson, A. 1959. "Empire or Anarchy: The Jamaica Rebellion of 1865". *The Journal of Negro History* 44 (2): 99–122.

Evans, S. 2009. "The Not So Odd Couple: Margaret Thatcher and One Nation Conservatism". *Contemporary British History* 23 (1): 101–21.

Fabian Society 1891. *Reform of the Poor Laws. Fabian Tracts 17*. London: John Heywood.

Farage, N. 2016. "Nigel Farage Delivers First Post-Brexit Speech to the European Parliament – in Full". *Independent*, 28 June. www.independent.co.uk/news/uk/politics/nigel-farage-brexit-speech-european-parliament-full-transcript-text-a7107036.html (accessed 20 December 2017).

Fay, C. 1950. *Great Britain from Adam Smith to the Present Day: An Economic and Social Survey*. London: Longmans, Green & Co.

Fenton, S. 2012. "Resentment, Class and Social Sentiments about the Nation: The Ethnic Majority in England". *Ethnicities* 12 (4): 465–83.

Fielding, S. 2003. *The Labour Governments, 1964–70. Vol. 1*. Manchester: Manchester University Press.

Finlayson, G. 1990. "A Moving Frontier: Voluntarism and the State in British Social Welfare 1911–1949". *Twentieth Century British History* 1 (2): 183–206.

Finn, D. 2015. "Welfare to Work Devolution in England". Joseph Rowntree Foundation. www.jrf.org.uk/report/welfare-work-devolution-england (accessed 20 December 2017).

Fisher, T. 2006. "Race, Neoliberalism, and 'Welfare Reform' in Britain". *Social Justice* 33 (3 (105)): 54–65.

Flaherty, J. 2008. "'I Mean We're Not the Richest But We're Not Poor': Discourses of 'Poverty' and 'Social Exclusion'". PhD dissertation, Loughborough University.

Flood, A. 2016. "Making Sense of the Brexit Tide of Reaction and the Reality of the Racist Vote". Workers Solidarity Movement blog. www.wsm.ie/c/making-sense-brexit-tide-reaction-racist-vote (accessed 20 December 2017).

Ford, R. & M. Goodwin 2014. "Understanding UKIP: Identity, Social Change and the Left Behind". *Political Quarterly* 85 (3): 277–84.

Forster, A. 2002. "Anti-Europeans, Anti-Marketeers and Eurosceptics: The Evolution and Influence of Labour and Conservative Opposition to Europe". *Political Quarterly* 73 (3): 299–308.

Fox, J., L. Moroşanu & E. Szilassy 2012. "The Racialization of the New European Migration to the UK". *Sociology* 46 (4): 680–95.

Fox, L. 2012. "The Pressing Case to Cut Both Taxes and Spending". *Financial Times*, 21 February. www.ft.com/content/2ee5b8de-5c8d-11e1-8f1f-00144feabdc0 (accessed 20 December 2017).

Fraser, D. 2009. *The Evolution of the British Welfare State: A History of Social Policy Since the Industrial Revolution*. Basingstoke: Palgrave Macmillan.

Fraser, R. 2011. "Race and Religion in the Victorian Age: Charles Kingsley, Governor Eyre and the Morant Bay Rising". The Victorian Web. www.victorianweb.org/authors/kingsley/rfraser.html (accessed 20 December 2017).

French, J. 1988. "Colonial Policy Towards Women after the 1938 Uprising: The Case of Jamaica". *Caribbean Quarterly* 34 (3/4): 38–61.

Garner, S. 2012. "A Moral Economy of Whiteness: Behaviours, Belonging and Britishness". *Ethnicities* 12 (4): 445–64.

Garner, S. 2015. "The Entitled Nation: How People Make Themselves White in Contemporary England". Sens Public. www.sens-public.org/article729.html?lang=fr (accessed 20 December 2017).

Geddes, A. 2014. "The EU, UKIP and the Politics of Immigration in Britain". *Political Quarterly* 85 (3): 289–95.

Gentleman, A. 2017. "Grenfell Campaigner Calls for Return of Local Assets as Reparation". *Guardian*, 13 September. www.theguardian.com/uk-news/2017/sep/13/grenfell-campaigner-calls-for-return-of-local-assets-as-reparation (accessed 20 December 2017).

Gifford, C. 2014. "The People Against Europe: The Eurosceptic Challenge to the United Kingdom's Coalition Government". *JCMS: Journal of Common Market Studies* 52 (3): 512–28.

Gilbert, J. 2017. "An Epochal Election: Welcome to the Era of Platform Politics". Open Democracy. www.opendemocracy.net/uk/jeremy-gilbert/epochal-election-welcome-to-era-of-platform-politics (accessed 20 December 2017).

Gillborn, D. 2010. "The White Working Class, Racism and Respectability: Victims, Degenerates and Interest-Convergence". *British Journal of Educational Studies* 58 (1): 3–25.

Gilroy, P. 2006. *Postcolonial Melancholia*. New York: Columbia University Press.

Gilroy, P. 2010. *There Ain't No Black in the Union Jack: The Cultural Politics of Race and Nation*. London: Routledge.

Ginsburg, N. 1992. "Racing and Housing: Concepts and Reality". In *Racism and Antiracism: Inequalities, Opportunities and Policies*, P. Braham, A. Rattansi & R. Skellington (eds), 109–32. London: Sage.

Ginsburg, N. 2000. *Divisions of Welfare: A Critical Introduction to Comparative Social Policy*. London: Sage.

Glasman, M. 2011. "Labour as a Radical Tradition". In *Labour and the Politics of Paradox*, M. Glasman, J. Rutherford, M. Stears & S. White (eds), 14–34. The Oxford London Seminars. www.lwbooks.co.uk/sites/default/files/free-book/Labour_tradition_and_the_politics_of_paradox.pdf (accessed 20 December 2017).

Glasman, M. 2016. "Why Should Labour Support the Undemocratic EU? The Case for Leave". Labour List. http://labourlist.org/2016/06/why-should-labour-support-the-european-union-the-case-for-out/ (accessed 20 December 2017).

Goodfellow, M. 2017. "The Connection between Grenfell and Finsbury Park". *Al Jazeera*, 21 June. www.aljazeera.com/indepth/opinion/2017/06/connection-grenfell-finsbury-park-170621075822519.html (accessed 20 December 2017).

Goodhart, D. 2004. "Too Diverse?" *Prospect*. www.prospectmagazine.co.uk/magazine/too-diverse-david-goodhart-multiculturalism-britain-immigration-globalisation (accessed 20 December 2017).

Goodhart, D. 2017. "Why I Left My Liberal London Tribe". *Financial Times*, 16 May. www.ft.com/content/39a0867a-0974-11e7-ac5a-903b21361b43 (accessed 20 December 2017).

Gray, N. & G. Mooney 2011. "Glasgow's New Urban Frontier: 'Civilising' the Population of 'Glasgow East'". *City* 15 (1): 4–24.

Grenfell Action Group 2017. "Combustible Cladding – Early Warnings Ignored!" Grenfell Action Group blog, 31 July. https://grenfellactiongroup.wordpress.com/2017/07/31/combustible-cladding-early-warnings-ignored/ (accessed 20 December 2017).

Griffith, P. & A. Glennie 2014. "Alien Nation? New Perspectives on the White Working Class and Disengagement in Britain". IPPR. www.ippr.org/files/publications/pdf/alien-nation_Oct2014.pdf?noredirect=1 (accessed 20 December 2017).

Griffiths, C. 1999. "G. D. H. Cole and William Cobbett". *Rural History* 10 (1): 91–104.

Grob-Fitzgibbon, B. 2016. *Continental Drift: Britain and Europe From the End of Empire to the Rise of Euroscepticism*. Cambridge: Cambridge University Press.

Guardian 2016. "Andy Burnham Sounds Alarm at 'Very Real Prospect' of Brexit", 10 June. www.theguardian.com/politics/2016/jun/10/andy-burnham-warns-remain-is-failing-to-reach-labour-heartland (accessed 20 December 2017).

Gulliver, K. 2017. "Britain's Housing Crisis Is Racist – We Need to Talk About It". *Guardian*, 6 July. www.theguardian.com/housing-network/2017/jul/06/britain-housing-crisis-racist-bme-homelessness (accessed 20 December 2017).

Hall, C. 1994. "Rethinking Imperial Histories: The Reform Act of 1867". *New Left Review* 208: 3–29.

Hanagan, M. 1997. "Citizenship, Claim-Making, and the Right to Work: Britain, 1884–1911". *Theory and Society* 26 (4): 449–74.

Hancock, L. & G. Mooney 2013. "'Welfare Ghettos' and the 'Broken Society': Territorial Stigmatization in the Contemporary UK". *Housing, Theory and Society* 30 (1): 46–64.

Handford, P. 2008. "Edward John Eyre and the Conflict of Laws". *Melbourne University Law Review* 32 (3): 828–44. www5.austlii.edu.au/au/journals/MelbULawRw/2008/26.html (accessed 20 December 2017).

Hanley, L. 2017. "Look at Grenfell Tower and See the Terrible Price of Britain's Inequality". *Guardian*, 16 June. www.theguardian.com/commentisfree/2017/jun/16/grenfell-tower-price-britain-inequality-high-rise (accessed 20 December 2017).

Hannan, D. 2014. "Enoch Powell's Monstrous Reputation Hides the Real Man". *Telegraph*, 15 December. www.telegraph.co.uk/news/politics/conservative/11294064/The-Conservative-Party-need-to-rescue-Enoch-Powells-name.html (accessed 20 December 2017).

Hansen, R. 1999. "The Politics of Citizenship in 1940s Britain: The British Nationality Act". *Twentieth Century British History* 10 (1): 67–95.

Harris, J. 1992. "Victorian Values and the Founders of the Welfare State". *Proceedings of the British Academy* 78: 165–82.

Harris, J. 2003. *William Beveridge: A Biography*. Oxford: Clarendon Press.

Haylett, C. 2001. "Illegitimate Subjects? Abject Whites, Neoliberal Modernisation, and Middle-Class Multiculturalism". *Environment and Planning D: Society and Space* 19 (3): 351–70.

Hayton, R. 2016. "The UK Independence Party and the Politics of Englishness". *Political Studies Review* 14 (3): 400–10.

Hazeldine, T. 2017. "Revolt of the Rustbelt". *New Left Review* 105: 51–79.

Heartfield, J. 2015. *The British and Foreign Anti-Slavery Society*. London: Hurst.

Heffer, S. 1998. *Like the Roman: The Life of Enoch Powell*. London: Weidenfeld & Nicolson.

Hellwig, T. 2005. "The Origins of Unemployment Insurance in Britain: A Cross-Class Alliance Approach". *Social Science History* 29 (1): 107–36.

Helm, S. 1995. "Brussels Chuckles as Reality Hits Mythmaker". *Independent*, 23 July. www.independent.co.uk/news/uk/home-news/brussels-chuckles-as-reality-hits-mythmaker-1592828.html (accessed 20 December 2017).

Henderson, J. & V. Karn 1990. *Race, Class and State Housing: Inequality and the Allocation of Public Housing in Britain*. Aldershot: Gower.

Hesse, B. 1997. "White Governmentality: Urbanism, Nationalism, Racism". In *Imagining Cities: Scripts, Signs, Memories*, S. Westwood & J. Williams (eds), 85–102. London: Routledge.

Heyrick, E. 1837. *Immediate, Not Gradual Abolition*. Philadelphia, PA: Philadelphia AS Society.

Hickson, K. 2013. "The Localist Turn in British Politics and Its Critics". *Policy Studies* 34 (4): 408–21.

Hill, M. 1969. "The Exercise of Discretion in the National Assistance Board". *Public Administration* 47 (1): 75–90.

Himmelfarb, G. 1966. "The Politics of Democracy: The English Reform Act of 1867". *Journal of British Studies* 6 (1): 97–138.

Hoggett, P., H. Wilkinson & P. Beedell 2013. "Fairness and the Politics of Resentment". *Journal of Social Policy* 42 (3): 567–85.

Hollis, P. 1980. "Anti-Slavery and British Working-Class Radicalism in the Years of Reform". In *Antislavery, Religion and Reform*, C. Bolt & S. Drescher (eds), 294–315. Folkestone: Dawson.

Holmwood, J. 2017. "Exit from the Perspective of Entry". In *Brexit: Sociological Responses*, W. Outhwaite (ed.), 31–40. London: Anthem Press.

Holt, T. 1992. *The Problem of Freedom: Race, Labor, and Politics in Jamaica and Britain, 1832–1938*. Baltimore, MD: Johns Hopkins University Press.

Horton, H. 2017. "Grenfell Tower Fire: Muslims Awake for Ramadan among Heroes Who Helped Save Lives". *Telegraph*, 14 June. www.telegraph.co.uk/news/2017/06/14/local-heroes-saved-lives-helped-residents-grenfell-tower-fire/ (accessed 20 December 2017).

House of Commons 1834. "Report from His Majesty's Commissioners for Inquiring into the Administration and Practical Operation of the Poor Laws". House of Commons Parliamentary Papers.

Hulsebosch, D. 2006. "Nothing But Liberty: Somerset's Case and the British Empire". *Law and History Review* 24 (3). www.historycooperative.org/journals/lhr/24.3/hulsebosch.html (accessed 20 December 2017).

Huzzey, R. 2012. "Minding Civilisation and Humanity in 1867: A Case Study in British Imperial Culture and Victorian Anti-Slavery". *The Journal of Imperial and Commonwealth History* 40 (5): 807–25.

Institute of Race Relations 2017. "Inequality, Housing and Employment Statistics". www.irr.org.uk/research/statistics/poverty/ (accessed 20 December 2017).

Inter-Departmental Committee on Physical Deterioration 1904. Report of the Inter-Departmental Committee on Physical Deterioration. London: Eyre & Spottiswoode.

Ipsos MORI 2016. "EU Immigration". www.ipsos.com/sites/default/files/migrations/en-uk/files/Assets/Docs/Polls/EU%20immigration_FINAL%20SLIDES%2020.06.16%20V3.pdf (accessed 20 December 2017).

Johnson, C. 1936. "The Conflict of Caste and Class in an American Industry". *American Journal of Sociology* 42 (1): 55–65.

Johnstone, C. & G. Mooney 2005. "Locales of 'Disorder' and 'Disorganisation'? Exploring New Labour's Approach to Council Estates". Presented at Securing the Urban Renaissance: Policing, Community and Disorder, Glasgow. http://citeseerx.ist.psu.edu/viewdoc/download?doi=10.1.1.456.3250&rep=rep1&type=pdf (accessed 20 December 2017).

Jones, G. 1983. *Languages of Class: Studies in English Working Class History 1832–1982*. Cambridge: Cambridge University Press.

Jones, G. 1986. *Social Hygiene in Twentieth Century Britain*. London: Croom Helm.

Joseph, K. 1974. "Speech at Edgbaston". Margaret Thatcher Foundation. www.margaretthatcher.org/document/101830 (accessed 20 December 2017).

Joshi, S. & B. Carter 1984. "The Role of Labour in the Creation of a Racist Britain". *Race & Class* 25 (3): 53–70.

Kay, D. & R. Miles 1988. "Refugees or Migrant Workers? The Case of the European Volunteer Workers in Britain (1946–1951)". *Journal of Refugee Studies* 1 (3/4): 214–36.

Kegel, C. 1958. "William Cobbett and Malthusianism". *Journal of the History of Ideas* 19 (3): 348–62.

Kelemen, P. 2007. "Planning for Africa: The British Labour Party's Colonial Development Policy, 1920–1964". *Journal of Agrarian Change* 7 (1): 76–98.

Kennedy, T. & T. Leary 1947. "Communist Thought on the Negro". *Phylon (1940–1956)* 8 (2): 116–23.

Kenny, M. 2012. "The Political Theory of Recognition: The Case of the 'White Working Class'". *The British Journal of Politics & International Relations* 14 (1): 19–38.

Kenny, M. 2015. "The Return of 'Englishness' in British Political Culture: The End of the Unions?" *JCMS: Journal of Common Market Studies* 53 (1): 35–51.

King, D. & M. Wickham-Jones 1999. "From Clinton to Blair: The Democratic (Party) Origins of Welfare to Work". *The Political Quarterly* 70 (1): 62–74.

King, R. & M. Wood 1975. "The Support for Enoch Powell". In *The Politics of Race*, I. Crewe (ed.), 239–63. London: Croom Helm.

Kohn, M. & D. O'Neill 2006. "A Tale of Two Indias: Burke and Mill on Empire and Slavery in the West Indies and America". *Political Theory* 34 (2): 192–228. https://doi.org/10.1177/0090591705279609 (accessed 20 December 2017).

Koksal, I. 2014. "7 Ways the Localism Act Is Shafting the Homeless and Precariously-Housed". Novara Media. http://novaramedia.com/2014/07/28/7-ways-the-localism-act-is-shafting-the-homeless-and-precariously-housed/ (accessed 20 December 2017).

Kundnani, A. 2000. "'Stumbling on': Race, Class and England". *Race & Class* 41 (4): 1–18.

Laville, S. 2017. "Government-Backed 'Red Tape' Group Looked at EU Fire Safety Rules on Morning of Grenfell Fire". *Guardian*, 22 June. www.theguardian.com/uk-news/2017/jun/22/government-backed-red-tape-group-eu-fire-safety-rules-grenfell-fire (accessed 20 December 2017).

Lawler, S. 2012. "White Like Them: Whiteness and Anachronistic Space in Representations of the English White Working Class". *Ethnicities* 12 (4): 409–26.

Lazer, H. 1976. "British Populism: The Labour Party and the Common Market Parliamentary Debate". *Political Science Quarterly* 91 (2): 259–77.

Levy, D. 2002. *How the Dismal Science Got Its Name: Classical Economics and the Ur-Text of Racial Politics*. Ann Arbor, MI: University of Michigan Press.

Lewis, G. 1996. "Welfare Settlements and Racializing Practices". *Soundings: A Journal of Politics and Culture* 10: 109–20.

Lewis, M. 2012. "Pictures of Revolutionary Reform in Carlyle, Arnold, and Punch". *Nineteenth-Century Contexts* 34 (5): 533–52.

Lewis, O. 1966. "The Culture of Poverty". *American* 215 (4): 19–25.

Lewis, R. 1979. *Enoch Powell: Principle in Politics*. London: Cassell.

Lewis, W. 1977. *Labour in the West Indies: The Birth of a Worker's Movement*. London: New Beacon Books.

Lindop, F. 2001. "Racism and the Working Class: Strikes in Support of Enoch Powell in 1968". *Labour History Review* 66 (1): 79–100.

Lister, R. 1996. "In Search of the 'Underclass'". In *Charles Murray and the Underclass: The Developing Debate*, R. Lister (ed.), 1–18. Lancing: The IEA Health and Welfare Unit.

Lister, R. 1998. "From Equality to Social Inclusion: New Labour and the Welfare State". *Critical Social Policy* 18 (55): 215–25.

Lorde, A. 1984. *Sister Outsider: Essays and Speeches*. Freedom, CA: The Crossing Press.

Lorimer, D. 1978. *Class, Colour, and the Victorians: A Study of English Attitudes toward the Negro in the Mid-Nineteenth Century*. New York: Holmes & Meier.

Ludlow, J. & L. Jones 1867. *Progress of the Working Class: 1832–1867*. London: Alexander Strahan.

Lund, B. 1999. "'Ask Not What Your Community Can Do For You': Obligations, New Labour and Welfare Reform". *Critical Social Policy* 19 (4): 447–62.

MacClintock, A. 1995. *Imperial Leather: Race, Gender and Sexuality in Colonial Context*. New York: Routledge.

Macdonald, R., T. Shildrick & A. Furlong 2014. "In Search of 'Intergenerational Cultures of Worklessness': Hunting the Yeti and Shooting Zombies". *Critical Social Policy* 34 (2): 199–220.

MacKenzie, D. 1976. "Eugenics in Britain". *Social Studies of Science* 6 (3/4): 499–532.

Mackenzie, J. 1995. "The Imperial Pioneer and Hunter and the British Masculine Stereotype in Late Victorian and Edwardian Times". In *Manliness and Morality: Middle-Class Masculinity in Britain and America 1800–1940*, J. Mangan & J. Walvin (eds), 176–98. Manchester: Manchester University Press.

Macmillan, L. 2011. "Measuring the Intergenerational Correlation of Worklessness". 11/278. University of Bristol: Centre for Market and Public Organisation.

Macmillan, W. 1936. *Warning from the West Indies: A Tract for Africa and the Empire*. London: Faber & Faber.

Macnicol, J. 1987. "In Pursuit of the Underclass". *Journal of Social Policy* 16 (3): 293–318.

Madden, A. 1979. "'Not for Export': The Westminster Model of Government and British Colonial Practice". *The Journal of Imperial and Commonwealth History* 8 (1): 10–29.

Magubane, Z. 2004. *Bringing the Empire Home: Race, Class, and Gender in Britain and Colonial South Africa*. Chicago, IL: University of Chicago Press.

Malinowski, B. 1929. "Practical Anthropology". *Africa: Journal of the International African Institute* 2 (1): 22–38.

Malinowski, B. 1945. *The Dynamics of Culture Change*. New Haven, CT: Yale University Press.

Malinowski, B. 1954. "Myth in Primitive Psychology". In *Magic, Science and Religion and Other Essays*, 100–26. Garden City, NY: Doubleday.

Mallalie, W. 1950. "Joseph Chamberlain and Workmen's Compensation". *Journal of Economic History* 10 (1): 45–57.

Mama, Λ. 1989. "Violence against Black Women: Gender, Race and State Responses". *Feminist Review* 32: 30–48.

Mama, A. 1992. "Black Women and the British State: Race, Class and Gender Analysis for the 1990s". In *Racism and Antiracism: Inequalities, Opportunities and Policies*, P. Braham, A. Rattansi & R. Skellington (eds), 79–101. London: Sage.

Mandler, P. 1990. "Tories and Paupers: Christian Political Economy and the Making of the New Poor Law". *Historical Journal* 33 (1): 81–103.

Mantena, K. 2008. "The Crisis of Liberal Imperialism". In *Victorian Visions of Global Order: Empire and International Relations in Nineteenth-Century Political Thought*, 113–35. Cambridge: Cambridge University Press.

Marshall, T. 1953. "Social Selection in the Welfare State". *Eugenics Review* 45 (2): 81–92.

Marshall, T. 1965. "The Right to Welfare". *Sociological Review* 13 (3): 261–72.

Marshall, T. 1992. *Citizenship and Social Class*. London: Pluto.

Martin, R. 1991. "Thatcherism and Britain's Industrial Landscape". In *The Geography of De-Industrialisation*, R. Martin & B. Rowthorn (eds), 238–90. Basingstoke and London: Macmillan.

Mason, R. 2014. "Nigel Farage Backs 'Basic Principle' of Enoch Powell's Immigration Warning". *Guardian*, 5 January. www.theguardian.com/pol itics/2014/jan/05/nigel-farage-enoch-powell-immigration (accessed 20 December 2017).

Maxey, K. 1976. "Labour and the Rhodesian Situation". *African Affairs* 75 (299): 152–62.

May, A. 2001. "'Commonwealth or Europe?': Macmillan's Dilemma, 1961–63". In *Britain, the Commonwealth and Europe*, A. May (ed.), 82–110. London: Palgrave.

May, T. 2016a. "Statement from the New Prime Minister Theresa May". Gov. uk. 13 July. www.gov.uk/government/speeches/statement-from-the-new-prime-minister-theresa-may (accessed 20 December 2017).

May, T. 2016b. "Theresa May's Keynote Speech at Tory Conference in Full". *Telegraph*, 5 October. www.independent.co.uk/news/uk/politics/theresa-may-speech-tory-conference-2016-in-full-transcript-a7346171.html (accessed 20 December 2017).

May, T. 2017. "The Shared Society". Gov.Uk. 8 January. www.gov.uk/government/speeches/the-shared-society-article-by-theresa-may (accessed 20 December 2017).

Mayhew, H. 1861. *London Labour and the London Poor*. London: Griffith, Bohn & Co.

McClelland, K. & S. Rose 2006. "Citizenship and Empire, 1867–1928". In *At Home with the Empire: Metropolitan Culture and the Imperial World*, C. Hall & S. Rose (eds), 275–97. Cambridge: Cambridge University Press.

McDowell, L. 2005. "Love, Money, and Gender Divisions of Labour: Some Critical Reflections on Welfare-to-Work Policies in the UK". *Journal of Economic Geography* 5 (3): 365–79.

McDowell, L. 2008. "On the Significance of Being White: European Migrant Workers in the British Economy in the 1940s and 2000s". In *New Geographies of Race and Racism*, C. Dwyer & C. Bressey (eds), 51–66. London: Ashgate.

McKibbin, R. 1984. "Why Was There No Marxism in Great Britain?" *English Historical Review* 99 (391): 297–331.

Michals, T. 1993. "'That Sole and Despotic Dominion': Slaves, Wives, and Game in Blackstone's Commentaries". *Eighteenth-Century Studies* 27 (2): 195–216.

Middleton, A. 2017. "The Second Reform Act and the Politics of Empire". *Parliamentary History* 36 (1): 82–96.

Mills, D. 2010. *Difficult Folk? A Political History of Social Anthropology.* New York: Berghahn.

"Minutes, 5th April" 1900. CO 318/299. National Archives UK.

Mooney, G. & S. Neal 2009. "'Welfare Worries': Mapping the Directions of Welfare Futures in the Contemporary UK". *Research, Policy and Planning* 27 (3): 141–50.

Moore, B. & M. Johnson 2004. *Neither Led nor Driven: Contesting British Cultural Imperialism in Jamaica, 1865–1920.* Kingston: University of West Indies Press.

Moore, M. 2008. "Immigration to Britain 'Will Be Capped'". *Telegraph*, 18 October. www.telegraph.co.uk/news/politics/3219776/Immigration-to-Britain-will-be-capped.html (accessed 20 December 2017).

Murji, K. & J. Solomos 2005. *Racialization: Studies in Theory and Practice.* Oxford: Oxford University Press.

Murray, C. 1996. "The Emerging British Underclass". In *Charles Murray and the Underclass: The Developing Debate*, The IEA Health and Welfare Unit (ed.), 23–52. Lancing: Hartington Fine Arts.

Nairn, T. 1970. "Enoch Powell: The New Right". *New Left Review* 61: 3–27.

National Housing Federation n.d. "How Public Money Is Spent on Housing". www.housing.org.uk/how-public-money-is-spent-on-housing/ (accessed 20 December 2017).

Nayak, A. 2009. "Beyond the Pale: Chavs, Youth and Social Class". In *Who Cares About the White Working Class?*, K. Sveinsson (ed.), 28–35. London: Runnymede Trust. www.runnymedetrust.org/uploads/publications/pdfs/WhoCaresAboutTheWhiteWorkingClass-2009.pdf (accessed 20 December 2017).

Ndem, E. 1957. "The Status of Colored People in Britain". *Phylon Quarterly* 18 (1): 82–7.

Nicholls, G. 1899. *A History of the Poor Law: Vol III.* London: P.S. King & Son.

Noble, D. 2015. "Decolonizing Britain and Domesticating Women: Race, Gender, and Women's Work in Post-1945 British Decolonial and Metropolitan Liberal Reform Discourses". *Meridians: Feminism, Race, Transnationalism* 13 (1): 53–77.

Norman, J. & J. Ganesh 2006. *Compassionate Conservatism: What It Is, Why We Need It.* London: Policy Exchange.

North, P. 2011. "Geographies and Utopias of Cameron's Big Society". *Social & Cultural Geography* 12 (8): 817–27.

NUS Black Students 2015. "Preventing PREVENT".

O'Connell, A. 2009a. "Building Their Readiness For Economic 'Freedom': The New Poor Law and Emancipation". *Journal of Sociology and Social Welfare* 36 (2): 85–103.

O'Connell, A. 2009b. "The Pauper, Slave, and Aboriginal Subject: British Parliamentary Investigations and the Promotion of Civilized Conduct". *Canadian Social Work Review / Revue Canadienne de Service Social* 26 (2): 171–93.

Olivier, S. 1933. *The Myth of Governor Eyre*. London: Hogarth Press.

Open Society Foundations 2014. "Europe's White Working Class Communities". www.opensocietyfoundations.org/sites/default/files/white-working-class-communities-manchester-20140616.pdf (accessed 20 December 2017).

Orde Browne, G. 1941. *Labour Conditions in West Africa*. London: HMSO.

Orrenius, P. & M. Zavodny 2008. "The Effect of Minimum Wages on Immigrants' Employment and Earnings". *ILR Review* 61 (4): 544–63. https://doi.org/ 10.1177/001979390806100406 (accessed 20 December 2017).

Parekh, B., Runnymede Trust & Commission on the Future of Multi-Ethnic Britain 2010. *The Future of Multi-Ethnic Britain: Report*. London: Profile.

Paton, G. 2008. "White Working-Class Boys Becoming an Underclass". *Telegraph*, 18 June. www.telegraph.co.uk/news/uknews/2151025/White-working-class-boys-becoming-an-underclass.html (accessed 20 December 2017).

Paton, G. 2012. "Private Schools Failing to Recruit Working-Class White Boys". *Telegraph*, 5 October. www.telegraph.co.uk/education/educationnews/ 9589978/Private-schools-failing-to-recruit-working-class-white-boys. html (accessed 20 December 2017).

Paul, D. 1984. "Eugenics and the Left". *Journal of the History of Ideas* 45 (4): 567–90.

Paul, K. 1995. "'British Subjects' and 'British Stock': Labour's Postwar Imperialism". *Journal of British Studies* 34 (2): 233–76.

Payton, M. 2016. "Brexit Legal Challenge: Only a Few of Nigel Farage's '100,000-Strong People's Army' March on Supreme Court". *Independent*, 5 December. www.independent.co.uk/news/uk/politics/brexit-supreme-court-hearing-article-50-nigel-farage-march-peoples-army-a7456406.html (accessed 20 December 2017).

Persky, J. 1998. "Wage Slavery". *History of Political Economy* 30 (4): 627–51.

Phipps, C. 2016. "British Newspapers React to Judges' Brexit Ruling: 'Enemies of the People'". *Guardian*, 4 November. www.theguardian.com/politics/ 2016/nov/04/enemies-of-the-people-british-newspapers-react-judges-brexit-ruling (accessed 20 December 2017).

Phizacklea, A. & R. Miles 1980. *Labor and Racism*. London: Routledge & Kegan Paul.

Phizacklea, A. & R. Miles 1992. "The British Trade Union Movement and Racism". In *Racism and Antiracism: Inequalities, Opportunities and Policies*, P. Braham, A. Rattansi & R. Skellington (eds), 30–45. London: Sage.

Porritt, E. 1912. "The British National Insurance Act". *Political Science Quarterly* 27 (2): 260–80.

Porter, D. 1991. "'Enemies of the Race': Biologism, Environmentalism, and Public Health in Edwardian England". *Victorian Studies* 34 (2): 159–78.

Potter, B. 1904. *The Co-Operative Movement in Great Britain*. New York: Charles Scribner's Sons.

Powell, E. 1967. "Speech to the Annual Luncheon of the Ealing North Conservative Women's Advisory Committee". POLL 4/1/3 Speeches. enochpowell.info.

Powell, E. 1969. "Speech to Conservative Women's Rally, Clacton". POLL 4/1/5 Speeches. enochpowell.info.

Powell, E. 1970. "Speech at Turves Green Girls School". POLL 4/1/6 Speeches. enochpowell.info.

Powell, E. 2007. "Enoch Powell's 'Rivers of Blood' Speech". *Telegraph*, 6 November. www.telegraph.co.uk/comment/3643823/Enoch-Powells-Rivers-of-Blood-speech.html (accessed 20 December 2017).

Preece, R. 1977. "The Myth of the Red Tory". *Canadian Journal of Political and Social Theory* 1 (2): 3–28.

Prescod, C. & D. Renwick 2017. "Fighting Fire". Institute of Race Relations. www.irr.org.uk/news/fighting-fire/ (accessed 20 December 2017).

Prest, W. 2007. "Law for Historians: William Blackstone on Wives, Colonies and Slaves". *Legal History* 11: 105–15.

Quinault, R. 1985. "John Bright and Joseph Chamberlain". *Historical Journal* 28 (3): 623–46.

Rae, A. 2016. "What Can Explain Brexit?" Stats, Maps n Pix blog, 25 June. www.statsmapsnpix.com/2016/06/what-can-explain-brexit.html (accessed 20 December 2017).

Ramdin, R. 1986. *The Making of the Black Working Class in Britain*. Aldershot: Gower.

Rayner, G. & C. Hope 2017. "Cut the EU Red Tape Choking Britain after Brexit to Set the Country Free from the Shackles of Brussels". *Telegraph*, 27 March. www.telegraph.co.uk/news/2017/03/27/cut-eu-red-tape-choking-britain-brexit-set-country-free-shackles/ (accessed 20 December 2017).

"Recommendations of the West India Royal Commission" 1940. CO 35/541/8. National Archives UK.

Reid, S. 2009. "The Great White Backlash: Working Class Turns on Labour over Immigration and Housing". *Daily Mail*, 10 January. www.dailymail.co.uk/news/article-1111151/The-great-white-backlash-Working-class-turns-Labour-immigration-housing.html (accessed 20 December 2017).

Renwick, C. 2014. "Completing the Circle of the Social Sciences? William Beveridge and Social Biology at London School of Economics during the 1930s". *Philosophy of the Social Sciences* 44 (4): 478–96.

"Report of the Ashridge Conference on Social Development – 3rd–12th August" 1954. CO 1045/296. National Archives UK.

Reynolds's Newspaper, 27 October 1850.

Rhodes, J. 2009. "Revisiting the 2001 Riots: New Labour and the Rise of 'Colour Blind Racism'". *Sociological Research Online* 14 (5).

Rhodes, J. 2010. "White Backlash, 'Unfairness' and Justifications of British National Party (BNP) Support". *Ethnicities* 10 (1): 77–99.

Rhodes, J. 2013. "Remaking Whiteness in the 'Postracial' UK". In *The State of Race*, N. Kapoor, V. Kalra & J. Rhodes, 49–71. London: Palgrave Macmillan.

Rice, A. 2010. *Creating Memorials, Building Identities: The Politics of Memory in the Black Atlantic.* Liverpool: Liverpool University Press.

Richards, S. 1999. "The New Statesman Interview – Gordon Brown". *New Statesman.* www.newstatesman.com/node/148975 (accessed 20 December 2017).

Ridley, J. 1987. "The Unionist Social Reform Committee, 1911–1914: Wets Before the Deluge". *The Historical Journal* 30 (2): 391–413.

Roediger, D. 1991. *The Wages of Whiteness: Race and the Making of the American Working Class.* London: Verso.

Rosamond, B. 1993. "National Labour Organizations and European Integration: British Trade Unions and '1992'". *Political Studies* 41 (3): 420–34.

Rose, S. 1993. "Gender and Labor History: The Nineteenth-Century Legacy". *International Review of Social History* 38 (S1): 145–62.

Rosenbaum, M. 2017. "Voting Data Sheds Light on Referendum". BBC News, 6 February. www.bbc.co.uk/news/uk-politics-38762034 (accessed 20 December 2017).

Runnymede 2017. "Reframing Racism: Explaining Ethnic Inequalities in the UK Labour Market". London: Runnymede Trust. www.runnymedetrust.org/uploads/Runnymede%20Reframing%20Racism%20TUC%20briefing.pdf (accessed 20 December 2017).

Rush, A. 2002. "Imperial Identity in Colonial Minds: Harold Moody and the League of Coloured Peoples, 1931–50". *Twentieth Century British History* 13 (4): 356–83.

Rustin, M. 2003. "The Making of Political Identity: Edward Thompson and William Cobbett". *Soundings* 24 (24): 131–52.

Samaluk, B. 2014. "Whiteness, Ethnic Privilege and Migration: A Bourdieuian Framework". *Journal of Managerial Psychology* 29: 370–88.

Scherr, A. 2003. "'Sambos' and 'Black Cut-Throats': Peter Porcupine on Slavery and Race in the 1790's". *American Periodicals: A Journal of History & Criticism* 13: 3–30.

Schofield, C. 2015. *Enoch Powell and the Making of Postcolonial Britain.* Cambridge: Cambridge University Press.

Schwarz, B. 1996. "'The Only White Man in There': The Re-Racialisation of England, 1956–1968". *Race & Class* 38 (1): 65–78.

Seligman, C. 1932. "Anthropological Perspective and Psychological Theory". *Journal of the Royal Anthropological Institute* 62: 193–228.

Semmel, B. 1968. *Imperialism and Social Reform: English Social-Imperial Thought 1895–1914.* New York: Anchor Books.

Seymour, R. 2016. "UKIP and the Crisis of Britain". In *Socialist Register 2016: The Politics of the Right*, 24–90. London: Merlin.

Shaw, B. 1900. *Fabianism and the Empire: A Manifesto*. London: Grant Richards.

Sherard, R. 1897. *The White Slaves of England*. London: James Bowden.

Shilliam, R. 2012. "Race, Class, and the Pan-African Congress in Manchester 1945". Robbie Shilliam blog, 12 July. https://robbieshilliam.wordpress.com/2012/07/12/race-class-and-the-pan-african-congress-in-manchester-1945/ (accessed 20 December 2017).

Shilliam, R. 2017. "Race and Revolution at Bwa Kayiman". *Millennium* 45 (3): 269–92.

Silverman, R. 2013. "White Working Class Boys Could Be Treated Like Ethnic Minorities by Universities, Says Minister". *Telegraph*, 3 January. www.telegraph.co.uk/education/universityeducation/9777067/White-working-class-boys-could-be-treated-like-ethnic-minorities-by-universities-says-minister.html (accessed 20 December 2017).

Singh, M. 2016. "The 2.8 Million Non-Voters Who Delivered Brexit". *Bloomberg*, 4 July. www.bloomberg.com/view/articles/2016-07-04/the-2-8-million-non-voters-who-delivered-brexit (accessed 20 December 2017).

Sivanandan, A. 2008. "Race, Class and the State: The Political Economy of Immigration". In *Catching History on the Wing*, 65–89. London: Pluto.

Sked, A. 1992. "A Proposal for European Union". In *Reshaping Europe in the Twenty-First Century*, P. Robertson (ed.), 3–21. London: Palgrave Macmillan.

Skeggs, B. 2005. "The Making of Class and Gender through Visualizing Moral Subject Formation". *Sociology* 39 (5): 965–82.

Skelton, N. 1924. "Private Property: A Unionist". *Spectator*, 3 May.

Slater, T. 2014. "The Myth of 'Broken Britain': Welfare Reform and the Production of Ignorance". *Antipode* 46 (4): 948–69.

Small, S. & J. Solomos 2006. "Race, Immigration and Politics in Britain: Changing Policy Agendas and Conceptual Paradigms 1940s–2000s". *International Journal of Comparative Sociology* 47 (3–4): 235–57.

Smiles, S. 1897. *Self-Help, with Illustrations of Conduct and Perseverance*. London: John Murray.

Smith, A. 1978. *Lectures on Jurisprudence*, R. Meek, D. Raphael & P. Stein (eds). Oxford: Clarendon.

Smith, A. 1986. *The Wealth of Nations: Books I–III*. London: Penguin.

Smith, J. (ed.). 1834. *The Shepherd*. London: B.D. Cousins.

Smith, J. 1994. "The Liberals, Race, and Political Reform in the British West Indies, 1866–1874". *Journal of Negro History* 79 (2): 131–46.

Smith, R. 1976. "Edmund Burke's Negro Code". *History Today* 26 (11): 715–23.

Snowdon, K. 2017. "Grenfell Tower Immigration Amnesty For Residents Slammed As 'Travesty' By BMELawyers4Grenfell". *Huffington Post*, 31 August. www.huffingtonpost.co.uk/entry/grenfell-tower-immigration-amnesty_uk_59a8466de4b0a8d14574072b (accessed 20 December 2017).

Snowdon, K., G. Bowden, L. Sherriff, *et al.* 2017. "Grenfell Tower Fire Lays Bare the 'Tale of Two Kensingtons' – A Borough of Extreme Rich and Poor". *Huffington Post*, 15 June. www.huffingtonpost.co.uk/entry/grenfell-tower-tale-two-kensingtons-borough-extreme-rich-poor_uk_594269e9e4b003d5 948d5116 (accessed 20 December 2017).

Social Justice Poverty Group 2006. "Breakdown Britain: Interim Report on the State of the Nation". www.centreforsocialjustice.org.uk/core/wp-content/uploads/2016/08/Breakdown-Britain.pdf (accessed 20 December 2017).

"Social Security in the Colonial Territories (Draft)" 1943. ACT 1/717. National Archives UK.

Solomos, J., B. Findlay, S. Jones, *et al.* 1992. "The Organic Crisis of British Capitalism and Race: The Experience of the Seventies". In *The Empire Strikes Back: Race and Racism in 70s Britain*, Centre for Contemporary Cultural Studies, 7–44. London: Routledge.

Squire, V. 2005. "'Integration with Diversity in Modern Britain': New Labour on Nationality, Immigration and Asylum". *Journal of Political Ideologies* 10 (1): 51–74.

Stanley, A. 1998. *From Bondage to Contract: Wage Labor, Marriage, and the Market in the Age of Slave Emancipation*. Cambridge: Cambridge University Press.

Stapleton, J. 2006. "The England of G.K. Chesterton". *Chesterton Review* 32 (3/4): 339–55.

Stephens, M., M. Fenger, J. Hudson, *et al.* 2016. "Housing Policy in the Age of Austerity and Beyond". *Social Policy Review* 28: 63–85.

Stone, D. 2001. "Race in British Eugenics". *European History Quarterly* 31 (3): 397–425.

Surridge, P., S. McAndrew & N. Begum 2017. "Social Capital and Belonging: The 'Citizens of Somewhere' Are More Likely to Be Pro-EU". LSE Brexit blog. http://blogs.lse.ac.uk/brexit/2017/11/13/social-capital-and-belonging-the-citizens-of-somewhere-are-more-likely-to-be-pro-eu/ (accessed 20 December 2017).

Sveinsson, K. 2009. "The White Working Class and Multiculturalism: Is There Space for a Progressive Agenda?" *In Who Cares about the White Working Class?* K. Sveinsson (ed.), 3–6. Runnymede Perspectives. www.runnymedetrust.org/uploads/publications/pdfs/WhoCaresAboutTheWhite WorkingClass-2009.pdf (accessed 20 December 2017).

Swales, K. 2016. "Understanding the Leave Vote". NatCen. https://whatukthinks. org/eu/wp-content/uploads/2016/12/NatCen_Brexplanations-report-FINAL-WEB2.pdf (accessed 20 December 2017).

Tabata, I. 1945. *The Rehabilitation Scheme: A New Fraud*. Cape Town: All African Convention.

Taylor, M. 2003. "Empire and Parliamentary Reform: The 1832 Reform Act Revisited". In *Rethinking the Age of Reform: Britain 1780–1850*, A. Burns & J. Innes (eds), 295–311. Cambridge: Cambridge University Press.

Taylor, N. 2015. "Perspectives on the Social Question: Poverty and Unemployment in Liberal and Neoliberal Britain". PhD Thesis, University of Warwick.

Telegraph 2009. "Government Has Neglected White Working Class, Says John Denham", 30 November. www.telegraph.co.uk/news/politics/6691426/Government-has-neglected-white-working-class-says-John-Denham.html (accessed 20 December 2017).

Telegraph 2011. "UK Riots: Text of David Cameron's Address to Commons", 11 August.

Telegraph 2015. "White Working Class Boys Are the Worst Performing Ethnic Group at School", 30 October. www.telegraph.co.uk/men/the-filter/11965045/White-working-class-boys-are-the-worst-performing-ethnic-group-at-school.html (accessed 20 December 2017).

Thane, P. 1978. "Women and the Poor Law in Victorian and Edwardian England". *History Workshop*, October: 29–51.

Thatcher, M. 1987. "Interview for Woman's Own". Margaret Thatcher Foundation. www.margaretthatcher.org/document/106689 (accessed 20 December 2017).

Thatcher, M. 1993. *The Downing Street Years*. London: HarperCollins.

Thompson, A. 1997. "The Language of Imperialism and the Meanings of Empire: Imperial Discourse in British Politics, 1895–1914". *Journal of British Studies* 36 (2): 147–77.

Thorne, S. 1997. "'The Conversion of Englishmen and the Conversion of the World Inseparable': Missionary Imperialism and the Language of Class in Early Industrial Britain". In *Tensions of Empire: Colonial Cultures in a Bourgeois World*, F. Cooper & A. Stoler (eds), 238–62. Berkeley, CA: University of California Press.

Todd, S. 2009. "Dressing the Part: The Body in/of the Diaries of Hannah Cullwick and Arthur Munby". In *New Essays on Life Writing and the Body*, C. Stuart (ed.), 108–31. Newcastle upon Tyne: Cambridge Scholars.

Tournier-Sol, K. 2015. "Reworking the Eurosceptic and Conservative Traditions into a Populist Narrative: UKIP's Winning Formula?" *JCMS: Journal of Common Market Studies* 53 (1): 140–56.

Townshend, C. 1982. "Martial Law: Legal and Administrative Problems of Civil Emergency in Britain and the Empire, 1800–1940". *Historical Journal* 25 (1): 167–95.

Travis, A. 2015. "Oliver Letwin Blocked Help for Black Youth After 1985 Riots". *Guardian*, 30 December. www.theguardian.com/politics/2015/dec/30/oliver-letwin-blocked-help-for-black-youth-after-1985-riots (accessed 20 December 2017).

Turley, D. 2003. "British Anti-Slavery Reassessed". In *Rethinking the Age of Reform, 1780–1850*, A. Burns & J. Innes (eds), 182–99. Cambridge: Cambridge University Press.

Tylor, E. 1920. *Primitive Culture Vol. 1*. Sixth edn. London: John Murray.

US Department of Labor: Office of Policy Planning and Research 1965. "The Negro Family: The Case for National Action".

Valentine, G. & C. Harris 2014. "Strivers vs Skivers: Class Prejudice and the Demonisation of Dependency in Everyday Life". *Geoforum* 53: 84–92.

Vincent, A. 1984. "The Poor Law Reports of 1909 and the Social Theory of the Charity Organization Society". *Victorian Studies* 27 (3): 343–63.

Virdee, S. 2000. "A Marxist Critique of Black Radical Theories of Trade-Union Racism". *Sociology* 34 (3): 545–65.

Virdee, S. 2014. *Racism, Class and the Racialized Outsider*. Basingstoke: Palgrave Macmillan.

Virdee, S. & B. McGeever 2017. "Racism, Crisis, Brexit". *Ethnic and Racial Studies*. https://doi.org/10.1080/01419870.2017.1361544.

Vobejda, B. 1996. "Clinton Signs Welfare Bill Amid Division". *Washington Post*, 23 August.

Vorspan, R. 1977. "Vagrancy and the New Poor Law in Late-Victorian and Edwardian England". *The English Historical Review* 92 (362): 59–81.

Vucetic, S. 2011. *The Anglosphere: A Genealogy of a Racialized Identity in International Relations*. Stanford, CA: Stanford University Press.

Wainwright, O. & P. Walker 2017. "'Disaster Waiting to Happen': Fire Expert Slams UK Tower Blocks". *Guardian*, 14 June. www.theguardian.com/uk-news/2017/jun/14/disaster-waiting-to-happen-fire-expert-slams-uk-tower-blocks (accessed 20 December 2017).

Walker, P. 2017. "Jacob Rees-Mogg: Hard Brexit Would Boost UK by £135bn over Five Years". *Guardian*, 14 November. www.theguardian.com/politics/2017/nov/14/jacob-rees-mogg-hard-brexit-would-boost-uk-by-135bn-over-5-years (accessed 20 December 2017).

Ward, R. 1978. "Race Relations in Britain". *British Journal of Sociology* 29 (4): 464–80. https://doi.org/10.2307/589661.

Waters, C. 1997. "'Dark Strangers' in Our Midst: Discourses of Race and Nation in Britain, 1947–1963". *Journal of British Studies* 36 (2): 207–38.

Watson, T. 1997. "Jamaica, Genealogy, George Eliot: Inheriting the Empire After Morant Bay". *Jouvert: A Journal of Postcolonial Studies* 1 (1). https://english.chass.ncsu.edu/jouvert/v1i1/WATSON.HTM (accessed 20 December 2017).

Webb, S. 1891. *The London Programme*. London: Swan Sonnenschein.

Webb, S. 1910. "Eugenics and the Poor Law: The Minority Report". *Eugenics Review* 2 (3): 233–41.

Webster, W. 2010. *Englishness and Empire 1939–1965*. Oxford: Oxford University Press.

Wellings, B. 2010. "Losing the Peace: Euroscepticism and the Foundations of Contemporary English Nationalism". *Nations and Nationalism* 16 (3): 488–505.

Wellings, B. 2014. "European Integration and the End of an Imperial Consciousness in Britain". *Australian Journal of Politics & History* 60 (1): 93–109.

Wellings, B. & E. Vines 2016. "Populism and Sovereignty: The EU Act and the In-Out Referendum, 2010–2015". *Parliamentary Affairs* 69 (2): 309–26.

Welshman, J. 1999. "Evacuation, Hygiene, and Social Policy: The Our Town Report of 1943". *Historical Journal* 42 (3): 781–807.

Welshman, J. 2005. "Ideology, Social Science, and Public Policy: The Debate over Transmitted Deprivation". *Twentieth Century British History* 16 (3): 306–41.

Whipple, A. 2009. "Revisiting the 'Rivers of Blood' Controversy: Letters to Enoch Powell". *Journal of British Studies* 48 (3): 717–35. https://doi.org/10.2307/27752577.

Whitehead, P. 1987. *The Writing on the Wall: Britain in the Seventies*. London: Joseph.

Will, H. 1970. "Colonial Policy and Economic Development in the British West Indies, 1895–1903". *Economic History Review* 23 (1): 129–47.

Willetts, D. 1998. "Conservative Renewal". *Political Quarterly* 69 (2): 110–17.

Williams, F. 1998. *Social Policy: A Critical Introduction*. Cambridge: Polity.

Wilson, W. 2009. "Foreword: The Moynihan Report and Research on the Black Community". *The Annals of the American Academy of Political and Social Science* 621: 34–46.

Winter, S. 2016. "On the Morant Bay Rebellion in Jamaica and the Governor Eyre-George William Gordon Controversy, 1865–70". BRANCH: Britain, Representation and Nineteenth-Century History. www.branchcollective.org/?ps_articles=sarah-winter-on-the-morant-bay-rebellion-in-jamaica-and-the-governor-eyre-george-william-gordon-controversy-1865–70 (accessed 20 December 2017).

Wolf, H. 1900. "Co-Operation in the West Indies". *The Cooperative News*.

Wolpe, H. 1972. "Capitalism and Cheap Labour-Power in South Africa: From Segregation to Apartheid". *Economy and Society* 1 (4): 425–56.

Wolton, S. 2006. "Immigration Policy and the 'Crisis of British Values'". *Citizenship Studies* 10 (4): 453–67.

Wood, M. 1999. "William Cobbett, John Thelwall, Radicalism, Racism and Slavery: A Study in Burkean Parodics". *Romanticism on the Net*, 15. www.erudit.org/revue/ron/1999/v/n15/005873ar.html?vue=integral (accessed 20 December 2017).

Worley, C. 2005. "'It's Not About Race. It's About the Community': New Labour and 'Community Cohesion'". *Critical Social Policy* 25 (4): 483–96.

Worstall, T. 2016. "Brexit Effects: A Deregulated City Will Thrive Outside the European Union". *Forbes*, 27 June. www.forbes.com/sites/timworstall/2016/06/27/brexit-effects-a-deregulated-city-will-thrive-outside-the-european-union/#41bb0f1f7993 (accessed 20 December 2017).

Worth, O. 2017. "Reviving Hayek's Dream". *Globalizations* 14 (1): 104–9.

Wrench, J. 1986. "Unequal Comrades: Trade Unions, Equal Opportunity and Racism". *Policy Papers in Ethnic Relations* 5. Centre for Research in Ethnic Relations, University of Warwick.

Wrench, J. & S. Virdee 1995. "Organising the Unorganised: 'Race', Poor Work and Trade Unions". *Research Papers in Ethnic Relations* 21. Centre for Research in Ethnic Relations, University of Warwick.

Wright, P. 2004. "Last Orders for the English Aborigine". www.patrickwright.net/wp-content/uploads/pwright-last-orders.pdf (accessed 20 December 2017).

Wright, S. 2014. "Lies, Spies, Cover-Ups and Corruption". *Daily Mail*, 6 March. www.dailymail.co.uk/news/article-2575174/Lies-spies-cover-ups-corruption-sickening-extent-Stephens-betrayal-police-exposed.html (accessed 20 December 2017).

Yeandle, S. 2003. "The UK Labour Market". In *Work to Welfare: How Men Become Detached From the Labour Market*, P. Alcock, C. Beatty, S. Fothergill, R. Macmillan & S. Yeandle (eds), 3–24. New York: Cambridge University Press.

Young, M. & P. Willmott 1956. "Social Grading by Manual Workers". *British Journal of Sociology* 7 (4): 337–45.

Young, R. 2008. *The Idea of English Ethnicity*. Malden, MA: Blackwell.

Young, T. 2016. "Who Speaks up for Poor White Boys When It Comes To Their Education?" *Spectator*, 6 February. www.spectator.co.uk/2016/02/who-speaks-up-for-poor-white-boys-when-it-comes-to-their-education/ (accessed 20 December 2017).

Zebel, S. 1967. "Joseph Chamberlain and the Genesis of Tariff Reform". *Journal of British Studies* 7 (1): 131–57.

INDEX

Somersett case, 13–15
Spencer, Herbert, 38
Starkey, David, 132–3, 161
Swing riots (1830), 19, 24, 26, 28, 29

Thatcher, Margaret, 106–7, 110, 112,
     113–16, 119, 123, 124, 126, 128, 133,
     135, 137, 147, 148, 151, 154, 156,
     158, 166, 170, 175, 176
Tiger Bay, Cardiff, 87
Tottenham
  Broadwater Farm (1985), 130–1,
     132, 177
  Mark Duggan, 130
Trades Union Congress (TUC), 50, 72,
     103–4, 146, 147
Tylor, Edward, 35
Tyndall, John, 42

Uncle Tom's Cabin, 36, 42
United Kingdom Independence Party
     (UKIP), 2, 100, 136, 145, 148, 152,
     153, 154, 155, 161, 162, 175, 176, 177,
     183, 190, 202, 205

Webb, Beatrice, 61, 62, 65
Webb, Sydney, 48, 62, 64, 65, 72
Welfare Reform Act (2009), 120
Welfare Reform Bill (1999), 120
Westway 23, 169–70, 181
whiteness, 4, 7, 103, 125, 126, 129, 134,
     155, 156, 160
Willetts, David, 3, 137, 144
William, Nassau Snr, 28, 30
Wilson, Harold, 95, 146
Woolf, Leonard, 69
workhouses, 19, 27, 29, 31, 48, 53